THE IMMUTABLY HOLY GOD
THE GOD WHO WANTS TO BE OUR HEAVENLY FATHER

———⁂———

EXPLORING ESSENTIAL DOCTRINES
OF THE CHRISTIAN FAITH

STEVEN G. MILLER

Revised, rewritten and expanded
Previously: Our Heavenly Father, The Immutable, Holy God

THE IMMUTABLY HOLY GOD THE GOD WHO WANTS TO BE OUR HEAVENLY FATHER
EXPLORING ESSENTIAL DOCTRINES OF THE CHRISTIAN FAITH

iUniverse books may be ordered through booksellers or by contacting:

iUniverse
1663 Liberty Drive
Bloomington, IN 47403
www.iuniverse.com
844-349-9409

ISBN: 978-1-6632-5350-7 (sc)
ISBN: 978-1-6632-5351-4 (e)

Print information available on the last page.

iUniverse rev. date: 06/14/2023

CONTENTS

Dedications vii

Introduction to the Book ix

Preface to the Revised Edition xi

Introductory Thoughts xiii

1. Reason for writing 1
2. The Journey 6
3. The Ultimate Reality 13
4. An illustration to demonstrate universal morals and
    unintended consequences of leaving Biblical truth 18
5. The basis of truth 27
6. Whose God is the real God 33
7. Looking at the values in a life without God 40
8. Exploring God's Perfect Nature 47
9. A divine dilemma 52
10. The need and reasonableness of the Gospel 58
11. The Gospel Message 63
12. God command for the church to fulfill the
    great commission 73
13. Understanding our call to be evangelistically obedient 83
14. Wrestling with thoughts about evangelism 91
15. The call of the church to be proclaimers of truth 103
16. Christian living in light of eternity 115
17. Our Prayer Life 123
18. The personal consequences of living in a fallen world
    and the hope of the Gospel 127
19. Legalism or Discipleship 138

20. Eternal Security and the spiritual stability of the believer 148

21. Eternal Security and the Gospel presentation 160

22. The consequences of the Bema Seat of Christ 166

23. Fatherly Discipline 180

24. Living with heartache and confusion 192

25. Types of Christians 199

26. Spiritual truths in 8 Mini Chapters 210

27. Reflection on culture 218

28. Walking away and coming home again 224

29. Ten and Ten 228

30. Summary Thoughts 241

31. What are our options? 246

32. Truth is truth even if hard to accept 252

The Author 257

Bibliography 259

DEDICATIONS

I first want to thank my Savior, Jesus Christ, for His willingness to sacrifice His life on the cross, so I can have an assured eternal salvation.

I want to dedicate this book to my cherished wife, Kim. Thank you for being my bride for over 40 years. I am thankful that I can traverse this life with you. It has not always been easy, but there is no one I would rather share the journey with.

To our three children: Jillian, Katelin and Christopher. Thank you for loving me as your dad. Your childhood passed too quickly, but it was the best part of our life.

Lastly, our grandchildren: Donovan, Daylen, Beckett, Quinn, and Brexley Ann. The joy of being a grandparent is the best. All the fun and few of the responsibilities. Hopefully, this list will grow, because grandchildren are the best.

INTRODUCTION
TO THE BOOK

In this book, you will find a straightforward answer to the way of Salvation; the satisfaction of God's Holiness, via the atonement, provided by our Savior: Jesus Christ. This need for our salvation is because we do not measure up to God's absolute and perfect holiness. He is immutable in His holiness: meaning He cannot change His nature. This book explains God's grand plan for the salvation of the world. It is an exclusive way through the God/man, Jesus Christ. He says: "For I am the way and the truth and the life. No one comes to the Father except through me." John 14:6 NIV

A beginning note: As you read this book, you will find repeated references to the holiness of God. As you continue through the pages, you may feel that I am overdoing the emphasis on this attribute; as it comes up repeatedly throughout the pages. It is addressed so often, that you may believe it is excessive, and overdone. This emphasis is often intertwined with my cognitive struggles over the implications of this aspect of God's nature; since it is a very hard concept to fully grasp. As I was finishing the manuscript, I took mental note of my usage of this theme. I am very aware of this emphasis. I even thought of removing some of my references to this aspect of God's nature, believing I may have overdone it. That it was too intensely emphasized. After additional reflection, I realized that it is impossible to overestimate the significance of this attribute. It needed to be left in the book as I had originally intended. How can we ever overemphasize this aspect of God's nature: His perfect immutable holiness, and those resulting implications?

PREFACE TO THE
REVISED EDITION

I knew when I published my original book it needed additional work. Now, after having been published, I have the benefit of feedback from readers. This has allowed me to reflect, add new theological thoughts, and make numerous corrections to the manuscript. All of which, I believe, add to the strength of the updated addition. Even now, I know the book is lacking the strength of a professionally written book. It was never a book to impress, nor to make money. I wanted to pass on the importance of my faith. When the first edition came out, I accepted the cost and gave the first hundred copies away as a witnessing ministry. I wanted -in particular- to have a permanent record of my insights into these critical truths. Spiritual truths that I could pass on to my children, grandchildren, and to other family members and friends. The Lord has given me numerous blessings, but without the salvation of my family, those blessings ring hollow. This was a major reason for my writing of this book. It was more in line with the thought: this is true, and I want you to know.

The feedback I received has been interesting. It was not as I fully expected. I anticipated some would disagree, without a clearly defined justification for why. That many would not like the ramifications of my conclusions. Most seemed to want to avoid thinking about the implications of what was written; I understand this thinking. I suspected that my conclusions would trouble many. I wondered if I was too raw, too honest, or if people were too uncomfortable with the subject. To be clear, I don't humanly desire these conclusions either. These ramifications are just the natural results of the Christian faith being true.

Even though I believe the implications of the Christian faith should be obvious for those who understand and accept the faith, they are hard truths to accept. I believe I laid out strong arguments to justify my conclusions. I recognized that some truths go to the soul of a person. But it is the most preeminent question of all time: where does one spend eternity? Furthermore, there is clear tension between this world we know, and our desires for the things of this world, and the sacrifices one is called to make because our faith is credible; this urgent need to advance the faith. We need to be constantly reminded that those efforts we undertake sharing our faith, may change the eternal destination of those to whom we witness; therefore, well worth the effort. I also present clear teachings on the enhancement of our glorification: by being devout followers of Christ. There are also serious warnings for those who neglect the faith, or compromise with the moral teachings of the scriptures. But within these warnings, there is presented the clear teaching, that these warnings do not include our eternal destiny. We are once for all saved at the very moment of faith in the person and work of Jesus Christ on the cross. I hope you take this journey with me. It takes an elevated degree of faith to see why the sacrifice of our personal comforts, for an unseen world, makes reasonable sense in light of eternity. If you accept my insights contained in this book, you will see the rationale for this assertion.

INTRODUCTORY THOUGHTS

I imagine there are a lot of people who desire to write a book. It could be their life journey they want to share with the readers, some learning they think is paramount for others to know, or some spiritual insights they think are worth expounding upon. In my case all three are somewhat true. I have been on a journey for over 35 years studying Christian theology, and now, I have a message I want to share about the implication of the Christian faith being true. Therefore, I wrote a book sharing these truths. Whether what I wrote is worth reading is up to each reader. I believe it will be worth your time, if you are willing to continue on into the substance of what I want to share? But it takes an investment, because I believe the book grows in substance as it progresses. I start the early chapters by laying the foundation for teachings to be developed later. The building of one principle upon another. As I develop a number of main themes, I keep returning to the central point, which is the imperative need to know the absolute holiness of our Heavenly Father. This comprehension opens our minds to the wonders of our eternal salvation provided by Jesus Christ. Hence the emphasis of verse 6, in chapter 14, of the Gospel of John. I repeatedly put forth this statement, made by Jesus Christ, of the exclusivity of salvation that is in Him alone. So in the chapters that follow, I will shoulder the responsibility to defend these claims. I will explain why Jesus Christ alone is the only means of obtaining eternal salvation. That He is the only way and the only source of absolute truth. The connotations of this claim are of extreme importance for both believers and nonbelievers, as I will contend.

There is simply no more preeminent subject than understanding God's loving plan for the redemption of mankind. But to really grasp the significance of this requires a knowledge of God's immutable holiness. Not exactly a common subject in today's Christian thinking. Most books are about the experience of the faith. What the faith means to them in their daily Christian walk. But something crucial is missing if the faith is limited to the experiences of the faith. There are truths regarding God's nature that need to be explored, and understood, to grasp the true significance of the Christian faith. I want to share my spiritual insights, with the hope that it will cause you to reconsider the real significance of who Jesus is, and what He accomplished on the cross. After the development of this revealed truth, I will continue into the reasons why we need to manifest a life of an authentic believer.

For many years, I have been engaged in Christian deliberation, contemplating aspects of what I believe. Over time, it became abundantly obvious to me that if the Christian faith is really true, the ramifications were far more significant than is being manifested by the average believer. We are exploring eternal issues. Those timeless truths, and the eternal ramifications which are inherently implied, by the faith. For example, there are facets of Christianity that are very comforting: the love of God is one. And there are Biblical truths that are terrifying: Hell as another example. Those two concepts are hard to reconcile in our minds. They are tied up in the very essential nature of God Himself. The issue becomes even more complex when we remember that God is also immutable. He cannot change: it is His intrinsic eternal nature. There never was, or ever will be, any aspect of God's nature that will change. He is eternally perfect in those attributes. With this in mind, I hope on this journey through the book, to help the reader to better understand the significance of God's immutable nature; with the goal of gaining a better understanding of what those attributes should mean to us. And to lay out a logical thought process that resonates the significance of the Christian faith being utterly true. The idea being, since the Christian faith is really true, we need to reconsider those resulting eternal ramifications. If we better grasp the full connotations of the faith, it should lead us to evaluate how we are living in light of eternity.

Therefore, I intend on using a contrasting style that looks at the implications of Christianity being true, or simply myths that have some practical value, but lack eternal significance. This is similar to some of the writing styles of Proverbs. Where thoughts are contrasted in some verses, and similar truths are parallel in other verses. Please keep that in mind throughout the reading of the book. And just like a good coach who teaches the fundamentals of a sport, I draw repeated attention to the key themes of this book; I don't want this study to be like a Sunday sermon that is preached with zeal, only to be too quickly forgotten. So I repeat the major themes over and over to firmly instill them into our memory. As an example, if the scriptures make a mention of a certain truth, it is fully true, even if only mentioned once. Think for a moment of the verses: John 3:16 or Ephesian 2:8-9. Either one alone would show the one condition to receive eternal life/salvation, is whoever believes the gospel. That truth would therefore be fully true, even if only mentioned once. However, the gravity of salvation by faith alone, is so important, that, while much of the Bible is written to believers, over 150x in the New Testament, the only condition to receive the gift of salvation is faith/belief/trust alone. This is particularly true in the Gospel of John, which is the only book of the Bible that is written to bring unbelievers to salvation. (John 20:30-31)

Ironically, one day as I was close to finishing up the final rewrites of the first edition, I was thinking about my three favorite books in both the Old and New Testaments. And I realized that this book of mine, for the greater part, is a summation of six books. My favorite three books in the Old Testaments are: Genesis which starts the process of describing the greatness of God. The almighty one. The cause of everything. The Creator. Or, as He describes Himself: I Am who I AM. (While the actual descriptive term is first used in Exodus 3:14, the foundation for the concept starts in Genesis) By using this description of Himself, God is declaring His self-existence without another cause. Next would be the book of Proverbs. The divinely inspired wisdom, which teaches us how to live wisely. And then the book of Ecclesiastes. The folly of trying to live a purposeful life without a God focused understanding of life. The vanity of terrestrial life. In the New Testament: the Gospel of John. Christ is the one. The only source of salvation. The God/man who is the Savior of the world. The basis and foundation of giving freely: eternal life. The One who is the cornerstone of everything written about in the Bible. In the OT everything looked forward to Him. (Luke 24:13-27) In the Gospels: this is Him. The balance of the New Testament, explores the significance of Him. Next in my list would be 1st Corithians. The highlighting of the temporal, and some of the eternal consequences, that will be manifested in how we live out the faith. Where the Bema Seat of Christ is explored, and the ultimate accountability of our Christian lives is revealed. Then as the book 1st Corithians continues, the significance of the resurrection is detailed. In addition to these crucial teachings, the Apostle Paul, includes some warnings about the consequences of sin in the life of the believer. Exploring some of the repercussions of living contrary to the revealed will of God. And lastly, the book of Hebrews, which highlights the One who is greater than all. There is no one, nor any belief system, that compares to the majesty of the Lord and Savior. It is Him or no other. To draw back from Christ is to depart from the greatest person to have ever lived. To adhere to any other system of beliefs or religion, is meaningless in comparison. I believe if you are willing to stay with me, the journey will be worth the effort, as we explore the theology of these six books of the Bible.

Later, in additional reflection, as I was finishing my second edition, I realized it is not really limited to these six primary books. There are very significant theological truths from other books, like: Galatains, Ephesians, Philippians, 2nd Timothy and James, that are highly utilized too. This is because they forward the purpose of the book. James emphasizes putting one's faith into action. Galations stresses that we keep the absolute freeness of the gospel in the forefront of every gospel presentation. The books of Ephesians and Philippians give crucial theological truths. And 2nd Timothy adds key truths that need to be pondered and incorporated into the Christian's walk. Therefore, while the first six are used as the primary theology, all eleven, and a few more, are blended into prominence. These are some of the essential theological truths that I believe need to be revisited and brought back into the minds of modern day Christians.

As with most people, we write like our personality. In this case, you will see that I am drawing out far-reaching truths of the Chrstian faith, without getting into the weeds of minor details. Making the central points the main points. But emphasizing them repeatedly to establish them solidly in our minds. However, this is not really a book on how to, but why these truths are so indispensable for living a life that is eternally relevant. By exploring the implications of the Christian faith, we see more clearly those key themes that are inherent in what we believe; and why it is so eternally significant. Those resulting insights should motivate us to be authentic life changing believers. If you are unsure if you even want to read this book, may I suggest reading a few select chapters, such as chapters: 6, 10, 11, 20, 22, and 23, or some of my concluding thoughts. I believe if you read a few of these selective chapters, you will want to engage with the rest of the book; because, I believe the book grows in value as it develops those central themes. By starting at the beginning, you will get the logical flow of the thought process that resonates with the importance of this book.

DISCLAIMER OF ORIGINALITY

One of the aspects of writing a book is trying to give credit to those so deserving. No knowledge is gained in a vacuum. There have been many helpful theological influences that contributed to the themes of this book. I took the nuggets of truth from numerous sources and developed them into the points I wanted to make. The difficult issue with this book is that most of the foundational material comes from schools of theology. Where hundreds, even thousands, hold the same views, and have articulated those teachings. Therefore, giving credit to just one is most difficult, since these theological views are held by the vast majority of those who have studied at those schools.

So please forgive me if I have not properly given every credit where it is due. There is always a fear that one may have read or heard something, and not recall the origin of the idea, or the view is held by too many to isolate credit. I believe I have gathered a plethora of thoughts and insights, and have developed them into those points of emphasis, I want to share with the reader. You will see in my recommended reading section at the end of the book, the many sources that I have studied and drawn insight from, but there are countless more. These theological truths that I am communicating are widely held within those schools that teach Free Grace Salvation.

MY MISSION

Therefore, the intent of the book is to take those theological concepts, and then evaluate the significance of those truths. I then argue that there should be a more resolute response by Christians, because the Christian faith is true! That our faith is far more eternally significant than is being practiced by most Christians. That in light of the temporary nature of life, our focus needs to be more on the eternal. It is like the stages of a jury trial. My reasonings are like the final arguments of a trial. (Not that I am alleging my book is the final say on these matters, it just makes a good illustration) Like the facts gathered from a trial, which then are argued to show the relevance of the evidence: the arguments set forth in this book. I am endeavoring to communicate that the central truths contained in the Christian faith are the most crucial truths ever given to mankind. If the fundamentals of the faith are true, then it means....

MY PRAYER

Prayfully, this study will cause all readers to evaluate the significance of God's immutable and perfect holiness. For the unsaved, to grasp their dire condition before an immutable holy God, who must exact perfect justice to remain true to Himself. This with the hope they embrace the simple offer of God's redeeming love: in the sacrificial death of Jesus Christ. For the believer, to develop bold confidence, because they understand their secure salvation that is in Christ; they can have this confidence, because of the trustworthy promises of God. Which then results in moving forward in courageous faith. Living a victorious life that is eternally significant, because we are already victorious in Christ. For the church, the body of Christ, to highlight once again the reasons why we need to recapture the urgency for evangelism, and then growing discipleship, as our primary mission. And for both the individual believer and church, to grasp a deeper understanding of the implications of the faith, so often ignored, so that in a hundred years, long after we are gone from this world, our faith made a lasting difference. All this with the goal that we develop into mature, well grounded, and duplicating believers.

That in light of God's absolute immutable holiness, we are equipped with an accurate understanding of the gospel, so we are able to bring the lost to saving faith, then help disciple them into maturity. So please venture with me. While this is a bit of a long clumsy start, I believe if you continue on you will find what is written, very worthwhile. Some thoughts about the Christian faith that are worthy of serious pondering.

Note: I truly believe that this book would have been better written if I used editorial help. You will notice that the flow of thought is not those of a skilled writer. I thought long and hard about having someone, or a few more gifted writers polish up the readability of the book. I recognize that I am not a skilled writer, as you will see. You will likely find numerous grammatical errors. Nonetheless, since I wanted to own the content of what I have written, to be a book of my spiritual journey into these essential truths, I am submitting it as I wrote it. It is not a professionally written book, but a book from the heart. It is somewhat like the game of golf. There are times it is fun to play a scramble game of golf, where numerous people contributed, which leads to a better score; however, in this case, I am accepting my deficiencies contained in this book, because it is intended to be a book written from my heart, and not a collaboration.

CHAPTER 1

REASON FOR WRITING

————⟨⟨⟨⟩⟩⟩————

Why write a book about such a deep subject? It does not fit with today's mindsets. In prior days, the desire to know systematic theology was of greater interest. They pondered more meaty subjects, like the inherent nature of God. They read the Bible with a greater degree of diligence, to explore these truths; our times and society have changed. We are now the entertainment and television generation. We are experientially focused in our religious practice. We gravitate towards feeling good upon leaving a worship service. We desire practical preaching that helps with living in a fast paced and stressful world. The normative, and desired Christian experience, is the experience itself; how does being a practicer of the faith, benefit their lives, and give their lives meaning. Most Chrisitans are pursuing a faith experience that helps them manage their stressful daily lives. It helps keep them grounded. No need to get into the deeper waters of theology; since it is often very divisive, and therefore, generally avoided in most churches.

Consequently, I believe there is a deficiency within the body of Christ, when we fail to comprehend some of the deeper truths about God. I am contending that until we grasp the true significance of who God is in His very nature, His eternal essence, the practice of our faith will lack an emphasis on what is eternally significant. Thereby, resulting in omissions regarding the implications of our faith. When this is the mindset, we will see the faith more as spiritual self-help, than eternally redemptive. This is primarily due to our failure to grasp the enormous significance of the immutable holy nature of God. Perhaps, the most significant attribute of God; and this attribute is thoroughly elucidated throughout the scriptures. When this revelation is understood, those aspects of God's divine justice are far more understandable. Moreover, it reveals the reason for the dispensing of His justice, that satisfies His inherent righteousness, and relates to both time and eternity. This insight is intertwined with His natural desire to express His loving kindness to us, the undeserving. Both of these truths coexist in God's nature, and neither can be compromised: either His absolute immutable holiness or His endless loving kindness.

Much of what I am writing is part of my personal journey. For many years I grappled with these aspects of the Christian faith. Finding assurance I was truly, and permanently saved, was always in the forefront of my thinking. I also struggled with the idea of Hell. I often wondered how we Christians could believe in an eternal Hell? That belief was always perplexing for me. I found myself struggling with these and other aspects of my faith. Even to the point that I had considered just abandoning the faith. I was frustrated trying to reconcile these aspects of my faith, feeling like my efforts to satisfactorily resolve these issues, were leading to an unsolvable conclusion, at least early on in my journey.

Over time, I gained insights that I believe provided a reasonable answer to my spiritual quest. I have not mastered them as a scholarly theologian, as I am self-taught. In that, I did not obtain an advanced degree in systematic theology; although, I do believe that after many years of diligent study, using many valuable resources, has helped tremendously. In a sense, I would consider myself as old school trained by Dallas Theological Seminary, even though I never took a single class there. I have gravitated towards those who were educated and/or taught there. It is not limited to DTS, since those educated at other schools, holding the same essential theology, were also intensely studied. This long and diligent pursuit of theological understanding helped equip me with a solid Biblical foundation for which to think through these difficulties. It was an extensive step by step process, and it continues....

The crucial beginning of my journey necessitated coming to a confident belief that the Christian faith was based on solid evidence. Included in this process was an assessment of some of the other faith traditions. Did they offer any solid evidence to substantiate their beliefs? From the beginning of my faith journey, I did not want to blindly assume my faith was true, without first probing into other faith traditions. Once reasonably satisfied that Christianity was based on solid evidence, this journey continued in the process of better learning what the Bible taught. (I was Biblically illiterate in those days) Often this process was simultaneously being pursued. This process continued as I studied various sources of Christian theology and apologetics. I also became an avid Bible reader; reading the Bible over and over. (It is hard to be Biblically literate if we do not actually read the Bible) This was all part of the process of learning essential theological truths. Those truths contained in the scriptures, once better understood, allowed me to think through some of these difficult questions. This led ultimately to my pondering the logical implications of Christianity. What does it mean, if what we profess to believe is really true? This is the major focus of this book: who is God in His very essence, what has He revealed, and why does that matter?

Let me make some acknowledgments before going deep into my presentation. First, this is not a book on the evidence for God's existence, or the apologetics for the Christian faith. Truth be told, there are far more capable authors that should be read on those subjects. (Some of those resources that are included in the recommended reading section)

Secondly, I am taking the Bible as the authority for my contentions and reasonings. I am asking you to assume these two truths for the purpose of what I am presenting in this book. First, there is a God, and secondly, he has spoken to us throughout the pages of the Bible. I acknowledge that if either of those two convictions are flawed, then everything I write is pointless. To be sure, the second assumption is dependent on the first. Should you personally wrestle with either of those two subjects? Then please take advantage of some of the suggested books and resources. (As noted, they are found at the end of the book, and are broken down in pertinent categories) A study of those resources will affirm that I am on solid ground to assume both of these for the purpose of this book. There are other topics that I will not pursue. As an example, there is the study of epistemology; which is the study of the means of arriving at truth. How do we come to believe, what we believe, is reliably true? This too is often included in the study of apologetics. As noted, these shall be left for more scholarly authors to explain. I am simply a lay Christian writing a book.

When referencing scriptural principles, I intend on giving my general summation of the Biblical concept, rather than an exegetical breakdown, or direct quotes. I am trying to make simple logical deductions of what the Bible teaches. Always asking: since the essential truths of the Bible are true, what are the implications? What does it mean, because it is true? As you will see, I follow the model of Jesus, and ask questions to illicit thoughts. As we progress, those truths are illuminated, as we apprehend the nature of God. What I have learned over the course of many years of study, I hope and pray, can be of value for your walk with our Lord; and a renewed motivation to live a Christian life that is honoring our Lord. With this insight, we would leave behind the overemphasis of some of our trivial temporal pursuits, and exchange them for those that are more eternally worthy. By gaining deeper insights into these truths, we would find the greater reason for living an eternally meaningful life; one that results in leaving an eternally relevant legacy.

With this background, let's focus on this journey into truths that are foundational for what we need to believe about God, and understand why it matters. You will see recurring themes that emphasize God's holiness, God's love, mankind's sinfulness, the master plan of God's redeeming love, and the resulting consequences of how we live out our faith. I hope to show that the implications of those truths are far more eternally significant than is appreciated by most Christians.

I plan on taking these chapters in a progressive and logical order of thought. The building of one truth, that leads to the logic of the next, to arrive at some conclusions; giving us a better perception of the intended Christian journey. Therefore, there are ideas woven throughout the book that should cause both the unbeliever, and the believer, to wrestle with the connotations of the Christian faith. While it is assumed that Christianity is true for the purposes of this book, I want to walk through the thought process as though you are evaluating the significance of the Christian faith for the first time, but not in a traditional apologetics manner. The desire is to look at the Christian faith afresh; so as, to see the actual implications of being true. I believe by the time you get to the end of my book, you will find some of my conclusions hard to embrace, but unavoidably true, if you accept the Christian faith as fundamentally true. With these additional introductory thoughts, let's start the journey in its logical order.

CHAPTER 2

THE JOURNEY

W ith this introduction, let's step back and start this thought process in its logical order, at least as I experienced this journey of mine. I think this is valuable since many will identify with this spiritual journey of mine. It all started with an epiphany of sorts. I remember one day, many years ago, I was pondering the Christian faith. I am sure it was more of a process, but one day in particular stands out to me. I was sitting in church on a normal Sunday morning and found myself thinking about the significance of the Christian faith. This thought is not the most profound thought ever to have passed through the mind of mankind. It was simply: what if Christianity is not even true? A simple deductive thought. Most of us have entertained that thought. This question could apply to either Christianity, or any religious belief. I suspect we all question our beliefs at times. It may even be good to question our faith. Since the process should lead to a stronger confidence in our faith, or reveal to us that what we are believing is not credible. Fortunately, for the Christian, this evaluation will reveal that there is strong and compelling evidence to substantiate Christian faith. In that case, the process can be very helpful. (Obviously, if Christianity is substantiated, then there is a need to know who this God is) In my situation, on that morning, I was asking myself if it was really worth my time spending my Sunday mornings in Church? I was very young in the faith. Actually, I am quite sure I was not yet a born again Christian. I knew some things about God and the teachings of the faith, but did not really understand the connotations of God's holiness, or provisions of the cross. I was culturally a Christian, but questioning the basis of the faith. In my mind, I was unsure if "my Christian faith" was even substantially true. I was mentally wrestling with the implications of being actually true, or simply a religious tradition. This thought, on that Sunday morning, generated a series of thoughts that led me on this journey.

I was mindful that there were numerous religious traditions. I was questioning why I practiced the Christian faith? Since it is true that most religious traditions are passed on within a culture. That is why certain religious traditions are grouped in particular societies or countries. (Even in the early formation of our country, most states were defined by their particular Christian identity) I was wondering whether my personal faith tradition was believed, simply because I was raised in the USA? It is unlikely I would practice the Christian faith, if I was born and raised in another county, one that held to another faith tradition. I realized that what I was taught to believe could be nothing more than our commonly held beliefs, because of our country's origin. Those beliefs passed on by our founding ancestors.

Furthermore, I was not seeing much substance or evidence, to convince me that there was much significance to the faith. It appeared to be a practice that encouraged people to be better people. A tradition of values that gave stability to our society. Religious beliefs that are part of our identity, but its true significance seemed to evade me. And, when measured in light of eternity, it did not match what I was seeing. My primary thought was: if our faith was fundamentally true, the alleged significance of the faith was not being manifested in most of the personal lives of those I was sharing this worship experience with, or in the priorities of the churches. My impression was: we were practicing in the shadows of the authentic Christian faith; we lacked an apprehension of the real implications of what we professed to believe.

These questions forced me to ask myself: what evidence did I have that Christianity was even true? What is the significance of believing in the Christian God? This led to a tremendous desire to explore the validity of the Christian faith. I needed to know if it was based on any solid evidence. For without the confidence that my faith is built on verifiable evidence, why practice the faith? I was questioning why I was even sitting in church? Why live a manner of life that does not always enhance my personal comforts or desired pleasures? Actually, I could surmise that "my faith" of that day did little more than make me feel guilty, so I would try to be a better person, and maybe, a bit more compassionate and kind, but other than that?

I was mindful that it was a fruitless endeavor to adhere to the principles of the Christian faith, if there is no credible evidence to suggest that it is even true. (At least from the perspective I held on that day) While I acknowledge that there are many good secondary benefits for our society. Maybe even some good self-restraining disciplines that provide stability for me individually, and protect me from those foolish decisions I was inclined to make. Those self-restraining inherent qualities of morality that emanate from Christian teachings, but no apparent vital benefits, unless the essentials of the faith were verifiably true. Then, in that case, the faith was of immeasurable value. These questions were part of the soul searching, and spiritual journey, I was grappling with early on in my quest of authentic faith.

So for over the last 35 years, I have studied and pursued this knowledge, in order to confirm the truthfulness of the Christian faith; and then to understand the implications of being true. I certainly am not an expert, but the end results of that pursuit has led me to believe what I was taught to believe, is in fact true; although, not as I was originally taught. And with this growing confidence that the essence of Christianity was true, caused me to see that these truths are eternally significant. I discerned from the onset of this journey that if Christianity is genuinely true, and it is, it is not being given the proper weight, either in the private lives of believers, or in the practice of the average local church. We are only living in a shadow of its reality. But I am getting ahead of the logical thought process.

It is fruitless to start a topic of this nature without first establishing some significance of God's existence. It is the foremost question of all time. The answer to that question magnifies everything. It either affirms that we have preeminent value as created humans, or it diminishes the very significance for our existence. Should the question of God's existence be affirmed? Then that being true: our lives have an intended meaning. It would affirm that we, as the central part of God's creation, must be paramount to God, since there is no other life form that is created in the image of God. And that would mean our existence is consequential. Furthermore, it would give hope for life beyond the present, since the message of the Bible is true, and trustworthy. Then, to that extension, there is assured eternal hope. For in the Christian Gospel, there is the assurance of eternal salvation, as I will explain as we proceed through the book.

The alternative is also true: a denial of God is ultimately an abandonment of real meaning. It is hard to argue we are significant in this universe, if we are only a link in the chain of biological evolution. I conjecture that one could pursue pleasure or power or fame in an effort to have fleeting meaning. There are many who do so. They are endeavoring to achieve a particular recognition in their community to find perceived significance. Those achievements could be in fashion or sports or financial success, or one of many other pursuits that lead to a desired community status. Only to realize in the waning years of life that those pursuits were hollow. I suspect we all do so to a degree. We often look for the affirmations of our fellow man to give our lives perceived meaning, by achieving some level of desired social standing. For too many, they will sacrifice what is truly meaningful, in order to achieve some community status.

But therein lies the conundrum of trying to live a meaningful life in a purposeless world. Many, at great personal cost, sacrificed a great portion of their lives, in order to achieve their personal quests, only to find it was ultimately unfulfilling. They are left with the realization that those achievements were often frivolous pursuits. The end result of these terrestrial pursuits is one is left with an awareness of the insignificance of what was pursued and accomplished. Think of winning the World Series in baseball. To some, a grand personal achievement, a goal of a lifetime. To others: so what. Most are indifferent to what some may feel was a grand personal accomplishment. In 20 years, the so what, is magnified. Few remember what you accomplished anyways. Those achievements are now, or will be, lost in the history of time. No matter how beautiful or successful or accomplished one is in sports, those moments of celebration are transitory and short-lived. We will naturally age. We will lose our beauty, or physical abilities, only to be replaced by a new younger generation. Those who then chase their terrestrial dreams, only to be later forgotten. This is a significant part of the theme of the book of Ecclesiastes in the Old Testament: the vanity of it all without God. This is the problem of existential living, for those who do not share our faith, or even a belief in God; ultimately, the achieved goal is meaningless, in light of eternity.

Therefore, the obvious conclusion is, that living a life in a surmised Godless universe, undermines any foundation for values, purposeful living, and disavows any hope beyond the grave. If we come to this conclusion? It results in an obvious sense of existential meaninglessness. Hopelessness! A vaper in our time of history is all we are. They are pursuits that lead to nullity. Meaning: a pursuit of no worth. In light of eternity, the existential questions one is forced to ask: What was it all about? What was all for?

This is particularly the reason why this topic needs to be considered carefully. Everything meaningful in life is dependent on the answer to the God question. To take the thought a step further: it is also dependent on the personality of God. Because who God is in His essence is absolutely crucial. Is He inept and/or distant? Is He knowable? Does He care about me or my situation? Is He a good God? Does He care about justice? Does He love me? Does He offer any real hope for our lives beyond the grave? These questions could continue. How these are answered will reveal what we believe regarding who God is. And how they are answered is dependent on who God is in His very essence. For us who are Christians, it will also permeate the practicalities of our Christian faith. If we understand God to be less than holy or loving or faithful or trustworthy or able, then there is no confidence to be had. His dependable nature is an absolute must if we are going to have confidence in what we believe. Because our faith in God is only valid if we have a trustworthy God. That is: He will always be true to who He has revealed Himself to be.

Furthermore, the rediscovery of those priorities are essential to our time in history, due to the rapid moral decline. It is clear that many Christians and churches have abandoned the basic teachings of Biblical truths. They are habitually foreign to most of the present day Christian's mindsets. Whereas, while the truthfulness of the Christian faith has been strongly established, it is not being grounded in our daily priorities, or held with actual real significance. And this awareness is essential to what I am trying to expounding upon. Since the arguments for what I am writing about are based on the truthfulness of Christianity, therefore, the inclusion of the study of apologetics is absolutely necessary, if there are doubts about the validity of one's faith. Even if you are not struggling with the truthfulness of the Christian faith, it may be for someone with whom you want to share your faith. Therefore, we need to be prepared with solid reasons for why we believe what we profess to believe.

However, as noted, traditional apologetics is not my focus. Once we come to the satisfying conclusion that Christianity is true, we need to move on into the implications of that truth. Therefore, we need to know the truth, then recognize that this truth is far more significant than is being portrayed by the body of Christ. We are living in the shadows of the faith.

Once we have come to reasonable assurance that our faith is strongly attested to by good evidence, we need to move to the next step: so what? This is the natural progression. It is the natural development of the next steps in the process: learning who is this God? Who is God in His essence? And then why does it matter? Let's return to the origin of this journey.

It was also during this long process, that I found myself struggling with the priorities in our churches. I was trying to grasp the insignificance of what was often being practiced. I was mentally processing how much of the present day preaching measures up in light of what the Bible teaches, the ultimate priority: one's eternal destination. This path returned to some of the difficult to understand, traditional orthodox teachings of Biblical truth, which led back to my struggle with the concept of Hell. A circular process of which I had little understanding how this could all be reconciled. It did not seem sensible to the human mind. How could Christians hold onto a doctrine that is so unconscionable. It was hard to accept how this could actually be true, at least in the beginning of this journey. (I will continue to wrestle with this notion throughout the book)

Some concluding thoughts on this chapter. All of this was dependent on knowing God's nature. This understanding is necessary to understand traditional doctrines of the faith. Those teachings that have lost their appeal to the modern-day Christians. The doctrines of the faith, which seem so unattainable in our thinking, which then are ignored or abandoned. Those aspects of the faith that answer the big questions in life: How do we qualify for heaven? Is there an eternal Hell? Will there be real justice? Does it really matter how I live? Are there consequences for the Christian too? And, can we have absolute assurance of personal salvation? To be sure: these were the big ones. To find satisfactory answers necessitates a knowledge of God Himself. And like any valuable relationship in our lives, knowing intimately the person is crucial. Because we can only have real confidence, if the person we are trusting has an dependable character; if we want to trust the person with our lives and future, this is an absolute. This is why the study into the nature of God is pivotal, especially for the Christian. The better we know our trustworthy Heavenly Father, the better we can cope with the difficulties of this life; and have the assurance that our devotion is a reasonable act of service. The confidence, that sacrifice of community status, and/or our personal comforts, in order to make the gospel message known, has the greatest urgency. In a world of many conflicting voices, it is crystal clear that knowing the truth is more important than ever. The time we invest in coming to know God personally, is a worthy pursuit. These struggles were part of my journey of faith, and it all started many years ago, with the simple question: is it even true?

CHAPTER 3

THE ULTIMATE REALITY

———✦———

Let's come to grips with an inescapable truth: we all will die one dayI This is an absolute certainty. It is the most undeniable of all truths. Some truths are so obvious -they are not worth arguing about. I know I am alive is an example. Some have alleged that our lives are just a mental illusion, this does not need to be refuted; we sober minded people know we are alive and real. So is the sobering fact that our physical lives, when measured in light of eternity, are just a mist. This is also a Biblical truth. (James 4:14) Regardless of what we do or accomplish, it is temporary. I have never met a 200 year old man. This reality of the brevity of life is also reinforced by a simple trip past a cemetery. There, as represented by the tombstones, is the reminder that there is an inescapable limitation to our lives.

I have visited cemeteries back East on historical trips, and locally, viewing the graves of those long lost. I have stood at the graves of loved ones and pondered life. Its brevity. In many of those cemeteries back East are buried some very historical people. Those we read about in our history books. I have contemplated what life was like for them. Realizing that their lives were more than just history, they were just as real as I am now. Undoubtedly, one day I will be joining them, I hope not too soon. In contemplating their lives, I wonder about how they live. The time in history in which they lived. Did they die for a cause like our freedom? Were they fortunate to enjoy the many blessings life can bring? Did they unjustly suffer? Did their lives include a lot of physical or emotional pain? Did their life have an immensely positive impact on those who knew and loved them? Or, did they waste their lives in pursuit of trivial, and often meaningless activities? Were they overtaken by the many vices of life? Did they invest their lives in meaningful learning, so as to impart lasting lessons of wisdom? The ponderings could continue. What is absolutely clear: we will all have a destiny with death.

It is also clear by reading the tombstones that many lived very short lives. They never lived long enough to have a family, or experience the precious love of family. Way too many children are buried there. Some gave their lives so we could have this freedom to write books expressing our faith. The speculations could continue. One thing is absolutely true: cemeteries are a sober reminder that life is temporary. Maybe something we all need to pause and reconsider, since it is in our future. Sometimes we need a little reflection to put life back into perspective, because while death is a natural part of life, it is so earthly final.

I remember a few years ago when I was approaching 60 years of age, it really struck me that this journey of my life was starting to wind down. Let's say for illustration purposes: I have a hopeful lifespan of 80 to 90 years. Should that be the case, then I was somewhere between 3/4 to 2/3 over with my life, and even that is not guaranteed. Not only is that true, but the normal trajectory of life usually results in declining health. Those times when we are forced to say goodbye to good friends and family. And to compound my reality with aging, I had read an article in Reader's Digest many years ago, that suggested that the best years of life were our fifties. If that was true? Then upon turning 60, this meant that the best years of my life were behind me. In my reflections, I was realizing that there were desired goals that I would never achieve. As most men who enjoy sports, it was clear that I would never achieve greatness on the field or court. I still take pleasure in beating my buddy Bob in golf, but most dreams of athletic greatness were going to be adolescent dreams that would never be satisfied.

Even as a parent, I understood that chapters of my life had passed, and would never be recaptured. I remember when our last child was leaving for college. (Our daughters had already ventured out) I knew a change was occurring, and our lives would never be the same. I sat in the backyard while my wife took our son to pick up some last minute supplies for college. (He was leaving the next day) I did not have a few tears: I sobbed. A tough realization that the day to day aspects of being a parent with children in the home had come to an end. A realization that there would be no more new experiences of them growing up at home. It was now forever changing. A chapter of my life had ended. The friends of our children being in our home. The sporting events. The vacations we took as a family. The apple orchards. The meals and homework that are a normal part of most of our lives. It was a very abdicating feeling, the letting go of my central role as a dad. I cherished being a dad with our children in the home. I would continue being a dad, but it would never be the same. I remember feeling those chapters of my life had passed too quickly. But also a reinforcing reminder to me, that everything in life had an ending point; the good ones, and those we would just as soon forget.

As I pause and evaluate my life to that point in time, depending on my focus, I could surmise that my life was reasonably successful, but too often, underwhelming. As with most lives, it was a mixture of both. I had moments that brought great joy and personal satisfaction. There are achievements that I can be proud of. There also were many choices, or actions, that left memories of regrets and remorse, those I wish to put behind me. Truth be told, all in all, life has been relatively good for me. I come from a good solid family. We had our normal family struggles. There were some hardships that I wished I did not have to traverse. But compared to the majority of people, I have lived a relatively good life. My wife and I have three adult children. All three turned out establishing successful professional, and for the most part, meaningful personal lives. We are blessed with a number of grandchildren. (Hopefully that number will continue to grow) We are fortunate that our children started having their children early, this is enabling us to enjoy quality time with them. The time to experience the joys of watching them traverse through their journey of life. Our grandchildren are fortunate that they have loving, devoted, and caring parents. But that does not surprise me, since their mother modeled that well for them. She is a good person and easy to be married to, for which I am very thankful.

But I have regressed. This is not about me, it is the reflection on life, for whatever it brings, it is temporary and fleeting. The inescapable fact is that life is temporary, and often contains more regrets and hardships than we had hoped, but certainly short in light of eternity! In a hundred years it will be doubtful if there will remain any significant memory of my life. Other than a tombstone! It was becoming clearer to me that nothing will outlast me: other than the faith and values that I passed on, and lives eternally changed by my sharing of the gospel. (These principles will be developed as we progress through the book) (If you want to do a fascinating study. Do some research on the influence of Jonathan Edwards. The profound impact his life had. What legacy are you leaving?)

Recognizing the reality of this truth, should cause everyone to reflect, as I have been doing. It is clear that we all will one day experience death. We will step into the world of eternity. There is no stopping its inevitable conclusion. We are all going to die one day. When it comes to the end of life, you can hold on with both hands, you can fight it, but the truth of the matter -it is going to come. For me, it was becoming clearer day by day that this life is starting to pass by, and I cannot stop the progression. Like most, I wish I could start over with what I have learned over the course of these years. There would be some choices that I would have avoided; nonetheless, life is a one way street, birth to death. As the shadows of my life slowly start to fade, I realize my time here on earth is not going to last in perpetuity.

The natural question is to ask: is there any rationale for real hope? Is there any reason to hold on to confidence that all our struggles and effort to make life meaningful, were not a fruitless effort? A mist that quickly passed with no ultimate purpose or reason. Is a destiny with the cemetery all we have to look forward to? So the obvious conclusion is that death is in my future, and sad to say, yours too! Regardless of how old you are, you will come to realize this journey is not going to last forever. We can deny it. We can ignore it. But it will come in its time. The inevitable truth - for everyone's life- is that it is temporary!

It has been estimated that approximately 150,000 die everyday on this earth. Someday, I will be one of them, someday, you will too! A very sobering reality.

This should lead everyone who is not sure of their eternal destination, to consider the most terrifying question: what then? Are you sure? For those of us who are believers, and have the hope of the resurrection, a chance to reflect and make sure we are living eternally fruitful lives.

It is not just a God question, but who is God, and what has He revealed that gives us this hope? This is the journey we are taking in this book. Let's continue to establish some spiritual principles that will give this book a deeper meaning. I will show that all real truth must be grounded in the immutable character of God.

CHAPTER 4

AN ILLUSTRATION TO DEMONSTRATE UNIVERSAL MORALS AND UNINTENDED CONSEQUENCES OF LEAVING BIBLICAL TRUTH

―――――⬥⬥⬥―――――

With these introductory thoughts and reflections, I want to continue to lay the foundation for the book. I hope to show in chapter four of this book, using an illustration, that *some* morals are generally agreed upon by the majority of society. That life needs to be lived in a moral universe. Even most atheists will acknowledge that they adhere to *some* standards in their lives, even if they do not hold to a Christian worldview. Even if one does not ascribe to the authority of the Bible, people have traditionally practiced many of those values that emanate from the Bible. For example, we can see even most atheists honor the bonds of marriage, a union established by God Himself. We also would agree that hurting a child for pure pleasure is wrong. The question in this chapter is the basis of our moral standards? Whose or what values are determinative? And, what does this mean for unbelievers and/or Christians? We all hold to *some* moral values, but whose, and why?

I think you will find this forthcoming marital illustration rather absurd, but it does drive home some points that I want to make. Therefore, there are a few purposes for the illustration. One is to show that as a society we generally need commonly held community values. This is necessary or we would find life intolerable. Can you imagine for a moment living in a society having no standards? One where everyone individually determines what is right or wrong. Look at the societies that lost that moral foundation, the chaos that ensued.

Ordinarily, we live out these values without really thinking through their societal merit. We naturally adapt to those community standards to remain socially acceptable. In general, these community values are usually a benefit to society. They provide for the flourishing of society. Like the strengthening of the family via the belief in the sanctity of marriage for one, and the natural protection of children is another. Even if one does not personally subscribe to the Bible as their moral authority, those Christians values did provide moral unity, and are a benefit to all of us. As an example: Our Christian heritage, that was held by the majority of our country's early founders, provided the undergirded foundation for the development of our country's strong moral leadership in the world, and our own prosperity. It was our Christian heritage, that was the impetus for the good we infused around the world. We were the great missionary sending country. (See the website: Wallbuilders, for historical evidence for these statements) Sadly, we are now the number one exporter of porn. There is a necessary moral foundation that instills virtuous living, so individuals behave with self-restraint, and allows for the safe enjoyment of life we all want. It also provides for the virtuous and healthy communities that thwarts the moral decay we are seeing. And as we progress in the book, we will see those desired values need to be anchored in a foundation that is always true, that is, the eternal attributes of God. These concepts will be developed as we progress in the upcoming chapters.

Consequently, there are unintended consequences when society slowly evolves away from the Biblically based, and moral foundational principles, that make a nation strong. When we leave this foundational highground, and we deviate from those Christian norms, we find that we have diminished our quality of life. When this is the progression: we see crime increase, families become unstable, substance abuse increase, mental health decline, and so forth. The progression of this trend is devastating to society. We need the foundation that is established by an objective standard. This is not achievable in a morally subjective society, where each member determines what is right or wrong; as I will pontificate on as we continue.

In this forthcoming illustration we will see twin truths. First, as has been noted, there is a need to live in a moral universe. I know it is not acceptable to walk down a street naked, even though it does not physically hurt anyone. And secondly, it will clarify the reason why we need to understand God's immutable nature, so our morals are anchored to some standard that is always true. This will become obvious, since God has conveyed standards that emulate out of His nature. The clear inference is that God's nature should set the standard that forms our morality. And be reflected as the standard for our moral conduct as a society. That is why God the Holy Spirit guided the writers of the scriptures to reveal His immutable perfect nature; so we can have our feet firmly planted on an everlasting foundation of truth. This standard of truth is needed to set forth a firm cornerstone for daily living; and as a determinative standard, for evaluating what is required to have a relationship with God. (Showing our need for salvation)

The alternative: we are left with our feet planted in midair, where all moral choices are formed by our own inherently sinful personal preferences. For those not holding to values based on the intrinsic nature of God, we will see that the forthcoming illustration is both logical and acceptable. Since in this view there are no transcendent values that define behavioral choices as either moral or immoral. It is up to each person to determine their own standards of morality.

Furthermore, we will see as we continue on in the book, there are consequences when there are violations of those standards: both in time and in eternity. If we properly understand God's nature, we will see why God has prescribed, and described them for us; they are for our good, and God's glory. (See Deuteronomy 10:13) These revelations will also show the unbeliever why they need a Savior, since they will see their inability to measure up to God's standards, which will highlight their need.

Lastly, should we as Christians practice the faith as intended, it will reflect God's nature in His born again children; so we as His children, manifest a bit of the nature of our Heavenly Father, to a watching world. (Hebrews 12:12) It is the practice and not just the beliefs that manifest this value to society. (See the book of James) It is very apparent that our moral foundations are crumbling, and this is being revealed in the brokenness of our society. We were once the hub of Christian truth. The great missionary country that sent out men and women to share the hope of the gospel and promote those Christian principles. We are now the hub of porngraphy, something has changed. This introduction for the illustration was a bit of a long winded, but necessary to set the stage for my illustration. Let's now contemplate the moral implications of what we believe with my illustration.

Let's say a man has a wife he truly loves, therefore, he desires her happiness. She comes home one day and confesses she is infatuated with another man she knows from work. The husband, desiring her happiness, gives his consent for her to have a weekly sexual encounter with this co-worker. So, once a week, she and her co-worker meet for a sexual tryst. At the end of that day she returns home and freshens up for dinner. They share a cup of coffee or a glass of wine, and discuss their day. They enjoy some companionship and a meal together. Later that night the two of them share a normal spousal relationship. The husband experiences a satisfying sexual experience. It could be even argued that his sexual experience is enhanced because she brings new experiences to their bedroom. They both experience an unfettered and more expressive sex life. Their daily lives go on as normal.

It can be logically argued that the husband has not been harmed. His sexual experience had been enhanced. He has lost nothing financially. He still has the companionship of his wife. They share quality time together at the end of the day. He was not physically harmed, nor personally deceived, since he willingly granted his permission. Even if it was argued he was harmed, how is it determined? There is no basis of morality to claim he has been cheated of his marital benefits, since in this perspective, there are no objective divine standards in which to assert a marriage is a uniquely sacred union. It is simply a relationship agreement both find acceptable. They enjoy the benefits of the relationship, without the normal exclusive sexual standards found in traditional marriages. It is like the friends with benefits concept. In this illustration, there is nothing that makes this relationship arrangement immoral –if there is no holy God! This is the logical and deductive reasonings that flow out of this thinking. By denying the divinely revealed moral standards, inherent in God's immutable holy nature, we deny any objective moral standard. This is what our society is presently doing, by removing the anchor of our moral foundations, which is God Himself. Thereby, claiming almost all expressions of sexuality are now acceptable, but are they?

However, should we affirm the reality of God and His inherent nature, then the relationship agreement is absurd! He has spoken. And He has clearly revealed His desire and purpose for marriage. This is the Christian understanding of God; an understanding of His design for traditional marriage. Therefore, we can see the incongruous marriage arrangement portrayed in the illustration. This is why this absurd illustration draws out the issue. It conveys whether marriage is sacred and has God given purpose, or subject to being redefined by society. It even determines what constitutes a marriage. That is why these progressive steps need to be thought through. Let's think through these progressive steps; it helps determine if there is a foundation for morality: 1. Is there a God? 2. Has He revealed His nature? 3. Has He spoken in a particular book, or revelatory way? 4. Why has He revealed these instructions? 5. What has He revealed about how we are to live? 6. What are the revealed consequences for how we respond to these teachings? 7. What are the revealed eternal consequences? 8. Is there a remedy if we fall short of these revelations? This is why understanding the intrinsic nature of God is so essential, even for everyday life.

This is not just some theological or philosophical argument; it has very practical real life ramifications too. What we morally infer about this illustration promulgates the basis of our values. It discloses whether we hold to divinely revealed values, or accept the subjective and ever changing values of culture. What we hold as the true foundation for our morals, will determine our view of marriage: whether it is sacred or subject to be redefined. It determines the cornerstone for all our morality. Let's continue looking at the logical implications of the illustration; the evolving negative consequences of deviating from God's standards.

We can see these changes in our society as illustrated through progressive mental pictures. A few years ago my wife and I were dog and cat sitting for our son and his wife. One evening we went downtown for some ice cream. There in the parlor was a picture, of what I surmised to be the opening of the original ice cream parlor, an old black and white picture. What particularly caught my interest -all the men had dress jackets on and every woman wore a dress. I remember appraising the time and culture of when the picture was taken. Jump forward mentally in time and recall the television show: *I Love Lucy*. A period that was likely somewhat close to the taking of this picture. If you recall seeing the bedroom? Remember, they were a married couple and had a son. What is striking is that the bedroom scene contained two separate beds. It was not appropriate to show a single bed even though they were married. It was reported that it was even unacceptable in those days to mention that she was pregnant on the show, even though they were married. Jump forward to many of the popular shows we now watch. The casualness of sexual relationships of those who are unmarried; and how normal we now accept that as the community standard. Jump forward again, and think of the impact of the internet age. The disturbing statistics on pornography viewing, even among Christians, and sadly, pastors. What has happened to us and our country? How did we drift so low in such a short time? To the point we hold few things as sacred anymore. This is *part* of the journey of this book. Regardless whether you are a Christian or not, it is clear something has gone astray. We are abandoning our trustworthy anchor, which results in losing our moral bearings.

Others, who do not hold our Christian values, will ask if our drift is really an issue. They will often assert that the problem is those restrictive traditional Christian beliefs. Some will even argue that we as a society are making progress by freeing ourselves from outdated beliefs. A freeing of our sexual expressions. This new perspective allows individuals to act as they please, without the unnecessary guilt that society has historically imposed on those who so acted; those who failed to live according to the expectations of the Christian faith. But these changing alleged benefits are not affirmed by any reasonable assessment of our crumbling society. The evidence is clear: crime is skyrocketing, divorce rates have grown exponentially over the last hundred years, more and more children are born out of wedlock, drug abuse is rampant, and there is an overall decline of our mental health, just to name a few. Furthermore, our children are struggling as never before with declining academic proficiency, and socially, because of the brokenness of their world. Their very innocence is being stolen by this progressive thinking. This decline is being accelerated, in part, by the promotion of very sexually expressive material to many of our children. It is even being promoted as a necessary component of education in some schools across the country; regardless of their parents' feelings on the matter. These descriptive examples are the byproduct of the removal of the inherent, self-restraining, character building morality, contained in our Christian heritage. Let's return to the main purpose of the illustration: the need for anchoring truth.

Regardless of the growing acceptance of our changing society, God has not changed. He is who He is: He cannot change. We have a moral conscience that is either formed by secular society, or is based on Biblical revelations. We swim with one or are anchored to the other. One is a sure foundation. The other leads to the devaluing of everything we previously esteemed. The end result of this decline: life itself eventually becomes so devalued, that very little is revered.

The stripping of our anchor from our long-held Biblical foundation has profound consequences. It is the loss of our moral glue that once gave society stability. This forsaking of Biblical morality, that formerly built our conscience, is being sheared from our former virtuous foundation. This is being pushed upon us by the media, educational systems, entertainment industry, and even our government; and results in a crumbling culture. This promotion of freedom apart from our righteous moral foundations, by the Godless secular left, is not producing the real freedom promised. The redefining truth to avoid guilt does not resolve the feelings of guilt, it only suppresses it. It only gives them the freedom to act with fewer inhibitions of their unrestrained carnal nature. (Romans chapter 1) The obvious solution is a return to the faithful practice of the Christian faith. The life renewing hope of the Gospel. (As explored in the upcoming chapters) A true righteous foundation our country needs; the resetting of our lives, according to the revealed truth in God's word.

Therefore, the question of which philosophy of life we should live according to, is all dependent on whether there are immutable truths. As the drift from objective truth continues, and Biblical truth is removed as the foundation for our society, and our personal lives, we see the organic consequences. The very fabric of our personal, and societal life, becomes unraveled. Even a superficial observation of our society makes this clear. So does the changing from dresses to pornography highlight how rapid we have transgressed the moral landscape. Where the previous Speaker of the United States Representatives proposed some rules in the House, where personal pronouns could not be used, because it may be deemed offensive to those who do not hold to traditional Biblical morality; and we casually accept it without too much pushback. Regardless of this evolving movement, I treasure being a son, a husband, a dad and a brother; I am not adopting those emerging perspectives simply because that is the drift of our current culture. God only created males and females. (Genesis chapter one) The idea that biological sex can be chosen, is just nonsensical. The science is absolutely clear: no one can change their X or Y. One may alter their body, but they can not change their DNA. I feel compassion for those who are confused about this reality; they are deceptively being led by the spirit of this age. It is as the person who observed, we are becoming a people whose feet firmly planted in midair, anchored to nothing. (My paraphrase) When this becomes acceptable, everything is permissible.

We could make the argument that the ethical nature of this relationship, as portrayed in this illustration, could be rationally defended. The determinative factor is whether God has spoken; if so, what has He revealed? Since if there is no God, then this lifestyle could be seen as a desirable option for some couples. They could argue that they have only added to their pleasures and lost nothing. But if God: then the whole discussion changes. This is why this illustration needs to be thought through; that is why I am exploring the implication of who God is, and what He has revealed about how we are to live our lives. There is a growing movement away from our classic understanding of who God is, and that has huge ramifications. Those revealed truths about God, which should determine my values and code of conduct, are dependent on whether He has spoken. He has and that has eternal implications. We are responsible even if we deny His authority and instructions.

I hope to show in the pages of this book that there are consequences for violations of God's decrees: both temporal and eternal. While different, there are inherent consequences for both the Christian and nonbeliever. There are implications of those revealed truths that determine our eternal destiny, those that we need to incorporate into society as our universal moral standard, and those we are personally responsible for in our own lives.

So let's explore in more detail why we need to examine the revelation of God, understand what He has said, believe it, and then put it into practice. In the pages of this book we will continue to explore aspects of God's nature, and those implications. Not only the practical aspects in this life, but by far, the eternal. You will notice that many of my thoughts are reiterated repeatedly, that is intentional. The purpose is to implant these truths solidly in our minds, so we seriously reflect on the implications of God's immutable holy nature. I do not want to breeze over what is intended to be far-reaching, and life changing truths. I want to keep refocusing on these essentials: the implication of authentic divine truth.

CHAPTER 5

THE BASIS OF TRUTH

W e all need to be committed to the learning of essential, and requisite Biblical truth, if we want to be well-rounded Christians; it is crucial for our spiritual evolution. All followers of Christ should be devoted students of the Bible, know the major doctrines of the faith, and those spiritual principles of the faith. Sadly, this is generally not the case. We have a crisis of Biblical ignorance in the Western church, and that to our shame! We have the resources available to us -beyond those of any group of believers have ever enjoyed; but our spiritual growth is only possible, if we are grounded in the scriptures. It is hard to live eternally meaningful lives, if we are not well versed in the scriptures, and skilled in the application of those truths.

However, as too often is the case, our desire is towards resources that will help us find solace from the stresses of our daily lives. Books offering to reveal the spiritual secrets for a tranquil and successful life; if we learn the newly discovered insights of the author. There are an abundance of books on the shelves in Christian book stores that promise the insights needed for personal success. My concern is some of those books are often promoting a false illusion of Christianity. Many even promote false doctrines. These are most notable in the theological vein of the prosperity gospel movement. Where they sell the naive

Christian a counterfeit understanding of the Christian faith, that usually is not fully Biblical. They make promises on behalf of God that are not grounded in the scriptures. This is because they have twisted the scriptures for their own prosperity, and not the cause of Christ

I have long wondered why we Christians struggle so much in our spiritual journey. It may be, in large part, because we have accepted a false understanding of the faith; one that is not fully scriptural. We have been taught the idea that Christianity is all blessing and should contain no suffering and pain. We are too easily influenced by spiritual gurus; who themselves are not solidly grounded in the scriptures. And when our lives do not measure up to this worldly illusion, we become disillusioned. When this takes place we miss the real call of God.

I certainly do not want to suggest the idea that our spiritual journey is not meant to be a joy filled and a meaningful journey. It should be. My concern is we are pursuing a worldly life that is less than God desires for His children. My point is: we need to be cautious that we don't spiritualize this world's values into our Christian faith, and be led to believe this is classic Christianity. We allow false concepts into Christianity, because we are not grounded in real truth. When we are not Bible readers, we easily accept a false understanding of Christianity.

There has been a spiritual drift away from the more substantive teachings. Those revelations from God, for which we are blinded to, because we are not grounded in the scriptures. We have drifted from those anchoring truths, that give foundational principles for all our moral decision making. In the absence of absolute truth, we can easily find ourselves adrift in our journey. We also lose our ability to leave a God honoring legacy; which is being exchanged for temporal pursuits of pleasure and comfort.

Therefore, it is essential that we are equipped, and grounded, so we are able to live out an eternally meaningful life. There is a difference. The former is being equipped with the knowledge of truth. It is hard to be fruitful, if we do not know what the scriptures teach regarding vital truths. The latter is, once we know the truth, and we are solidly grounded, we can then be effective witnesses for God. We can move forward, since we now better understand the gravity of what is true. This is key. We need to know the truth and then put it to use. This is what James, our Lord's younger half brother, wrote about in his book. He criticized them for looking into the mirror and quickly forgetting their face. In their case, they knew the truth, but they were quick to set it aside. They were not putting it to practical use. This is a major point I am trying to make: if our faith is well established and true…. Let's continue.

We now need to move on to consider the implications of some of the more essential truths that the Bible illuminates. Those eternal verities that we naturally shy away from. These implications should be entirely anticipated if we accurately perceive God's nature. If we know God's essential nature: His immutable and infinitely perfect nature. Therefore, this exploration of divine truth, is a process of coming to know God Himself. In particular, the comprehension of our God, who is immutable holy. I believe if we as a people of God would contemplate the implication of what we profess to believe, it would change how we live, and anchor our lives in the eternal. But that process will not take place until we take the time to know God as He has revealed Himself; not as He has been so falsely proclaimed in many of our churches. Where they alter the Christian truth, into their desired truth. Many tend to do this, because the real truth is not always agreeable with their desires. So they substitute the real truth about God, into the image of God they want; the God, they want God to be. Regardless of their desired God, it is often an alteration of the God of the Bible. Let's continue to think this through.

Over the years I wrestle with how a compassionate and loving God could have a Hell? Most Christians do. It can be an inconceivable thought. An eternal Hell is unthinkable even to consider. But there are other issues that I have struggled with at times, like the lasting and/or temporal benefits of being a good person. Some of the most prosperous people in this life are those who do not always play by the rules. Being good does not always appear to be pragmatically beneficial. Understanding that life is so short, we may question if being good is always the most prosperous way to live; those restrictions that limit my personal pleasures or desired goals? There are two primary views. The one with our feet anchored in mid air; where truth is defined by personal preference. The other, where truth and morality are anchored, in the very nature of God. These perspectives have significant ramifications, and they extend beyond today, into eternity. Where each viewpoint has unalterable eternal ramifications. Furthermore, each perspective reveals how we view life, and what we believe is true about life. And what is absolutely, and always true, can only be anchored in the intrinsic nature of God. Since that is the only essence that never changes.

This does not mean I like the repercussions of certain truths! However, my grappling with these eternal verities, eventually lead to a greater appreciation of the magnitude of God's immutable holy nature. While the consequences of Hell for the unredeemed is undeniably hard to accept, it is a rational outcome of God being infinitely holy and just. Disliking the consequences of a truth, is not the same, as the necessary inevitable results of being true. The fact remains: the origin of absolute holiness is inherent in the very nature of God. By growing in our comprehension of the immutable nature of God, we learn what He does, is ultimately according to His nature; and therefore, just and fair for all of eternity. These ramifications are not usually according to our personal sense of fairness. Consequently, what we believe is just, is not the same as God's need for absolute justice; therefore, our understanding of divine justice, should be in accordance with the unwavering righteousness of God.

Therefore, I am urging the unbeliever to continue on in this study, so they better understand the nature of God, and why it matters. The unbeliever needs to see the implications of God's holiness, which should result in seeing their need to be delivered from the inevitable consequences of their sin: the necessary righteous judgment of sin. The upholding of the absolute righteousness standard that is inherent in the very nature of God. This is one of the principle reasons God has revealed Himself, so we can know Him as He is. That standard is revealed, in part, so you understand your predicament, and hopefully, and accept the salvific solution. We all need revealed truth. An unchangeable standard that is not subject to every whim and personal preference, since this knowledge will show: we all need a Savior!

For the believer, it is hopeful that this revelation we are exploring will motivate us to share with confidence, the hope we have in Christ. To be gospel oriented as ambassadors of Christ. To further motivate us to be authentic in worship. To move past the superficial and often meaningless routine of our Christian walk, into eternally purposeful living. This insight will show that every detail of our lives matters to God; both now, and with the results of how we are living, manifesting in eternity. This is why a clear understanding of God's nature opens up the understanding of the gospel. These implications will be developed as we continue in the upcoming chapters.

(My reflections) I wanted to share with you that some of my struggles with these revelations were difficult to accept. My personal feeling was that I might be happier if I just abandon the Christian faith. A freeing thought! Many believers have found these truths so unacceptable, that they have walked away. That may resolve the existential struggle, but the end result is we lose our hope, because our hope is tied to the assurance that our faith is true. That God made promises that can be trusted because of His character. Furthermore, it does not resolve many of the issues that are troubling us: there is still death, injustice and pain. Whether there is Hell or not, does not depend on my feelings about it. To think that there would never be final justice, or settled fairness, does not give any peace either. Reminding me that even without my Christian worldview, life can feel very unfair. Furthermore, there was very little that would change, if I did decide to walk away. It would only put my life on a path that would make my existence: inconsequential. A temporary pursuit to avoid discomfort and find pleasure, but losing the hope in the gospel.

These reflections are all part of the mental process I have labored to work through. The more I reflected on the intrinsic nature of God, the greater my insight into the implications of those attributes. In particular, the aspect of God's nature that stood out to me was the absolutely holy nature of God, who is also immutable. That set the standard. That defined the issue. Which led, naturally, to the reassuring hope we have in the gospel of Jesus Christ. But that conclusion came later in the resolution stage of my thinking. I still believe thinking through the process of deductive reasoning is beneficial. To suggest a conclusion, without the logical progressive reasoning, short changes many of the benefits of arriving at the conclusions. The conclusions remain the same in the end, but we may not fully understand why. By taking this systematic approach, we will arrive at an understanding that is both logical and rational. If we short change the process, we will need to go back and fill in the gaps in our thinking. Therefore, I think there is a lot of benefit to the chronological process of thinking this through, even though I am clearly Christian in my worldview. Now therefore, having established the necessary need to have a basis of truth, let us return to the deductive process: the resolving who is the real God step. Because only the real God is the basis for real truth. You cannot find absolute truth in a God who is not the one and only.

CHAPTER 6

WHOSE GOD IS THE REAL GOD

I have often seen the bumper stickers on the back of vehicles that show numerous icons of the various major religious faiths. Oftentimes, the symbols spell COEXIST, or a form of that. With the symbols of major religions spelling the word. There is an implied suggestion by this emblem that all religions are equally true. The choice of which one to follow is a matter of personal preference. This insight was seen by Blaise Pascal, a great theologian and mathematician of the 17 Century, who remarked that: "People almost invariably arrive at their beliefs not on the basis of proof, but on the basis of what they find attractive." It is further implied by the message being portrayed, that we need to be accepting of others beliefs, and non-judgemental of their merits. That it is disrespectful to these other faith traditions -to claim one's own beliefs are true- and another belief tradition is fallacious. It may even be supposed by some, that alleging that one particular faith as true, over others, is uncharitable; thereby, offensive to those who hold to those alternative beliefs. The emphasis being portrayed by these icons is that all beliefs hold equal merit, and we ought to "COEXIST" without alleging we alone hold the truth. But this perspectives deny any hope of arriving at actual truth, since they have digressed to preferred truth. Baselessly, they hold to their personal beliefs, without credible evidence to support those beliefs.

Therefore, to assert my conviction that the Christian faith is actually true, logically indicates that the other beliefs are not, or they are lacking crucial elements of truth. However, is that not being inferred by those of other faith traditions, with their professed beliefs? By adhering to any other religious tradition, they are in essence saying what they believe is true. It is illogical to practice a set of beliefs, if one does not believe those beliefs are genuine.

How did we get to this place where there are so many alleged beliefs without supporting merit? There are a number of reasons why people hold to a set of particular beliefs. It may simply be unexamined customs, or beliefs that are familiar to their culture, and thereby, assumed to be true. They are simply accepted because it was what they were taught, without any examination of their merit. It is simply their cultural identity. Alternatively, for those not raised in a particular faith tradition, they may believe that all faiths have some merit, but their personal preference satisfies an emotional or spiritual need in their life. One that extends some sense of meaning of significance, beyond their existential struggles, in an otherwise meaningless world. Lastly, for those who have deconstructed from the Christian faith, it may be the unacceptability of some of the harder truths inherent in Christianity. Which leads them to abandon the fundamentals of the Christian faith, and modify their beliefs; so they are more acceptable with what *they* want to believe. Those who have left the Biblical faith, for what they believe is a more fair-minded view of divine justice, may simply be unwilling to accept the notion of Hell, as an example. This is often described as progressive Christianity. A form of Christianity that denies some of the undesirable elements of the faith and promotes the universal equality of all faiths. Yet, they often want to maintain their identity as a Christian. They have determined, they know better what is fair and equitable justice, more so than God.

This does not mean that there are no intellectual and emotional struggles with the Christian faith. There are, but that does not mean the Christian faith is not entirely trustworthy. We need to think through those alleged problems to resolve these alleged contentions. I realize there are numerous reasons people become disillusioned with the Christian faith. I am sure we all have felt this at some point in our Christian walk. It may be unanswered prayer, or the loss of a loved one. Either can lead to the feeling that God, who is reportedly faithful to His promises, was not in our time of great need. These are only a few of the emotional struggles we all experience with the faith. Nevertheless, these enigmatic struggles are not always truth struggles. While these are true enigmas, they are not fatal to the faith. The means for coming to an assured and trustworthy faith requires one to assess the merits of our core beliefs, not by believing all our problems disappear when we become a believer, but whether it is evidentiary true. This is one of the resulting problems of not thoroughly examining the abundance of evidence for the Christian faith. Once we establish the validity of the Christian faith, we are then better equipped to resolve some of those emotional enigmas. This is part of the reason for this book: we are examining why God must act, as He does, in light of who He is.

Notwithstanding these struggles, there are considerable difficulties with this contention that all religions are generally equal. The first obstacle to overcome is that it is impossible to reconcile the alleged truths of the various faiths, one faith with another. It is transparent that all can be less than fully true, but they all cannot be entirely true. One's religious truth claims cannot be completely true, and any of the other faith claims be completely true at the same time, since they teach contrary beliefs. A truth claim cannot be fully true and not fully true at the same time. I know of the moral fall of Ravi Zacharius, but he did a really nice job of explaining this dilemma. Many other Christian thinkers also make compelling arguments on why the differences between different faith traditions can not harmonize. It cannot be done when their core beliefs are in disagreement. This problem of logic is called the *law of noncontradiction*. Which is simply: a truth claim cannot be true and not true at the same time. That is, what one believes can not be contradictory, and still be true.

These various assertions of truth are relevant for us Christians to consider, because we too make truth claims. Take for example: the Gospel of John, chapter 14 verse 6. In the New International Version, it reads: Jesus answered, "I am *the* way and *the* truth and *the* life. No one comes to the Father except through Me." As Dr. Andy Woods has noted in one of his sermons, take note of the definite article, "the." He is "the" way, He is "the" truth, He is "the" life. Jesus does not say He is "a" way. So while all religions can have aspects of truth in what they teach, they all cannot be fully true, since, once again, they contradict each other! So our question is: did Jesus tell the truth? If He did, then all other faith traditions are in their very essence, less than fully true. Simply because, what Jesus said, is irreconcilable with all the other faith traditions. What He claims is: He is "the" only way. He is "the" truth. His truth claims are simply irreconcilable with the other beliefs. Either He is telling the truth or He is not! What we believe should not be because of our personal preferences. Since what people believe are often without real merit, and what we believe does have eternal consequences. What we trust in, or reject, determines our eternal destiny. Since not only does Jesus claim to be "the" truth, He claims: He is the only way to the Father! He uses the exclusive claims of, "no one" and "except through Me," as the only way to God the Father. He is claiming to be the exclusive path to God the Father. It has eternal ramifications in His very claims.

Of course, we need to show Christian love in all circumstances, but that does not mean that we accept every alleged belief as valid. Truth is truth regardless of our individual desires. This is also why we Christians need to be suspicious of those who claim to have visions or special revelations from God. A major world religion and the Morman faith both started with an alleged vision from an Angel. And yet they differ greatly from each other. But remember: Satan too masquerades as an angel of light. There are some litmus tests to validate our faith; we who hold to the truthfulness of Christianity. Consider, as an example: the claims of the deity of Christ, His bodily resurrection, and the sufficiency of His death on the cross; which is the basis for salvation. All are absolutely necessary to be considered a born again Christian. The complete authority of the scriptures is high on that list too. But ultimately, it comes down to: who is Jesus Christ? A great teacher of moral principles or Almighty God in flesh? Our only legitimate redeemer, or a fraud?

These truth claims should also determine the reason we fellowship as a body of believers. The unifying aspect of joining a local Christian church is that we agree with the nature of God, the doctrine, and mission given to the church. At least it should be! It should be more than the preference of music, and likability of the people, or even the charisma of the pastor. The unity around those core beliefs should determine the reason we gather as a body of believers. Therefore, a denial of those core tenets of Christianity, and the exclusive claim by Jesus in John 14:6, undermines the legitimacy of one who claims to be a Christian. When we abandon these core Biblical truths, we lose the very reason for existing as a body of believers. We were called to be the beacon of light in a dark world. That light grows dim when we depart from the truth; when we join the chorus of religious voices –those who deviate from the truth –we have nothing of substance to offer. When this takes place, we as the body of Christ, lose the core reason for existing. We would have no message of eternal worth. No real truth to proclaim. We become nothing more than a subset of culture. A group of individuals, who foster what they desire to believe, but not the actual truth.

When the truth of what we believe is abandoned, waterdown or neglected: we have lost the reason for the gospel. How do we value the work of Christ on the cross, if we do not grasp the immutable holiness of God? If we compromise our understanding of the absolute holiness of God, we lose our rationale for sharing the faith. Why share the gospel if there is no need? The assured hope contained in the gospel message becomes unnecessary if we deny a real Hell.

Even when churches desire to maintain a quasi evangelical presence, so they can retain the claim to be an evangelical church, the abandonment of core teachings often leads to erroneous gospel presentations. I have listened to sermons advocating the need for the unbeliever to be saved. (A salvation message) Only to have the pastor mistaken on the core elements; those necessary aspects of the faith that must be understood, for salvation to be received. There are fundamental truths that are necessary to know, and believe, to become a Christian. How does one appropriate the merits of what Christ did on the cross when the salvation message is vague and confusing? The merits of Christ's sacrifice are magnified when the mind is opened to essential core truths of the Christian faith. These are tied together into inseparable truths. And when these are not held together: we lose the gospel to confusion. And this all starts with whose God are we following. A message has no chance of being salvific, if we start on the wrong track, with the wrong understanding of who is God. But even when we are on the right track, with the right understanding of God, many distort the clarity of the gospel.

A few examples to show what I mean:

Often the gospel is presented as asking Jesus into one's heart. What does it mean to ask Jesus into one's heart? Where even is that verse in the Bible? It is a confusing and unbiblical message! (See Pastor Dennis Rokser's book on this subject from Grace Gospel Press) Or, the necessary need to make a commitment to Christ to become a Christian. The first question should be how much of a commitment is sufficient? This is needed information to have assurance of salvation. This unqualified and subjective standard would be very troublesome for me. Anyone who truly assesses their own moral life in light of God's immutable holiness could never have confidence that they are saved. How do you qualify a human commitment with the infinite? When is it enough? Remember when Christ called His disciples to abandon everything and follow Him, not to even look back. If absolute commitment, as called forth by Jesus, is a condition for salvation, I have never met a true Christian! To compound the problem with requiring a commitment for salvation, there is not one verse that calls an unbeliever to make a commitment to be saved. There are many verses that call for believers to make a deeper commitment to fervent discipleship. To become mature saints, we need to be diligent in our discipleship. Stay with me, as I will further develop these subjects, as we progress in the book.

These subjects are immensely important to this whole conversation. When we deviate away from the established teachings of classic Christianity, or even who is God, we lose the assurance we have in the Christian gospel. We also need to be cautious that we don't invoke the warnings of the Apostle Paul as recorded in his letter to the Galatians: adding or distracting anything to the gospel message has eternal repercussions. It can bring an anathema (severe judgment) to the one sharing this erroneous message. (Galatians 1:8-9) That is why knowing God's attributes are absolutely essential. This is not just how well we live as Christians. It is much more than that. It is having the *right* answer to the most important question ever asked: where will you spend eternity?

The legitimacy of everything we profess to believe, is based on who, and what is, "the" truth. Therefore, the truth about which God we are worshiping, and a clear understanding of the attributes of God, need to be magnified, for there to be an understandable gospel. For one to receive the gift of salvation, an accurate gospel message is undeniably necessary. For without this accurate gospel message, we are left with a useless message. Our spiritual eyes would still be blinded to what needs to be understood and believed to receive the gift of salvation. The end result is: we would have no effectual gospel message. Moreover, we lose our reason for sharing the message. The only trustworthy message that gives assurance of eternal life. Is this not what we are seeing in the American and European churches? I will fully address the essential salvation details in the upcoming chapters.

(My editorial) It is my assertion that Christians have been neglectful in their pursuit of the indispensable knowledge of the nature of God. There are aspects of God's nature that are crucial to understand if we want to be theologically sound Christians. Unfortunately, many pulpits are often silent on these essential truths that make Christianity, authentic Christianity. What greater knowledge can there be for anyone, but to know who is the real God, and what is His immutable essence. Everything related to our practice and mission is dependent on this understanding. A faulty understanding of who God is, leads to a faulty understanding of "the" truth. When that happens, our message will be devalued, or worse, even accursed. The first area to suffer is likely going to be the exclusivity of who Christ is, and what He did. (John 3:16, 5:24, 14:6) If we don't understand the pending consequences the non-believer is going to encounter upon death, we will have nothing of substance to offer: the assured hope of eternal life. A byproduct of this, for the born again Christian, is finding ourselves proclaiming a deficient salvation message. To avoid this, it all starts by ensuring that we have a correct understanding of God. No other alleged religion besides Biblical Christianity has these credentials, nor an accurate understanding of who is "the" truth. An exclusive claim from the very mouth of our Lord Jesus Christ. I address salvation principles in chapters 8, 9, 10 and 11.

1. Sermon by Dr. Andy Woods @SLBC Andy Woods Sermon on the Gospel of John 14:5-7

CHAPTER 7

LOOKING AT THE VALUES IN A LIFE WITHOUT GOD

I briefly want to look at a few more reasons why we need to make sure we are on the right path, before we move on into the meat of this book. I do not intend on spending a significant amount of time on this subject. There are countless books on how to live a life that is meaningful -one that is ultimately purposeful. It would be like chasing a rabbit, Zig and zagging, without getting anywhere relevant. And a pursuit of that nature would take us beyond the scope of this book. Although, how we live as Christains, is one of the secondary emphasis of the book. For those who desire to live a life that avoids unnecessary self-created troubles, and an enduring positive impact, a few additional thoughts might be helpful.

If one returns their thoughts to the marriage illustration in chapter four of this book, we see the implications of living a morally relevant life in light of God's holy design for marriage. Marriage is defined by God as a sacred union: intended solely for a man and his wife. A union that only makes sense when understood in this light. Outside of this God given purpose, the marriage union could be seen as little more than a sexually limiting arrangement. Your view on whether or not to hold to marriage as a sacred union, depends on the premise of one's morality. This premise returns once again to what is the foundation for all our morals, which we Christians should know, is the inherent nature of God. So to those who do not hold our perspective, we may ask in the form of a question: why be moral? A simple, but far reaching question. A simple but very probing question. The response to the question will vary based on one's reference point for morality. That is why I am asking! I am trying to force the believer and non-believer to ponder their basis for morality.

One may answer, for numerous sociological reasons, and there are many. It is clear that the stability of society is strengthened by traditional marriage. As an example, it is clear, children do much better in every aspect of life, in a loving, supportive, and Biblically based stable home. That each, a man and women, bring attributes of their own that benefit the development of an emotionally strong child. Particularly, when each member is manifesting those qualities that emanate from being solidly grounded in the faith. Therefore, even outside the Biblical mandate, society has valid reasons to support traditional marriages. It is the optimal way to live for both a healthy society, and the emotional wellbeing of children; which is dependent for a large part on the stability and quality of their parents' marriage. Even later as adults, the stability of their parents' marriage continues to give stability to their lives. It is clearly God's plan, which always works best.

The alternative is also true: if there is no God to ultimately answer to, why is marriage an exclusive relationship that needs to be honored? Why object to the previous illustrated marriage arrangement in chapter 4? If I am going to live a short meaningless life, and then die! Therefore, these merits of our morality are all dependent on: is there a God and has spoken? As I previously argued in the illustration, there are no reasoned moral violations in the marriage illustration, if there is no God. The logic is solid: the man and women both, it can be argued, have benefits from the agreed extra marital relationship. She has the freedom to explore her sexual urges, to pursue her lustful desires. He has benefited from a more expressive sexual encounter. No immoral inference can be logically alleged if the holiness of God is removed from the equation.

The natural consequences are those that relate to the jealousy of the partner. But what is jealousy? Many will assert that there are ethical problems with the relationship. However, where do these ethics derive from? Who decides? Why don't we all pursue this arrangement as illustrated? Seriously: sex is enjoyable! Why not explore sex to the max? In light of the temporary nature of life, this could be seen as a reasonable and logical course. That thinking should be the logical conclusion of those who reject the moral teachings of the scriptures. Those who are atheist. I still would not suggest that course of action, because the results are never good, but there is logic to the thinking. The question always returns to: what has God said? And why has this been revealed in the scriptures as the only pattern for marriage? It can be simply stated: God designed marriage. It is His idea. Therefore, a reflection of Him, and the best way to live secure and stable lives. Otherwise, there is no anchor on which to base our morality. It is leaving this foundation that has rippled through our society, particularly, when we lose this foundational perspective. These ill conceived reasonings are called: "Reductio Ad Absurdum". These ideas, when taken to their logical conclusions, show how absolutely absurd they really are.

This is a temptation that many face as they age. They see the better part of their life slipping away, and they reach for fleeting satisfaction. They feel the heavy burdens that life often brings, and they want to escape. They fall into a feeling of weariness due to the daily grind. The day to day burden of responsibilities and struggles, just to survive. They want a vacation of freedom from the mundane aspects of life. They want to recapture the titillating stage of their youth. When this mindset takes hold, some will foolishly start on a path, only to realize that it caused irrevocable regret and pain. What looks like renewed freedom, only results in remorse and regret. And most often results in a broken relationship. This is also destructive to the lives of those around them. We do not live on islands. Every choice has ripple effects. Do you really want another man or woman raising your children, while you are still paying for their keep? Having someone else raising them or disciplining them in a manner that you would disapprove of? Or, teaching different values than you desire to impress upon them. Of course, by abandoning your pledge to your spouse, you have already devalued your moral influence. Furthermore, if you are in a later stage of life, do you want to give up half of everything you have labored for all your life? In addition to these factors, there are issues regarding holidays and special family events. You may find yourself sharing holidays with those that are not our own, while your own biological children spend those cherished times with biologically unrelated relatives of the other parent's new spouse. Or, sadly, one is left trying to celebrate those major events alone. This is why leaving the foundations of Biblical faith leads to so many unintended negative consequences.

In addition to those potential consequences: why do we resist these impulses? Is it simply because of expective societal norms? It may even be argued that for society, it is better to be moral and hold to the sacredness of marriage, but not in my individual interest. Again, in light of the temporary nature of life, this may seem logical. Why subject my egocentric sexual interest for the benefit of society? Considering there is no moral underpinnings to consider this wrong, that is, without proper view of God. Is it simply our culture imposing a code of moral expectations that limit my sexual experiences? A few contrasting thoughts on the reasons for fidelity to the marriage in light of knowing the nature of God. There is a divine plan for mankind. The practical aspects of our lives are affected by our moral reasoning, regardless if one is a believer or not. God's plan just works better for all.

The further we drift from Biblical morality the more acceptable these perverse ideas become. The decision of whether to adhere to the fidelity of one's marriage commitment, is becoming more influenced by current cultural norms, and less on the moral expectation established by God. As John Stonestreet contended in a Colson Center Podcast: He remarked that marriage was previously more like gravity, meaning an absolute. Now society treats marriage as a speed limit, subject to the changing values of culture. What was once a traditional stabilizing value has now become a fading Christian standard. This is because we are being influenced by those emerging values, as our culture changes, and not by God.

As noted, it is interesting that even those outside the normal Christian identity, in general, hold to the expectation that marriage is to be exclusive and a faithful standard between a man and woman. But I keep asking: why? This is a functioning relationship in the illustration. What is there to object to? That is, if both parties agree with this arrangement. For that matter, what harm is there if these activities occurred, and no knowledge of the affair was discovered? It is the knowledge of the actions that causes the emotional pain for the one betrayed. The unsuspecting spouse is not emotionally harmed, if they are unaware of others activities.

However, for the Christian, God knows. He holds the marriage bed as sacred. And He will hold us accountable: either in this life, or at the Bema Seat judgment, or both. (1st Thessalonians 4:6) (Both of these consequences will be discussed later) Furthermore, there are the real practical consequences of being caught. The guilt and the hurt inflicted by the betrayal. The betrayal discovered has lasting consequences, forever altering the basis of trust. Solid, Godly, and lasting marriage, is clearly the desired plan of God. It promotes the stability of society. It allows us to sleep peacefully at night knowing we are living according to the revealed standards of our Heavenly Father. God has equipped us with a conscience, and guilt is a difficult emotion to live with. One of many aspects of the Holy Spirit's ministry is the conviction of sin. What the world too often accepts, will always be considered gravity for us Bible believers. Over the last hundred years as the church and society have drifted from Biblical truth, the more prevalent, and acceptable these lifestyles have become. This corresponds with the removal of Bible reading and prayer in school in the early 60's. Take some time and study the results to our country when we abandon those moral foundations. It resulted in the explosion of the sexual revolution. The resulting consequences to our nation, and to us, individually. It has been detrimental to the sacredness of our sexual lives. Making the sacred: common. It becomes a pursuit of sensual pleasure, and less the bonding aspect of a sacred union established by God.

Regardless of the changing values of society: God's immutable standards do not change. This is why we need to renew our minds, so when we start to meander and entertain lustful thoughts, we remember that there are consequences to choices. We then pause and quickly count the cost! What society may now find acceptable, will always be a firm principle from our Heavenly Father. Those principles reveal His nature. He will not alter His opinion just because society has.

I certainly believe in God's forgiveness. I believe He can rebuild broken lives, but it was never His original desired plan. In the beginning: God created man and woman to become one flesh. God has done amazing things in many fractured relationships, but the pain should have been avoided. That is why God has spoken. His way is always the better way. It is the only way to eternal life, and the best way to live an eternally significant life, a meaningful life.

It is not always easy, those value commitments we make in life, but we personally sacrificed. My wife stayed home with the kids when they were young. I am not saying it was the only way, but I never regretted giving up some material things to have my wife home. She loves being a mom. It gave stability to the home. It was a chapter in our lives. Later my wife went back to college and became a RN. She was able to pursue a desired goal and find fulfillment in a career. But there were priorities we held as of greater importance. Our focus was to sacrifice some of our material blessings as an investment into the lives of our children. It took a lot of hard work. I believe we did a reasonably good job. This is evident in the fact that they are no longer dependent on us for their daily subsistence. That's also the hard part. The letting go at the end of the process. You are successful, in part, if you are not depended upon for their daily substance. Our children are all self-sufficient, and are managing life well as adults. They are continuing our heritage by passing on many of the values that they were taught as children.

It is losing the daily interaction with them that we thoroughly enjoyed, while they were living at home, that is hard to let go of, but it is the natural progression of life. They move forward in their journey of life. Thankfully, we continue to maintain a good relationship with them. But like chapters in a book, those chapters of their childhood at home have passed. They are now focused on their careers and their family responsibilities that come with parenthood. It is the way it should be. I told each of them that when they started having families of their own, that every emotion they would ever have, will be magnified as a parent. This is the journey of life. The foundation for a healthy society is the home and the values that are taught there. The other perspective results in detrimental consequences; those that naturally result, when we diminish the inherently good foundational values of the Christian faith.

Hopefully, one can see the intent of my argument. The ramifications inherent in the marriage illustration should be clear. There are natural consequences that flow out of our moral underpinnings. When we abandon a Godly moral foundation, we see the rippling effects in our society. Those values that are established by God, when violated, have natural consequences. A meaningful life is a purposeful life, that is lived with God's perspective in view. I am going to leave this subject a bit unfinished. (I am not sure if it was a chapter worth leaving in the book? However, since the necessity of a moral standard is crucial to my arguments, I decided to leave it in) I will argue as the book progresses, the reasons why we individually, and as a body of believers, and as a society, should understand these subjects in light of God's unchangeable holiness. The most urgent is our need to be brought into a right relationship with God. There is simply no subject more important than where we will spend eternity. This is the theme we will explore in the next four chapters.

If you wonder why I use sex as one of my main illustrations for mortality? This is because it is the quickest way to clarify the basis for personal morality. Since some see sex as morally neutral, its expression is reduced to one's personal preference. Whereas, others see sexual standards as established by divine decree. Therefore, this is a very quick, and simple way to illustrate my points.

CHAPTER 8

EXPLORING GOD'S PERFECT NATURE

G ranting my conviction that God exists, and the Bible portrays the only reliable description of His nature, let's continue the thought process. We all know this earthly journey has built in limitations. There is an unavoidable day when each member of the human race enters eternity. Therefore, there is an unmistakable need to know God's relationship requirements. What will He require of each one of us to be in His presence? To help in this understanding, it is crucial that we have some understanding of the standards of God. We also need to know what determines those standards. For this to be understood, we need to know God's attributes; we need some theological descriptions of those attributes. I have eluded to them a number of times in the previous chapters. I now need to give greater clarity to these divine attributes. Not only do these need to be understood, these need to be kept in the forefront of your minds throughout the reading of this book. My expressed arguments in this book are dependent on these truths. These are my lay interpretations, not scholarly, but I believe them to be accurate just the same.

The first is holiness: the only attribute of God that is used in the Bible, trifold. The use of this description of God is in the books of Revelation and Isaiah. It is the descriptive emphasis of God's unique and total separation from anything sinful. And, therefore, it may be argued that it is the most essential attribute, since it is the only described attribute of God that is used trifold. Holy is simply what we would commonly understand by the term. While God is by nature loving, it may be said that His holiness is central to who He is, because of the usage in those two books. The theme is emphasized throughout the scriptures. This is seen in Isaiah 57:15, where His name is holy and that is His described identity.

When man is exposed to God manifesting this revelation of His nature: it results in praise, relevant fear, the awe, the worship, and adoration of God's being. It is being taken back by the fact that God is: Holy, Holy, Holy. Here are some illustrated examples, embodied in the Bible.

First, I am thinking of 1 Chronicles, chapter 13. The Israelites were moving the Ark of God and it became unsteady. Uzzah placed his hand on the Ark to steady it, and was instantly killed. He transgressed the holiness of God. Even though it may have appeared his actions were noble, God's holiness cannot be compromised, or infringed upon; even if it is done with the right motives.

Secondly, would be the requirements for entering the most holy place of the temple. Where only the High Priest, and only once a year, could enter to meet with God. Thereby, indicating that this was not something to undertake haphazardly, or presumptuously. That entering God's presence was sacred, and needed to be done with utmost respect, and in a very prescribed manner and only in God's described manner.

Thirdly, this is seen in the description by Jesus of John the Baptist, whom He called the greatest of all prophets. Yet, John, understanding the holiness of Jesus, declared he was unworthy to even untie Jesus' dirty sandals. (Mark 1:7) Think for a moment about that contrast. The greatest of all prophets was unworthy to untie the dirty sandals of the Lord Jesus Christ. There are countless more. Complete books would not be enough to explore this profound attribute.

But clearly, one of the best descriptions of God's nature, is that He lives in unapproachable light. Think about this for a moment before moving on: living in unapproachable light. (1 Timothy 6:16) And, therefore in reflection, certainly what we honestly lack. It is ludicrous to think that in any aspect I could consider myself holy. If we believe we are holy or righteous, in the absolute sense, it indicates a very faulty and fundamental misunderstanding of the absolute holiness of God. This is also the standard by which He will one day judge us. He Himself is the standard. Since the standard is God Himself, to be in His presence, requires a standing equal to that absolute holiness. Most every aspect of life has a means to measure, to see if what is being measured is up to a defined standard. God Himself is the standard. Unmitigated holiness is inherent in His very nature. Let's be clear here: you and I do not measure up!

The second is that He is intrinsically holy in His nature. Webster defines intrinsic as belonging to the essential nature or constitution of a thing. What something is in its very essence. God is who God is! He is perfect in every and all aspects. He has a nature that is absolutely holy, and the nature God possesses, is incomparably holy to any other being. God in His essence is in a class by Himself that has no comparison. In the Old Testament, He simply describes Himself as: I Am who I Am. The mild difference may be described as: holiness is an attribute possessed as God, and that attribute is the intrinsic nature of who He is as God. It is inseparable from who He is! Think of this way: I may have attributes, but that does not mean I have them intrinsically in myself, as God does. I have been given this created nature by God, but He has that nature intrinsically.

Thirdly, and just as essential: God is love. It is another aspect of His intrinsic nature. Love originates in the very nature of God. Therefore, as the origin of love, God is a loving and compassionate God. It is an aspect of being the triune God. His nature is just that: loving kindness. This attribute is portrayed in His long-suffering kindness, which is expressed repeatedly throughout the scriptures. As the source of love, the greatest expression of love is the cross of Christ. He is not wanting anyone to perish, but all to come to repentance (change their mind), and accepting the gift He is offering. This gift that is being offered, is the gift of eternal salvation and forgiveness of sin. That gift is made possible because the Lord Jesus Christ, Himself, paid our sin debt on the cross. Which upon personal acceptance by a believing sinner, results in our eternal salvation. (As we will explore in more detail in the coming chapters)

Fourthly, is the understanding that He is immutable. This is the idea that God cannot change: ever. Not only is His nature intrinsically holy, it is an unchangeable righteous nature. He will never get better, nor decline in that attribute. He is by nature, who He is, and to change would cause Him to be less than the incomparable, immutable, and intrinsically holy God; as described in the Bible. This is an eternal state. He will never ever be other than who He is, or ever can be, eternal and immutability, holy! This is one that really grabbed my attention over the last few years. An immutable holy God. And this understanding is absolutely essential if we want to truly grasp the significance of the gospel. He cannot compromise His nature, and it will never ever change! He is an eternally perfect being. He can never change or compromise any aspect of who He is. There is an absolutely uncompromising aspect of His nature. He is perfect in all aspects of His nature, especially His Holiness.

Next, for the purpose of this descriptive focus: He is omnipotent. The description starts in the very beginning, in the book of Genesis. From the very beginning: God created. The creative, and majestic power of God, can be seen in the act of creating the whole universe simply by His command. It is unfathomable to grasp the power that God possesses. He has the power to do whatever He desires as long as it does not conflict with His nature. This is very significant for us to understand. While it may at first appear to be an unsolvable tension; it does have a divine solution. There is a means for which God can be simultaneously: both immutably holy and immutably loving. This without ever compromising either essential attributes.

Lastly, to help in the foundational understanding of what I am attempting to communicate in this book, is that God is omniscience. He will never learn anything. He knows everything and is indefectible in that knowledge. Not only is His nature immutable and holy: He also possesses absolute knowledge of everything. He knows every detail about your life, including the very hairs on your head. (Matthew 10:30)

I am always learning and relearning, not so with God. God knows both actual and potentially, everything. The idea that God does not know every aspect of my life, both potentially and/or actually, misunderstands omniscience. This means every thought too. To think that someday, I will stand before this Almighty God, and have any hope that He will not be totally mindful of my behavior, or can overlook any of my sinful actions, is wishful thinking. It is certainly not a Biblical truth. Think about that the next time you entertain a thought or engage in an action that is not consistent with who we are called to be as Christians. Alternatively, if you have not come to benefit from the person and work of Jesus Christ on the cross, this knowledge of your behavior is still subject to the absolute standard: God Himself. This idea that God does not remember every minute detail about our lives is not a Biblical truth. He does, and the standard for judgment is still the same: His immutable holy nature!

The Gospel of Jesus Christ will never be fully understood, and appreciated, until these concepts are clear in the mind of believers; and to a lesser degree, unbelievers. Since unbelievers need to understand their need for salvation, before they can understand the redeeming work of the God/man: the only Savior, who is Jesus Christ. Therefore, it is of the utmost importance that these truths are understood, and repeatedly emphasized. He is absolutely holy; that is His intrinsic nature, and it cannot change, ever! He is the unchangeable and incomparable holy God. A bit redundant, but necessary to get these points established. These concepts are the principle building blocks for everything I want to address in this book, particularly, in the next few chapters.

1. The difficulty using particular references for these chapters is that this information has been found in dozens and dozens of books that I have read. I used a generalization of all that material. Please check out the Bibliography. In general they all address the same salvation themes.

CHAPTER 9

A DIVINE DILEMMA

There is only so much we can know about God, just by the visible observation of the world. It is easy to see God's creative power, open your eyes, and stare at the sky on a clear night. Look through a microscope at the wonders of God's intricate creation. But most other characteristics of God's nature can only be understood via revelation. Since if He did not reveal Himself, we could only speculate on His nature. Thankfully, He did reveal Himself, in the pages of the Bible. Which is our only trustworthy source, for personally knowing the Creator, our Heavenly Father. There are essential attributes of His nature that simply could not be known without that divine revelation. For example, we would not know He is holy. We may see the injustices of this world, and then surmise that God is extremely powerful, but imperfect in moral character; if nature and humanity are a reflection of His nature. We may see unanswered injustice and not know that He is the ultimate source of justice. Without that divine revelation, we would not know that in eternity, every wrong will be made right, and perfect justice will be finally administered; which is oftentimes hard to perceive in light of the fallenness of this world. This knowledge is even more meaningful when we are the victim of injustice. We naturally desire accountability and justice when we have been victimized. We may not always comprehend that He is a righteous God, who is also loving and compassionate to those who are hurting. A God of eventual justice, who will make all wrongs right, but also extends His loving kindness when we are struggling. We may see glimpses of His loving kindness; hopefully, expressed by His children. But the real assurance of His final justice does not come, until we are assured that eventually He will wipe every tear away, and restore His creation back into a state of perfect righteousness. This growing insight becomes even more comforting, when we understand He has a plan for the renewed perfection of his creation: in the coming Eternal Kingdom. (Revelation chapter 21)

Thankfully, from the beginning of creation, God chose to reveal Himself for our benefit. For without that revelation, we would not understand the dilemma that we were exploring in the last chapter. Always keeping in mind: He has revealed clearly that He is holy, but is also a compassionate and loving God. Which is encouraging to know in this very harsh world in which we live. However, when we started this journey into an understanding of His nature, our initial response to the revelation of His absolute holiness, as described, is likely dread, maybe even outright fear. This should be the expected reaction, because we intuitively know we do not meet this standard. Yet, this is the necessary first step in understanding our need. It is almost like pain. Pain is what often drives us to the doctor, whereby we are diagnosed, and get needed treatment. If we do not know our need, we likely would not seek a solution. We need to know our utter sinfulness, before the justice seat of a holy God, before we would seek deliverance from a qualified Savior; otherwise, we would die in ignorance. Can you imagine dying in an unsaved state, and meeting God, and for the first time you understand His nature and yours: a problem discovered too late.

Let's start with some more introductory thoughts: a review and preview of this situation. This is a crucial need, because of the eternal significance. Without this basic knowledge, most people are depending on their own perceived goodness, which is a faulty standard to gauge one's qualifications for heaven. This is why these chapters are so extremely important. Because when we fail to grasp this essential understanding of the unmitigated holiness that is inherent in God, we are oblivious to the problem. His unapproachable holiness: which is the standard that God must uphold to be true to Himself. Consequently, without this knowledge, unbelievers have no perception of the required status needed to be in God's presence. Then when the event happens for the unsaved, as it will for all of us, that someone steps over the line into the world of the dead, and finds irrevocable horror: it is then simply too late. The consequences are irreversible and forever. I am trying to help you think this through with some preliminary thoughts, even if it is repeatedly discussed, it is just that important! So let's continue our exploration of this subject, even if it appears to be an overly excessive evaluation of the theme.

I want to go over this one more time, because we need this diagnosis of our problem, for us to understand the vital solution. This is really indispensable information. There are countless individuals who will pontificate on their understanding of what is necessary to meet God's standards. Their surmising about the qualifications for entrance into this final state: how they hope to qualify for heaven. Oftentimes, they can be even a bit self confident; surmising that they in themselves are deserving of heaven, but it is just speculation on their part. They don't have a valid reference point to gauge the qualifications for that acceptance. Their gauge of goodness or acceptable righteousness, is their self-comparison to the culture around them. They surmise that they are better than most. They point to some good qualities in their life as evidence for this opinion. However, this is a faulty understanding of required holiness. Societal standards were never the standard with God: His divine nature is! Those trusting in their own subjective goodness have not come to understand God's perspective of holiness. Tragically, most don't even pursue this understanding. (This is the foremost reason for me writing this book on **God's immutable holiness**) They will spend more time planning a vacation or retirement, than inquiring about what God says about these qualifications. One can be a relatively good person, but not holy, not in the absolute sense. I know many really good people. I have never met one who is absolutely holy. The standard is the intrinsic and immutable holiness of God, which is the very essence of His nature. This is what God will require: complete perfection! I am sorry to tell you: holiness is not inherent in you! You need it to be granted to you, because it is an unattainable standard to achieve on your own.

Let's pause for a moment and remember once again the undeniable truth about life: we will all eventually enter the next stage of life, the eternal. It is coming. No stopping it. Death is as sure as anything we will ever experience in this life. And the matter is generally ignored for the pursuit of personal, but temporal fulfillment, even in our churches. We are okay with general goodness, we just feel extremely uncomfortable with preaching on the holiness of God. But what God demands to be in His presence is absolute perfection. When we first come to this knowledge, it is like, oh crap, I have an enormous problem. A huge, and at first appearance, an apparently unsolvable one; at least one we have the ability to solve on our own.

May I step back and reflect for a moment: truthfully, at times, I wish there was a different way. A general goodness that was acceptable by God. I had once thought that the removal of these perfect standards would be easier to mentally live with. The basic goodness that we generally find in most of our friends and neighbors. I desired to set aside the thoughts of an absolute perfect standard for salvation, and simply enjoy the goodness of life. I personally prefer relative morality, we all do! But if that were the case? How would we define that standard? At first, it may appear to be a relief that I am able on my own to achieve the standard God requires. However, when you start to ponder, how to gauge if one measures up, that would give little comfort. We could never know for sure. What if I was wrong in my assessment? Thinking that I have merited this good standing, only to be wrong in the end, horribly wrong. In deeper reflection: I prefer the perfect standard, knowing that it is not I who is able to meet it, but Jesus Christ and His completed sacrifice on the cross who does it for me. Then I can have the confidence that is assured. An assurance that is dependable, and eternally trustworthy. Please give me the time to elaborate on those ideas as we continue. I wanted to review for a moment, to ensure we are all understanding this crucial truth.

Let's resume with the logic of the reasoning. I am left with this dilemma: I believe the Bible gives an accurate reflection of God's perfect standard. His standards are a reflection of His nature. Having come to this insight, which makes perfect sense, as I would expect nothing less from God. Who wants to worship an compromised and less than perfect God? Who would want to worship a sinful God? One that is flawed like us. There would be no ultimate basis for justice. Even the rapist would have a defense against God's justice. One could claim in their defense: you too are a sinner like me, so by what ultimate standard gives you a right to judge me? (Then again, how does one even define evil, if there is no immutable perfect standard? A perfect standard that is inherent in a perfect person. Just reflecting, I do that alot, that is why I am writing a book) The clear revelation in the Bible, regarding God, is that He is: Holy, Holy, Holy. There is simply no other way of understanding the revealed nature of God, other than He is who He is! He is, and always will be, immutably holy. Let's continue....

Coming to grips with this is difficult, but is logically expected, if one considers what a perfect God must be like. It is also the revealed truth by the Holy Spirit, and not able to be understood without this Biblical revelation. So whether by gentle persuasion, or terrifying truth encounter, this is the plain truth about God. And that truth has eternal repercussions. (That is why I am writing an evangelistic book with this heavy emphasis on holy. It is an extremely important truth, about an extremely important subject, but not an easily to accept truth)

I had thoughts of what it would be like to cross over to the other side (enter eternity) and come face to face with the infinitely holy God, who knows everything about everything. He knows our thoughts and our actions and our motivations, and then being rejected! Can you even contemplate for a moment what it would be like to be irrevocably rejected. There will be no argument or defense. What can one argue before an all knowing God? He CANNOT change His standards. What a horrifying thought. Read about the rich man in the Gospel of Luke in chapter 16. The agony of His experience was actual and irrevocable. Interestingly, he suddenly became interested in evangelism, which is a little late now! There is no more horrifying thought that could ever be considered by man, than being irrevocably lost for all of eternity. I don't like it. I hate the notion. Philosophically, I wrestle with how this can be true? There is no way to soften this reality. Generally why Chrisitians and churches ignore this topic. It is hard to grapple with the implications. Who even wants to consider the possibility! We are embarrassed even to admit this is what we believe, so we quickly move on to a new subject;

even though this is the premiere question of all time. Nonetheless, while difficult to accept, due to the implications, its importance is undeniable.

This is why a better understanding of absolute holy is so crucial, for both the believer and the unbeliever. And why this needs to be clearly taught in our local churches. It is also why we individually need to accept the reality of God's distinctiveness, even though we may feel a bit repulsed by the ramifications. It is who He is and we are not. It is the reality of the situation. We don't have a say in the matter. Our preferred opinion does not matter, nor does what we want to believe matter. He cannot change who He is.

Furthermore, this understanding defines our missions as a body of believers. And should give pause to the unbeliever to reconsider their implicit need for deliverance from their precarious situation. How to escape the eternal consequences of their inevitable, which is their lack of standing before the justice seat of God. Until this understanding is realized, there appears no reason to look for a potential solution. Why look for a solution? If there is no awareness of the coming consequences? This results because we lack an accurate knowledge of God's righteous standards. And when this understanding is lacking: we miss the central message of the Bible. It could be summarized in three steps of truth. The first is obvious: this life is temporal, and death is inevitable. The second two need divine revelation. The first of these second two is: the revelation that God is absolutely holy, and cannot alter His standards. Lastly, He loves us enough to create a complete solution to our inherent sin problem. Or, as I like to do, and ask in the form of a question: how can an immutable holy God have a relationship with an inherently sinful man? The answer magnifies a person and a mission: the Lord Jesus Christ, coming in the flesh, and His sacrifice on the cross. So we start by coming to an understanding of the nature of the problem: the dilemma! Let's continue to explore God's marvelous solution to this unavoidable predicament: how to qualify for heaven?

1. The difficulty using particular references for these chapters is that this information has been found in dozens and dozens of books that I have read, and podcasts listened to. I used a generalization of all that material. Please check out the Bibliography. In general they all address the same salvation themes.

CHAPTER 10

THE NEED AND REASONABLENESS OF THE GOSPEL

———⌇⌇⌇———

This comes back to my primary focus in this book. This is not a new profound revelation, some grand insight that I just learned that nobody else has discovered. It is a simple return to what has been the historical understanding of God. I am only drawing attention back to some classic truths of the faith that have been forsaken for a variety of reasons. Both in the church, and practically, by most individual Christians. These next two chapters are likely the most significant chapters in my book. It is the one subject that has too often been minimized: how to find deliverance from the consequences of our sin. There is simply no greater need for mankind, than to know the need, and then, accept the means of deliverance. The eternity of one's soul dependents on it. Knowing the problem is the first step: God is immutably holy and we are not! Let's continue with the progression of the thought process.

One would think that the obvious, that is, our need to know our eternal destiny, that this requisite knowledge would be the ultimate pursuit. The, I need to know, that I know for sure, where I will spend eternity. There is no question in life that should be of greater concern: what happens after death? Because the consequences are so final. There should be a presumed natural desire to know if there is an answer. A quest to know if there is a God, and if He has designed a plan to solve our humanly unsolvable dilemma. I have already alluded to the answer in the previous chapters. It is now time to focus more intently into the resolution of our problem: the answer. Since it is clear we have no way to bridge the chasm between us. We are sinners by nature and deed. We do not have the means to resolve our hopeless situation, or change our sinful nature. If there is a solution, it is up to God, because we literally need a divine solution.

These are the questions: How does God set forth the restoring of this broken relationship? What was God's dilemma when it comes to restoring His relationship with mankind? How could God express His love and not compromise His holiness? The proper understanding of His nature is undeniably, and essential, to understanding the problem. Actually, it was a solution God possessed in His mind, in the timeless past. He just needed to reveal it, so we could have the opportunity to respond.

While man is the one who is facing the consequences of the sin problem, only God has the ability to solve it. After a perfect creation everything changed. Adam, the father of all mankind, who once was in a perfect relationship and fellowship with God, became broken by willful sin. By sinning, he became a sinner, and thereafter, passed that nature on to us. (I will clarify the difference between the two later: relationship and fellowship) The Apostle Paul addresses this crucial issue in the book of Romans, chapter 3. There Paul writes about God needing to be just, and also the justifier. Notices that He does not change His standards: He is just. Another indicator of His holy nature and disposition, or state of consummate righteousness. He is just, because by His nature it is who He is. A judge who does not administer justice is not just. And in this case: absolutely and forever, perfect righteousness is the standard. A terrifying thought, no doubt. Please understand by repeating these themes, I am trying to secure these truths solidly in your mind. These are eternally crucial truths!

Furthermore, the clear indication of that verse is: only He is able to justify the sinner, since it is clear we cannot undo our sinful condition, nor reverse those we already committed. To further our predicament, not only can we not erase our sinful past, nor stop from sinning, we are not inherently righteous. We are completely unable to measure up to His never-ending perfect state of consummate righteousness. The reality is: we are in an humanly unresolvable situation. Thereby, indicating only God can change the status that is needed in the life of the unbelieving sinner. We need God to be our justifier!

When I was teaching in my jail ministry, (before covid) I would use this illustration to demonstrate the contrast. This is the litmus test that will tell if we are understanding the predicament correctly? I would explain to those in my class using this contrast: a litmus test. When one understands that God is so holy, that the most insignificant, the most seemingly trivial, or benign sin, is enough to keep one from being in God's presence for all of eternity, they are just beginning to understand His intrinsic holiness. And His justice requires an atonement, an payment, as a consequence for violating His standard. He requires absolute and complete justice. His nature requires an uncompromising separation from the sin, since sin and holiness cannot coexist. Therefore, whatever unatoned sin exists, would remain forever in an unforgiven state. He who possesses a sin nature: must endlessly be separated from the presence of God. Before becoming saved, our only relationship with God is: He would be our Judge someday.

However, and thankfully, the work of Christ is so complete: that the most vile, the most evil and/or disgusting sin, is fully atoned for by the all sufficient work of Jesus Christ on the cross. That is the litmus test of both the holiness of God, and the sufficiency of the person: the God/man, Jesus Christ. It reveals the indispensable need for the payment of our sin, by the God/man on the cross. It is crucial to understanding these twin truths; since it is the essence of what makes the Gospel so grand. Both the satisfaction of the required holiness of God, and the payment for the sinfulness of man, are resolved only by one person: Jesus Christ, and His sacrifice on the cross. When those are understood: the gospel is esteemed and treasured. It also should heighten the urgency to share this marvelous hope. The hope we have in the gospel. Once thoroughly understood, it should become the central mission of the church, and for individual believers! (As we will explore in later chapters) Helping people resolve interpersonal issues is important, but pales in comparison, in light of eternity.

Therefore, without a doubt, this is the ultimate question for each individual. The question for all time, because it determines our place for eternity. Either God is or He is not. Either He is eternally and intrinsically and immutably holy, or we have a defective and less than perfect God. Truthfully, those thoughts used to terrify me, knowing that I could have entered a state of eternity, and there would have been no recourse, nor any hope of ever escaping His absolute and perfect eternal justice. There are no adjectives that fully describe this potential reality. But notice the tense of my words: I "used" to fear this pending judgment, a literal Hell. I have now come to have a full assurance of my salvation, because I have accepted the full salvation, given to me, via my faith/ trust in the payment of my sin, by my fully qualified Savior. I am now resting on the fact that God, who cannot lie, has made this promise. I can, therefore, forever rejoice in the assurance of my unchangeable salvation status.

(A reflection) This is also the key consideration for teaching the security of the believer. If I am not permanently saved, then this concern for my eternal destiny will be a recurring fear that will come up again and again. A potential that I would need to be fearful about. Because, while I may be safe now, there is no assurance that I may not have to face this dilemma of unresolved sin in the future; if in fact, I am not eternal and securely saved. (This too will be explored more in the coming chapters)

This message of salvation is historic Christianity: it is Biblical Christianity. We can deny it. We can ignore it. I have considered that option, since it is often a thought too heavy to keep in the forefront of our mind. The alternative is: I would need to abandon the faith, and by abandoning the faith, I would give up all hope. Furthermore, I would lose any meaningful reason for living; since, I will still die one day. And my leaving the faith would not change whether it is true or not. It only removes the consideration from my mind. I actually think I would be freer, but it is a denial of truth, and reality. No matter how unpleasant the thought, it is the paramount of reality, and it is the truth!

Now let's continue to consider the original salvation litmus test that I used in my class. This test opens our understanding of God's holiness and the completeness of Christ's salvific work on the cross. God cannot tolerate or accept anything short of absolute perfection. He cannot, because to do so would compromise His intrinsic nature, and compromise would be to change His nature. (Again, being intentionally redundant, since this is one of the major themes of my book) This is our eternity we are discussing: our eternity! And it is our only hope! I really do not believe I can overdue emphasizing the importance of this subject!

1. The difficulty using particular references for these chapters is that this information has been found in dozens and dozens of books that I have read. I used a generalization of all that material. Please check out the Bibliography. In general they all address the same salvation themes.

CHAPTER 11

THE GOSPEL MESSAGE

In our conception we inherited a sin nature. We sin because we are by nature: sinners. The evidence for this is any two year old child or teenager. In my case, a simple evaluation of my life. I sinned because I did so according to my nature. Actually, when I am honest, I would say there were many times I enjoyed my sins. I later regretted most of them, but at the time they were desirable, or why would we do them. Additionally, God's revealed nature also magnifies my awareness of my sinfulness. This is part of the reason for the law: to define sin. To give an awareness of our sinfulness. A reflective way to have a measurement of a standard. When we come under conviction, via the work of the Holy Spirit, generally through the word of God, I have an initial understanding of my need: I am a sinner. Therefore, the obvious need for a personal Savior, a deliverer. Someone who is able to rescue us from our sin penalty dilemma. We need someone that can meet our needs, if there is such a person? Thankfully, there is one, who is fully qualified. His name is a name above all names, the Lord Jesus Christ.

There are a host of things God does for the believing sinner to qualify him/her for heaven. (Always remembering that one must be positionally perfect to be in the presence of God) Therefore, the absolute need of the cross, and the application by the Holy Spirit of those benefits. I will not give an exhaustive examination of those necessary requirements, but enough to bring confidence to the believer; so that one can know with settled confidence that they are fully acceptable. That every demand of the required justice before God has been fully satisfied by Jesus Christ. Which should result in stable peace to those who believe. A settled confidence that I am forever right with God. That the struggle to measure up to the standard of God has been fully satisfied. That the uncertainty of my eternal future is now assured, that is: SHOULD I BELIEVE, AND PERSONALLY ACCEPT WHAT JESUS DID FOR ME ON THE CROSS: THE MESSAGE OF THE GOSPEL!

Before going too far with the requirements for salvation, I should indicate that we have a qualified Savior. If we need a complete salvation, we need a Savior who is completely qualified, and Jesus Christ is such. He is eternally God, just as is God the Father and God the Holy Spirit. Jesus Christ, satisfied the Old Testament qualifications, by coming from the tribe of Judah, in the Priesthood of Melchizedek, and is the promised heir of the Kingship of David's line; but was always eternally the Son of God, the promised Messiah. Actually, His deity is the basis, and the foundation for our salvation. (John 1:1-2, John 8:24) In John, chapter 8, when Jesus refers to Himself, He is claiming to be the: I Am who I Am. This is the one and same Yahweh of the OT. This description is seen repeatedly throughout the Gospel of John.

He was born via a virgin, by the name of Mary, without the help of a biological father. He was conceived by the Holy Spirit in Mary. (This information for those who do not know the basic Christmas story) He eternally existed and only added human nature at conception. He is the exact representation of the eternal self-existent God: God the Father. (Hebrews chapter 1) By being a man, He could stand in our place as a human, our representative. He therefore can be our Kinsman redeemer. The idea that one can stand in the place of another, because He/they have legal rights as a member of a group. (Ruth chapter 4) In this case, Jesus humanity gives Him standing as a representative of mankind. As fully God, He could make a payment, an atonement for sin, that was infinite in value. This is why the genealogies of the Gospels of Matthew and Luke are so significant. One gives His legal rights and the other gives His birth rights to be our substitute. Both are necessary to be our Kinsman redeemer. Our qualified sinless Savior: who is fully God and fully man in one person. This is the message: the Son of God became man, so by faith in His payment on the cross, we could become sons and daughters of God. We can become children of our Heavenly Father. (John chapter one)

His life proved His sinlessness. (Just read the four gospels) He is qualified to be our bridge to God the Father. (Although, I don't fully like the bridge idea, since it may imply a need for me to do something, i.e. walk) While in the gospel, it is God who prepares a bridge, and He crosses it to us. Since Jesus Christ was the one that came to the earth (had a human body), and resolved our needs by dying on the cross. Jesus Christ's sacrificial payment is the only –and the full satisfaction –of God's requirements for justice. When God the Father accepted the anticipated, and then completed sacrifice, which Christ proved was acceptable by resurrecting from the dead: God was forever satisfied with the payment. His resurrection also shows He conquered death, by resurrecting from the dead. This is the victory that Jesus Christ accomplished; a completed salvation. (1st Corinthians chapter 15) A once for all time payment. Never to be repeated, never needing to be repeated. A sacrifice of infinite value. We have an infinitely righteous Savior, who was able to atone for all sins, of all time. (Just read the NT epistles)

This was verified by His resurrection, which was witnessed by hundreds, and written about by those who meet with Him after his death. And, as a little apologetics: the fulfillment of hundreds of prophecies and types in the Old Testament, which predicted the mission on which He was sent. (Jesus confirmed this in Luke 24:25-27) Which is nearly mathematically impossible to be a happenstance. (Again there are better able scholars who will defend this statement. See some of the suggestions at the end of this book)

Now believing is the only acceptable response that God honors or accepts. Knowledge about Jesus is not enough. Knowledge is the understanding that an airplane can fly. Faith is the understanding, not only can airplanes fly, but that I get on the plane. I trust in that belief. This is "a" definition of faith. A trust that gets me on the plane. Faith may come with some apprehension, but is trusting what I believe to be true, in that apprehension. There is no contribution that anyone can make that is acceptable to God, outside of accepting what Jesus Christ has already accomplished. There is no action or deed that measures up to God's infinite standards. We simply trust/ believe the revelation of God; as revealed in His only book, the Bible. There is a clear, one and only requirement: believe/accept what Christ completed on the cross on our behalf. This is God's instruction, and only requirement. To add anything to what God demands, or requires, is not acceptable. (Some will claim that the lack of faith is what keeps people from heaven. I don't think that fully grasps the totality of the issue. I believe that both personal and inherited sin is what is keeping us from heaven. It is the failure to exercise faith in Christ's sacrifice, that is the reason why the sin issue remains. Those who remain unsaved are unsaved because they never partook of the solution God offered)

Pause, and seriously think this through. What could an inherently sinful man/woman offer to God, that would in any way, be acceptable to meet His standards. Never forgetting that His standards are a reflection of His immutable righteous attributes. My need is literally an infinite one, that only God could satisfy. We need both mercy and grace. There is a difference. Mercy is not getting what we deserve, that is: punishment for sin. Grace is a step beyond that: It is the giving of something we have not earned, but receive as a free gift. A gift that God is offering by His gracious hand. We have grace upon grace in Christ Jesus. The gift of God is a grace gift. Unearned! Just received!

Upon believing in the person and work of Christ, I am given eternal life. By general understanding: eternal means forever and forever. I possess at the very moment of faith: the gift of eternal life. Now having been a probation officer for many years, I understand what probation conditions are. This is not what John 3:16, 5:24 or 6:47, and so many other passages teach. I have at that very moment of faith: eternal or everlasting life. The very righteousness of God imputed to me. The descriptive words that God the Holy Spirit guided the writers of scriptures to use, have intended meaning. God means what He says. So let us keep this real simple: eternal is forever, and forever is eternal. If I could lose this received gift of eternal life, then it was not really eternal from the beginning. God our Father is not a probation officer, nor works in a divine probation department. (I will develop this too, later in the book) It is a very simple message. And we would be wise to stay with what God requires and accepts. Do not add or subtract to what God says. That is what Eve did in the garden. The gift of God is eternal life. It is received simply by accepting the payment Christ made on our behalf. And upon receiving, it is a present possession, and lasts forever and forever. Pretty simple, right?

Another benefit of believing the gospel is we are born again. In the 3rd chapter of the Gospel of John: Jesus says this is an absolute requirement. One must be born again or born from above. Just like natural birth, this is a one time and non-repeatable event. One is never born again, then later, needing to be born again again. There is not a hint of this ever being required a second time in the scriptures. This is a one time event that happens at the very moment of faith in the gospel. This birth gives one acceptance into the family of God. A forever acceptance! Now that knowledge alone should give a wonderful and peaceful mindset. The knowledge that God has accepted me into His forever family. This concept is also described as regeneration: the concept of spiritual regeneration or renewal. A new birth into a new family. These results are not two steps, but one act of faith, which results in numerous necessary benefits. Since faith has no merit, it is simply accepting what God has offered. A pre-paid, free to us, salvation. This is God's Grace! This is also expressed in the phrase: that either one is born twice (physical and spiritual), in which case they will only die once (physical), or people who are only born once (physical), will die twice (both physical and spiritually). This spiritual death is not the cease to exist death, but an eternal separation from God. (Death in the Bible means separation)

Not only are we accepted by new birth, we are adopted into the family of God. The first gives me supernatural birth into the family. We are born again by the Spirit of God. Our acceptance is further described as full adoption. Adoption is the given legal rights, as a son or daughter, into a family that they were not originally born into, but now having the same rights and standing as one who was born into the family. This is true since we were born as sinners outside the family of God. We were born into Adam's sinful race. We are now, at the moment of faith, fully adopted into the very family of God. A member of the household of God. We have the full standing as a son or daughter into the family of God: both in new birth and adoption.

Another great truth of the salvation gift is justification. The cornerstone of the reformation. It has been said that justification is the idea, as though I had never sinned. But I understand it a bit more than that. I see it as God's declaration: He has declared me *just* in his sight. A legal term. A legal declaration of my righteous standing before the bar of God's justice. A perfect standing of righteousness before a perfect God. God is the ultimate Judge of the universe, and this is His declaration of me, upon my faith in Christ Jesus as the God/man, and my acceptance of the completed sacrifice of Jesus Christ on the cross as a full payment for my sin. (Romans chapter 5 and 8, and Galatians and Ephesians first few chapters)

These wonderful truths continue. It is seen in the first chapter of both of the books of Ephesians and Colossians, where the Apostle Paul talks about redemption, the forgiveness of sins. It is addressed in other places too, like Hebrews chapter 9, verse 12. Where it is described as an eternal redemption. The understanding is that *in Christ* we have been redeemed and forgiven. It is a relief of a problem we had, that is undeserved, just received. A freeing thought! The truth that the benefits of Jesus Christ's death on the cross, upon my faith alone, are applied to me, and results in my secure redemption. His sacrificial death payment made those benefits mine upon acceptance. The purchase price was fully paid for me on the cross, and once accepted, results in my eternal redemption; which makes me His forever. God does not overlook sin just because of His loving kindness. He forgives because the debt has already been fully paid, and therefore, He is free to forgive. The price has been paid, for all of us: have you accepted it? It is like an uncashed check. It has potential value, but its real value is only good upon cashing.

These truths continue. There is a theological truth called propitiation: which means God's righteousness has been satisfied. God is forever satisfied with what Jesus Christ did on our behalf. If we have partaken of those benefits: then God is forever satisfied. There is nothing for us to do in regards to securing salvation; He did it all. We simply need to respond by accepting the offer.

There is also a standing that is necessary for all mankind; that is the standing of absolute righteousness before God. Now at the very moment of faith: we are forgiven of all our sins, gifted with eternal life, accepted into the family by new birth, adopted into the family of God, redeemed by the blood of Christ, and justified before God. But that is not all. We are also clothed in the very righteousness of Christ. He who bore our sins now cloths us with His untarnished righteousness. I am in Christ and He is in me. His perfect righteousness has been granted as an imputed gift of righteousness, if we accept His offer. We are now clothed in the very righteousness of Christ. That knowledge should cause a shout of praise, not that it is required.

I hope you have come to understand these marvelous truths. They need to be known and embraced. They are well taught by many gifted scholars. As I have learned from many, including those like Dr. Andy Woods, in his Soteriology series. (Found at SLBC Dr. Andy Woods, under Soteriology) That in Adam lineage we were all imputed with the sinfulness of the first man, Adam. His sinful nature is being passed on to each and every person. On the cross: Christ was imputed with all the sins, of all mankind, of all time. Upon believing, I have been imputed with the very righteousness of Christ. I have full and complete righteous standing in the family of God. As mentioned: there are two aspects, one is adoption, and the other, new birth. It is an eternal standing and sonship. An absolutely secure eternal salvation. Think about that before moving on. We often read profound truths, and then quickly move on to the next thought. This is a thought that needs to be pondered, anchored into your soul, and kept firmly in your mind. If you want the presence of God's peace, and have settled assurance, meditate for a moment on these truths. In Christ, I am as righteous as Christ, because I have been clothed in His righteousness. I have imputed righteousness. Therefore, I have the right to be in the presence of the Holy God, because I am, in my new positional righteous standing. I am now fully accepted! These truths understood are the first step in real worship! Authentic worship! The Almighty God has accepted me into His forever family.

And you would learn, in a more thorough study of the scriptures, the many more blessings that are granted upon the acceptance of what God did in the person of Jesus Christ, and via His sacrifice. What he undertook because of His love for us. How He made us potentially acceptable to Himself. Now is the time, with what has been written, to ask: have you believed? Have you accepted what God did for you when He gave His only begotten Son for you? Have you accepted His gift of salvation? I truly hope so! Because His standards will never change. There is not another option for us or for God. He is immutable, and cannot change the standards; even God cannot do somethings! He cannot change His righteous standards just because He loves us. His love motivated Him to undertake this redemptive plan, but His immutable holiness does not allow another option. He has accomplished His plan. He has made "the" payment for you in the person and work of Christ. There are no other options or solutions to our sin problem. He is holy and we are sinners. We cannot change our inherited sin nature, but thanks be to God, by being born again, He has. This happens when we are spiritually born again. Then at physical death, the old nature is forever gone, and we continue on in a state called glorification. Until then, we are simultaneously both sinners and saints. Sinners in some of our actions, in our flesh; but Saints by position, because of our new birth.

The redemptive plan for our salvation is finished. And our eternal redemption is a great truth to keep firmly in our minds. He made us redeemable when He paid our sin debt. When we trust in Christ's finished sacrifice on the cross, we are then redeemed. His death is the satisfying payment. His work is forever completed, never to be done again, never needing to be done again! Therefore, upon believing, all the aforementioned blessings, and many more are fully and freely granted to you: at the very moment of faith! And, upon receiving, they never need to be repeated to remain a forever child of the living God. Please, don't forgo the opportunity to believe! Now is the day to receive the offer of salvation. Now is the time to accept the most magnificent gift. The free gift from God! Accept the finished work of Jesus Christ on your behalf and join the forever family of the eternal God. Because the work of Christ is only potentially salvific. You must personally accept this for yourself. Then it is a forever reality! God has no grandchildren. Your eternity is dependent on this decision. Let this sink in! We appreciate what happened on the cross, when we understand we deserve eternal Hell; which is more terrifying than anything you could ever fear, but I will say it again: that will never ever happen, if we simply accept the gift of eternal salvation the Lord offers. I am very intentionally being an evangelist now! This is the urgent reason for the book. To share this hope. And hope in the Bible is the confident assurance of what has been promised. It is not a wishful hope, but an assured hope. In chapters to come, we will see the church's, and our individual expected role, in this divinely given responsibility to share this hope. Not to do so: neglects the very faith we profess to believe. This does not mean we are not saved. It means we are denying our discipleship responsibilities. If we are real Christians: this is Christianity! It is the assurance of our salvation, via His finished work on the cross: the Gospel of Jesus Christ:.

You may think that I am overdoing it with the repeated emphasis on this theme. Yet: this is a book that is addressing the weakness within the body of Christ to really grasp the significance of the unapproachable holiness of God. But ultimately, it is a book, with the intent to bring hell-bound sinners into the family of God. This subject is just that eternally important. Furthermore, I am also trying to impress upon the reader the understanding that the gospel will be neglected, if we fail to grasp the seriousness of what we profess to believe. While it is primarily an evangelistic theology book, it also evaluates the importance of living out our faith according to the sound teachings of Biblical theology. The Bible should be the foundational truth for the way we live as a Christian. There is also the theme that should permeate throughout the book that simply asks the question: what are the real implications, if it is true? I am trying to force every believer to consider the real significance of what we progress to believe. While I am not trying to defend the faith through traditional apologetics, I am trying to force the reader to grasp the implications of Christianity being absolutely true. Since if Christianity is not a dependable depiction of absolute truth: then everything I write is a wasted read, and was a wasted time to write. Furthermore, life is then lived as a vapor without actual meaning, or hope.

Therefore, if you conclude with me that the Christian faith is based on strong evidence, and it is, then there is no more urgent message to proclaim than the hope of eternal life in the gospel of Jesus Christ. Consequently, this is ultimately a book that lays out the logical implications of something being true: God is immutably holy, and we need a complete solution to an eternal destination problem. This exclusive offer is best seen in chapter 14, verse 6, of the Gospel of John. This is why I emphasized that verse in this book. It forces the reader to face the exclusive claim by Jesus Christ. Only He is the way of salvation. It clarifies the outworking of the litmus test. The exclusive claim that only Jesus Christ is fully qualified to save us from the deserved wrath to come. Since my conviction is that this is true, I am alleging there needs to be a more robust evangelistic response to these truths; since these implications are really forever. This is why my emphasis is on pushing the truth to its logical conclusions, by reinforcing the central points.

Lastly, I have spent numerous Sunday mornings in worship service, then later go golfing or meet up with friends for coffee. I have this occasional habit of asking what the Sunday message was about. Often it is with those, with whom, I attend the same church. Only to have them struggle to remember the content. Often a very solid message, but very little lasting impact. Therefore, if I want to make a few unforgettable key points: I need to come back to the central themes over and over to make sure they find a secure place in our memory. Like any good coach or proficient instructor, those who train the fundamentals, so they are solidly grounded in what they need to know.

One thing should be absolutely clear: that one who is born again, cannot be more justified than they are at that very moment, but they can be more radically saved in their sanctification, which results in a great glorification. Please keep on reading to better understand some of the reasons this truth is not impacting us, as suggested, by the significance of what has been discussed. I will leave this chapter with this observation from the great Christian thinker, C. S. Lewis: "All that is not eternal is eternally useless."

1. Dr. Andy Woods found at SLBC Andy Woods, The whole Soteriology series.
2. The difficulty using particular references for these chapters is that this information has been found in dozens and dozens of books that I have read. I used a generalization of all that material. Please check out the Bibliography. In general they all address the same salvation themes.

CHAPTER 12

GOD COMMAND FOR THE CHURCH TO FULFILL THE GREAT COMMISSION

I am contending in this book that we as a body of believers are failing to grasp the weight of the unapproachable holiness of God. That it is a vastly neglected teaching in our churches. Most Christians will accept the basic premise that God is holy, but accepting the full implications of God's absolute holiness is a different matter. They grasp that God is holy, but neglect to give that truth its natural implications. For example, when it comes to the urgency of evangelism, there are a growing number of professed believers, who now believe there are other means of entering the heavenly abode. This is confirmed by recent polls that reveal a growing number of pastors now believe heaven can be earned by good behavior. This is further seen in the *body of Christ,* where a growing number of Christians -those who identify themselves as Christians- now believe one can enter the heavenly abode via another religion. The long held belief in the exclusivity of Christ alone is being abandoned by many Christians. This is largely because they fail to grasp the full significance of the litmus test I previously gave in chapter 10. This is the reason why I used my litmus test. It clarifies for an individual, whether they are understanding of the unmitigated holiness of God, and sufficiency of Christ's work on the cross. It defines the issue. If there is another way, then, Christ died in vain. (John 14:6 and 1ˢᵗ Corithians chapter 15) Resulting in Christianity being reduced to secondary benefits like feeding and clothing the poor.

That is why an understanding of God's immutable holiness, while difficult to fully accept, is absolutely crucial; if we are going to be motivated to fulfill the Great Commission. (Matthew 28:19-20) For without this comprehension, the church loses the reason to pursue its primary mission, to reach the lost with the Gospel of Jesus Christ. The litmus test reaffirms that there is only one hope. There is only one name that is able to save. (Acts 4:10-12, particularly verse 12) Tragically, for the lost, this is generally not the mindset of today's progressive church; which too often compromises the exclusivity of the faith alone in Christ alone, as the only means for salvation.

For most, to consider the status of the lost, is too unthinkable to even consider in today's popular culture; so it is replaced with more palpable messages. There is growing pressure on pastors to provide more desirable messages, those messages that massage the conscience, but avoid some of the orthodox doctrines of the faith that are hard to accept; those inherent truths of the Christian faith. For without the litmus test, one may believe he is able to achieve acceptability with God. This failure to understand the contrast between God's righteousness and our sinfulness, diminishes our ability to explain what Jesus accomplished on the cross. This neglect to grasp what is true about God's nature, results in a growing disinterest for evangelism. I believe this is because of a number of reasons. Here are a number to consider: 1. Most people do not want to face their own mortality. 2. The implications of God's holiness are too hard to accept. 3. They are uncertain about what really happens at death, therefore, they contrive their own theory. 4. They believe they somewhat merit salvation, so the need for a Savior is ignored. 5. They hold the view that these aforementioned judgements of God are preposterous, so they determine their own merit based standards for heaven; thereby, denying the litmus test connotations.

Consequently, the pursuit of the implications of who Christ is, and what He accomplished by His death on the cross: is either denied, diluted or ignored. Most professed evangelicals, still accepted as doctrine what we have traditionally professed to believe: that Christ alone is the sole means for salvation, but dilute the certain eternal connotations. Whereas progressives deny the exclusivity of Jesus Christ for salvation, based on the merits of Christ alone, but often continue to practice a shadow of the Christian religion; which is a denial of the merits of what Jesus did. Notwithstanding these perspectives, since Christianity is demonstratively true, and considering the consequences of where we will spend our eternity, evangelism should be the most urgent mission of the church. For those of us who claim the name of Christ, this should be our premier priority.

There is a journal entry by the late missionary, Jim Elliot, that reads: "He is no fool who gives what he cannot keep to gain what he cannot lose." That principle could be applied to the usage of our monetary resources, knowing that upon death, they have no remaining value to the owner. But a better understanding of this principle, would be to invest one's life fully into evangelistic service for the Lord; since there is nothing we can take with us beyond the grave, besides those eternal investments. So investing your life for what will last forever, is the most astute manner in which to live. Jim Elliot believed that principle to the point that it cost him his life on the mission field. This was the Apostle Paul's perspective too. (Acts 20:24-27)

Unfortunately, this is not the present mindset of the ordinary believer today. According to a 2008 Pew Research, and many other newer polls, a growing number of Christians now believe that people can enter heaven apart from the gospel message. That belief is irreconcilable with the historical understanding of Biblical Christianity: the gospel that Jesus, the Apostle Paul and the others taught. And is one of the mainsprings that should flow out of an understanding of the absolute immutable holiness of God. The cornerstone of the Biblical faith. Should we conclude that Apostle Paul's evangelistic motivation was a rational response, based on the compelling evidence for the actual physical resurrection of Christ, as described in the Gospels, and his grasping the eternal ramifications, then that same urgency should be more pronounced in our church ministries. He understood the urgency, so strongly, that he was willing to sacrifice all his personal comfort, to get out the message. It showed in his passion, as described by Luke in the book of Acts, and often written about in his epistles. (Acts 20:24-27)

I know most will be very uncomfortable with this notion in their personal lives. They desire to be good people, that is noble, we should be good people, but they prefer not to have it emphasized too much in their places of worship; it is too unsettling for most to even consider. Most do not want to think about this aspect of our faith, so it is ignored.

Accordingly, this neglect to perceive God's intrinsically holy nature, has resulted in a lukewarm church. (Revelation 3:14-21) The more we drift from the litmus test contrast, the more irrelevant the church. The church loses its distinctive message: the promise of eternal life in Christ. It is obvious that the church has drifted significantly over the decades. Churches that were once established on these truths contained in the scriptures, who once comprehended the eternal consequences of the proclaimed faith, are now being replaced by churches that promote a mystical spiritual experience. Where peoples terrestrial interests have taken priority over those with eternal ramifications. One of the church's first missions to suffer neglect: the priority of purpose driven evangelism. The weight of this urgency has now been replaced with social programs and those of self-help, which are more appealing to many congregations. Those prefer programs, which are more desired over the hard realities of our eternal destinies; and therefore, they are pursued because they are more acceptable to the conscience. They also avoid the stigma of what we have historically believed. Consequently, over focusing on the temporary quality of one's life, to the neglect of the eternal, results in a practice of our faith that is often void of eternal impacting endeavors.

Be sure, the Bible gives a Christian a roadmap for how to live a meaningful life. It addresses every conceivable aspect of life. If one wants a good foundation for living a meaningful life: Christianity is the best place to start. Since every conceivable vital aspect of life is taught in the Bible. However, no matter how one computes the importance of living a meaningful life, always remember, that every temporary pursuit in this life has an ending point; it is fleeting, since the way of all men is death. Therefore, if there is one question that absolutely must be resolved before entering the state of eternity, it is not the quality of your life, or what you were able to accomplish outside of Christ, it is the assurance of one's eternal destiny; and then, endeavoring how to live a life that leaves an eternal legacy. And only the Bible is a reliable source for how to be assured of Heaven, and how to avoid Hell. Then subsequently, how to live an eternally relevant life; what is required for this to be realized in each person's life. The Bible is the only book that teaches these principles in light of what is really worthy. It addresses both the temporary, and more importantly, the eternal. Those contrasting truths of the litmus test are not being taught. When that distinction is not being preached: the church omits the reason for evangelism. But when we fully accept that eternity is dependent on the acceptance of those truths, their eternal destiny, it reinvigorates the church to fulfill that mission.

Therefore, the great commission, as commanded in the Gospel of Matthew, should be the central mission. It should be the premier priority for every church. The sanctification of the believer should follow the evangelism of the lost; which too, is an aspect of the great commission. The development of mature disciples of Christ. The changing of the world, one person at a time through evangelism, and then personal discipleship. Unfortunately, this is generally nowhere to be found in many bodies of believers. Where are the deeply mature believers who are able to minister individually to those in the body? First, equipt to bring the lost to saving faith, then grounded in the faith, so they can help disciple men and women into effectively duplicating saints themselves. Christians who are able to teach the principles of God's word, and then disciple effectively. Our story of redemption should become our ministry of sharing with others the way of redemption.

I believe if we want effective and mature believers, interpersonal issues need to be addressed and worked through. It is part of making people whole and well rounded saints. When this desired aspect of discipleship, which should be part of the mission of the church, is lacking, then so are mature saints. So please don't understand me here. I am not indicating the present struggles should be ignored. I am suggesting that an over emphasis of pursuing temporary success, to the neglect of the eternal, is foolish in light of eternity. When these take too much priority, the church compromises its greater call, to reach the lost with the ultimate hope: the Gospel of Jesus Christ.

The issue remains: this life is temporal. There is no escaping that reality. Upon death, there is no recourse to our condition. If anyone neglects the free offer of salvation, there is no second chance. This could be a horrifying consequence, that I am not willing to risk. I want that absolute assurance of what the eternal future holds. As often been noted, we will spend considerable time planning our once in a lifetime vacation, but ignore a once in lifetime event that has eternal consequences. The implications are undeniable. There is an inescapable truth of our pending death; that is a reality that we can not ignore. We will make diligent efforts to make sure our retirement is secure, not even knowing if we will be alive to enjoy it, and ignore the requisite knowledge needed for our eternal destiny. I have known good friends who spent a working lifetime planning for a stable and promising retirement, only to die prematurely, and pass on those benefits to someone who did not earn them. This too is vanity. Again, read the book of Ecclesiastes, which looks at the vanity of many of our temporal pursuits, with a God-centered perspective of what it means to live a meaningful life.

I have often heard pastors discuss their frustration with the lack of involvement by the members in their local body of believers. It is an accurate observation. There are at least three reasons I believe contribute to this situation. The first, in many ways, the body does feel there are two tiers of ministry. Those that are recognized with a title, and then the congregants. The "professionals" enjoy the benefits of clerical support and have resources available to them that are needed for lay ministers too. The leadership in the church needs to focus on the teaching of priesthood of all believers. And developing the more mature believers into roles that elevate them to teaching and sometimes preaching, provided those are their gifts. The idea that there is always a greater degree of Biblical wisdom, that is only possessed by the professional, is often fallacy. I have found many well read and gifted believers that are not being utilized or developed to their fullest. They are not being disciplined to be effective lay ministers. They are too often limited in their roles, because it is believed they do not have an qualifying official title. But even in the pastoral books of the Bible, the elder is one who must be able to teach the doctrines of the faith. If that is a requirement to be an elder, then it is also a responsibility, or an opportunity that should be afforded to those so gifted. No one man is the source of all knowledge or spiritual insight. One pastor preaching week in and week out as though he is the only fountain of Biblical wisdom, may not be utilizing all of the body's talents. No one man is that deep in endless knowledge. We are a body of believers, each with different skills and abilities; those should be better utilized.

The second, is pastors have done an inadequate job of teaching maturing believers how to be duplicating ministers of the gospel. The message we have needs to be taught to others with the desired effect, that they too, can minister to individuals in their unique contact situations. Pastors generally don't have the broad access to the unsaved masses that the congregational members often do, through their work, business, or other natural contacts. This diminishes the expansion of the gospel into their communities. This is a major focus in the book of Ephesians, chapter 4. The equipping of the saints for the ministry. Preaching to the body is not discipleship. Sunday school or Wednesday night services are not discipleship if they are not discipleship making sessions. And part of discipleship is duplicating mentorship, one generation to the next. The equipping of the present generation to carry the message forward, then equipping the next in the fundamentals of the faith. This was a big theme in both testaments. By various means, believers were called to be ambassadors of the faith, by passing on the truths of the faith, once for all given. (See the book of Jude)

This leads to the third factor affecting the lack of growth in the body. Where are the mature believers who are able to mentor the hurting. If there are marriage issues, where are the successful and stable married partners who are able to mentor the young, or more mature, but struggling couples. It is certainly a principle that Apostle Paul discussed in his pastoral letters to Timothy and Titus. This applies to both men and women with some conditions. Older women teaching younger women on how to be good mothers and wives. Men who are able to teach other younger men how to man up, and be stand up men of the faith. Teaching them how to properly love their wives. Personal discipleship was the practice of Jesus. He discipled men in the faith who later became apostles and evangelists. Principle upon principle, with the goal of maturing the faith in new believers; then duplicating the faith to the next generation.

It needs to start as an emphasized priority in the pulpits. If pastors want to be a mature and multiplying ministry, they need to create that emphasis. Setting forth the principle that this is the mission of the church. Emphasizing frequently that the gospel changes the eternal destiny of the unbeliever. Then the intentional engagement with the new believers, mentoring them in the discipleship process. The taking of a babe in Christ, then disciplining them into mature and duplicating members of the local body. Anchored, and able to defend and proclaim the hope we have in Christ. This results in the greater part of the body having a mindset to be ministry orientated; at least it should be! This is the process of evangelism to discipleship the Bible lays out. Whole movements have started this way. Like the emergence of Sunday school programs, which now misses the mark of real discipleship making. Those sessions have emerged into little more than acquiring additional Christian knowledge, without equipping the saints in how to spread the life changing message. We have gone from the Great Commission to the great omission.

Think about the churches that are shadows of their past founders. The driving passion that gave rise to these denominations. Those who felt the call to change lives with the gospel; a burning desire to reach the lost. Many of these churches have now become shadows of their past zeal. If we don't properly assess our declining situation as an evangelical church we are headed to irrelevance. We will be simply reduced to being soup kitchens. Churches that once were a bright light of truth, and had a passion for the life changing gospel, are now just communities of well fed but lost souls. Our impact on the community is slowly becoming nothing more than a social support system. When the light of truth grows dim, so goes the society; manifesting in our communities, in the form of moral decay. Sin has personal and community consequences. The devaluing effects of sexual sin are hard to restore in the life of those deceived by the lies of culture. The resulting consequences to our society, those having been deceived by the allure of unrestrained sexual freedom. Only a clear understanding of the newness of life, that is possible in Christ, can give the hope needed to start anew as a newly born saint. It starts with evangelism; then progresses as we learn how to live out of our new identity as a child of the King. It starts with the gospel and continues in discipleship.

What greater call is there for the church than to bring the lost to Christ and then build them up in the faith. Equipping them so there is a lasting change in their personal lives, and also in their families. The unified effort to bring lost, and hell bound sinners, into a right standing with God. This statement seems so harsh and odious, but it is literally and Biblically true. It is a hard concept to accept. It is certainly a theme that I would prefer to ignore. But I am left with the recurring dilemma: either the faith is built on solid evidential foundations, or let's all eat and drink and be merry, because this transitory life is just that. Most will simply ignore, or greatly dilute the implications, because it is a more diverting mindset to have. But we can't honestly justify that mindset when the litmus test is a valid distinguishing test? The inherent truth that God is absolutely holy, and the gospel is absolutely sufficient to save even the worst of sinners, clarifies the reality of the situation.

This is why I believe this message of this book is so needed today. It was not an easy book to write. I like my life for the most part. I have a nice marriage. I enjoy my time with our children and grandchildren. I have many good quality friends. I generally enjoy life. I really don't care to be overtly evangelistic, it is very unnatural for me. And even though I am writing a strong evangelistic book, the realities of what I am contending are still difficult to fully accept. I too have a hard time accepting all the implications of what I am writing about. I would prefer a loving God with more accepting and adaptable values, it would be so much easier to live with. The warm fuzzy God that many have conceived God to be. But that is not the God of the Bible. The revealed God is a holy God. Therefore, the question remains: is it true or not? If not, then let's eat, drink and be merry, for tomorrow we die; I mean I am in my 60's. My life journey is starting to fade as the years go by. It really comes down to the simple truth claim made by Jesus in John's gospel, 14:6. Either we wrap our arms around the truth of this message, which results in an assurance of our eternal destiny, knowing that the best is yet to come, or give me a cold beer, and let's set aside this conversation and have a good time. Those who are strong fundamentalist may find objection with my last statement. But is it consistent with what the apostle Paul wrote in 1st Corinthians, chapter 15. Paul writes: if for this life only....

CHAPTER 13

UNDERSTANDING OUR CALL TO BE EVANGELISTICALLY OBEDIENT

(Editorial note. As you read this chapter, it will appear, I am jumping back and forth repeatedly with the same contrasting thoughts. Wait until the end of the chapter and you will see my reason for taking this approach)

In the previous chapter, I discussed the churches need to make evangelism, then duplicating discipleship, the central part of the mission. (Matthew 28:19-20) This chapter is focusing on the exhortation by God, to each individual Christian, of our personal responsibility to fulfill the great commission. There should be an obvious urgency for that mission, to reach the lost with the gospel. When an Christian ponders the connotations of eternity, then the rationale for engaging in evangelism should be obvious. And our degree of motivation reveals whether we are really grasping the consequences of the litmus test. This is the case I have been making throughout the content of this book. There are the profound implications inherent in the gospel message of Jesus Christ's death and resurrection; the total satisfaction of our sin debt.

Most individuals customarily enjoy our annual Christian traditions. We look forward to the seasonal celebrations of the birth of Jesus Christ (Christmas), and His death and resurrection (Good Friday and Easter). These traditions are often treasured occasions for most families. A time to gather and celebrate our Christian heritage. However, these momentous events in history seem to have lost the real merit they should demand. There seems to me that there is an immense disconnect between how we outwardly celebrate these holidays, and having a genuine appreciation of what we are celebrating. For example, consider the importance of the resurrection of Christ, it may be the most important event in human history; since it has real eternal repercussions. It should be far more paramount, than the average American gives credence. Instead, it is often treated as a nostalgic seasonal celebration. This is also true for the birth of Jesus. The idea that God Almighty entered humanity as a man, is far more significant than is generally appreciated. This is a bit bewildering for me, if we are giving the weight of these events their due. I have spent considerable time pondering why this is so. It is clear we are failing to grasp the full inference of these momentous events: the entrance of God into humanity, the death of Jesus Christ, and His actual physical resurrection. While other holidays are significant, they are not in the same category as God entering His own creation so He could atone for the sins of the world. May I suggest there are a number of reasons why this might be:

The first is we have adapted a form of universalism. The idea being held by too many Christians is that Chrisitanity is the best way but not the only way. Those that hold this view believe it will somehow work out for the others. Surely God did not mean a real literal Hell, and if He does, it is only for the most evil of mankind. (The Hitlers of the world) Or, we may reluctantly believe it may be true, but are not entirely convinced. We only give these events the weight that our faith allows. We are not willing to sacrifice our desires for what this world offers, for something that may not be literally true. We hope it is true; we want it to be true; but we are not convinced. We shallowly hold it as our hope for heaven, but not to the radical degree of actual sharing the gospel.

Another factor for some is simple disbelief. People cherish the traditions, but are suspicious of the truthfulness of Christianity. They believe it happened so long ago, they wonder if they can trust the stories as real events in history. Lastly, some are simply caught up with living life, pursuing the preferred life, and the inference conflicts with that desired lifestyle. They like the traditions, but they are spiritually blind to the actual significance of these events. In all these cases, people are not asking the most pertinent question: whether it is absolutely true or not. In all of these cases, it is clear they have never come to the point of weighing the magnitude of the claims of Jesus, as alleged in John 14:6. They don't understand the litmus test. They never settled in their minds the real eternal ramifications. Those that are inherent in the very claims by Jesus Christ: His claim of deity (John 8:24), that salvation is by faith alone, in Him alone. (John 14:6) But there are a few other factors too:

They believe in the plane's ability to fly but have not taken a seat on the plane. Meaning, they have not exercised trusting faith. They may believe it is possibly true, but have stopped short of trusting in the gospel personally as their only hope. They may reluctantly believe it is true, but don't like the implications, so they minimize it to make it more palatable. We Christians are often embarrassed to admit to those outside the faith that this is what we really believe. We lack the courage to take a stand on the fact this is what we actually believe. Lastly, we may falsely believe we can merit heaven with faith and good works; a combination of our good deeds and God's grace. Therefore, the cross is minimized, because some people believe they are somewhat earning the right to heaven. Regardless of the reason, the significance of those events are devalued. Two and two do not equal four anymore. What we celebrate is not given its real worth.

Regardless of these perspectives, what people know and believe is eternally significant. I know most non-fundamental Christians have various conceived ideas of what is required to get into heaven. They may believe all one can do is to hope for the best. Besides, it is generally believed by most, that all reasonably good people will be accepted; whatever heaven or the next life holds. Their belief is that God is a good and accepting God. They surmise that He is an accepting God, if He even exists? They believe as long as one has some faith, and a general goodness, that is all that will be required. In general, they believe this is their primary life. To suggest there is a literal Hell to avoid and a Heavenly paradise to gain, is seen as a bit of an extreme position to hold. Many believe it is all speculation anyways. Maybe holding to the perspective that nobody really knows for sure, so don't take it too seriously. Most are befuddled thinking people, with no place to put their feet. They have no solid ground of truth. We are becoming a people with no anchor of truth: just preferences.

But is it wishful thinking that for the vast majority the door to heaven is very wide and generally open to all? That only the most deplorable and completely faithless will experience an heavenly denial. Can the majority really take comfort that those normal, and generally good people, can have a confident assurance that God is a loving and accepting God. That He will grant entrance into His Kingdom, to those who are generally good; even as the Pope now appears to be alluding too. That even the atheists can hold on to a hope that the door to heaven is open to them too; if the intent of their heart is good.

Regardless of what we *prefer* to believe, the question is still: is the Bible trustworthy and true? Was Christ telling the truth when He said that He was the only way to the Father? Remember the central claim He made in the Gospel of John, chapter 14, verse 6. The question is will we accept what He said? The fact is that He will never ever change. We treat our sins like something we *should* avoid, and not as an eternal destiny issue. Most prefer to ignore serious consideration of the possibilities, since it is undesirable to even consider. It is a concept we generally want to avoid thinking about, so we put aside any serious consideration. We create in our minds, what we think are those heavenly accepting requirements. But when someone holds that mindset, they are blinded to the truth. They are denying the exclusive claims of Jesus Christ. It is a failure to make a decision, based on the facts supporting the deity of Christ, and the evidence for His death and resurrection from the dead; and it will cause them for all eternity. There is an exclusive claim by Christ: that it is Him alone, for our eternal salvation! Everyone must decide, but the consequences remain.

This is where the insight into the God Immutable holiness returns to the equation. If, as I am alleging, that God is unalterably holy, and due to His intrinsic nature, he cannot change - then the whole question is magnified. The expectations of most will be greatly misplaced. The inevitable will meet the reality of all of life. People do die, and are met with the situation that they are not prepared to meet God. They are not positionally holy. They have not met the perfect standards of pure righteousness. What a horrifying consequence! And, when this reality manifests itself to those trusting in other options, there will be no recourse. They will find that throughout all of eternity that God remains unalterably and immutable holy, and His justice is being satisfied. The question remains: did we each accept the offered righteousness, because of what Christ did for us, or are we each accepting the consequences of our deficient merits, which will be shown to be absolutely inadequate for all of eternity. Both results last for all of eternity. (Matt 25:46) In either case, there will be divine justice. One a declaration of our righteousness, made by God, because of what Jesus did for us; one, administered by God, because of willful ignorance or pride.

As I previously noted, I have long struggled with the thought of an eternal Hell, and so does everyone I know who will spend any time considering its implications. It seems so unnatural and extreme. Unfair to the highest degree. It's like, really: Hell? An eternal and forever place of consequence for sin. How can a loving God have such a place in His plan for mankind. A real destiny for those not covered in the righteousness of Christ. The only answer that is even somewhat conceivable, even remotely understandable, is when we return to the revelation of God's immutable holiness. This is the intrinsic nature of God. He cannot tolerate, in His presence, sin to any degree, ever.

(Some reflections) As a person who made his living in law enforcement, I know there are consequences for illegal and immoral choices. The intent of the law is fairness: blind justice. A consequence equal to the offense, and equally applied. But Hell appears to be anything, but fair! In my humanity, and as one who likes people, I want to push back against the whole concept, because Hell appears to be an injustice in the highest degree! What kind of God would send someone to Hell? Let alone: one that is eternal in duration. While objectionable and hard to accept, it is logically understood only as one gets an vision of immutable holy! Not only intrinsically holy, but also immutably holy. So the status remains, at anypoint should God alter His standards, He would no longer be the revealed God of the scriptures. He would no longer be immutable. He would be like one of us -in the sense- He would be relatively good. His justice would be subjective. Yet, regardless of our desires to have a God we prefer, the nature of God is not subject to change. The litmus test remains: sin unatoned for at death, remains unatoned for all eternity, and so do the consequences.

I wish there was another way. I truly dislike this whole notion of an unchangeable God, who will never be other than He is; and therefore, cannot adjust His holy standards to suit my preferred standards. I do not get to make God in my own preferred image. It is God who is the creator. He made man in His image. When man does not measure up to that stated standard, the door is closed to having a relationship with Him. It will never alter! I need a permanent declaration of righteousness. One that provides an acceptance that will never change. Since outside this perfect eternal standing, should I ever fall short of that infinite standard, the relationship would be rebroken. I would no longer be qualified. I need a permanent salvation. To compound the problem even more, I was born with a sin nature, so I am only doing what is according to my birth nature. So even if I would try my very best to be a good person, I am not positionally holy. I need Christ's permanent righteousness credited to me. (Again, repeating these points by intent to emphasize their importance)

I fully understand why we dislike evangelism. I have mentioned repeatedly that it is disagreeable to me. It does not fit my preferred or natural personality. I am really an easy going and hopefully likable person. I am one of those guys who says hi to just about everyone: "Hey, how are you doing?" I like the environment that is portrayed on the old Andy Griffith show. Sitting on the porch on Sunday afternoons and enjoying fellowship with those passing by our way. Folksy people who care for each other. Hanging out at the street curb, and chatting with our friends, as we inquire into their well-being and catching up on their family. Where most everyone is a decent person. I think you are getting the picture. This is a desired part of being human: enjoying warm fellowship with our fellow man. Regardless of this preferred life, it does not nullify the truth of what I previously wrote; therefore, there is an urgency to share the gospel. But I know the uneasiness of the whole subject.

As I have noted a few times, my dislike of the implications is so strong at times, I have even savored the idea of setting aside the whole kitten caboodle. Just turning off the idea of being a Christian, at least in the evangelical sense. I have entertained the idea more than once. Just get on living and forget the whole subject. Be a fun loving guy and enjoy my life.

However, to do that I must set aside those unavoidable questions that we all must face: simply, what happens at death? Is there real truth? And, if I determine that the Christian faith is based on verifiable facts, can I just ignore them? I have my "ticket" to Heaven verified and my destiny is secure. I could enjoy the fellowship of a local body of believers and engage in acts of kindness. That would give me a sense of purpose and may satisfy my desire to be a positive difference maker. Helping people transverse through the journey of life with as little discomfort as possible. Helping people become whole and happy. I have considered dropping out of the race; all because I do not enjoy the existential discomfort of sharing my faith, and I like to be liked. But the eternal implications and truthfulness of the faith do not really allow that option.

Therefore, to avoid the call of evangelism, I must set aside those issues of Heaven and Hell, and the eternal destiny of those I love. And furthermore, this would result in my neglecting to influence the eternal destiny of those that I love. Is not the greatest love of all the willingness to self-sacrifice? Am I not willing to set aside some of my desired comforts in this life, if I really believe it is true? This is the tension! Between what I want from life, and what I believe is ultimately true. What are we going to do with the claims of Christ?

Be mindful, that we will be held responsible for our evangelistic efforts, or lack thereof. In the 20th chapter of Acts, Apostle Paul, is recorded as saying that he was free of the blood of all men: since he did not hesitate to preach the gospel. Later in the book of 1st Corithians, in chapter 9, verse 16, he writes: woe is me if I do not preach the gospel. This is similar to the watchman in the book of Ezekiel. The failure to warn the unrepentant to change their ways leaves the unrepentant still responsible for their own sins. However, as in Ezekiel's warning, those who shrink back, are responsible for not warning them. This is not a Heaven or Hell question for the believer. But it is a warning for all of us who are commissioned to share the faith. It is an accountability issue with the Lord. For the New Testament believer, it is likely that this accountability will be addressed at the Bema Seat of Christ, or by Fatherly discipline in this life. If we get caught up too much in this life, don't be surprised if God removes some of those cherished items from our lives. We are commanded to go and make disciples. That is even a step beyond evangelism. The question is: do I love people enough, knowing the eternal consequences, that I would set aside my desire to always be appealing to them, in order to share this hope we can have in the gospel of Jesus, even though it is often uncomfortable? How can we Christians claim Christianity is true: if 95% of all professed believers never lead one person to saving faith? We become bolder in our faith when we go from superficially believing, to counting it fully true in all its ramifications. I understand the dilemma, it is hard.

As you can see in this chapter, it was not so much about how to share our faith, but to understand the implications of the faith. Since few really enjoy the inherent responsibility that naturally comes with implications of the gospel. It can be very uncomfortable to even consider stepping out and engaging with others over their eternal destiny. Most people feel ill equipped to share. Those who so desire, there are some really good resources that can help. (Some really bad ones too: those that promote a false gospel) The thought of engaging in evangelism is a very unnatural feeling for most of us. So in this chapter, I wanted to recognize the stigma we all feel with the call to evangelism. I was trying to capture the mental anguish we all grapple with over sharing our faith. This is why I was back and forth mentally wrestling with the connotations of the faith. The rationale for evangelizing only makes sense because it is absolutely true, and because this life is guaranteed to be short; like a mist that appears, then is gone. Ultimately, it is too eternally crucial to neglect: because it is true! If for this life only….. As the Apostle Paul wrote.

CHAPTER 14

WRESTLING WITH THOUGHTS ABOUT EVANGELISM

I f you are grasping the central theme of this book, you should feel a renewed motivation to share the gospel of Jesus Christ. You should see more clearly the striking contrast between real Heaven and a literal Hell, and realize you are not doing enough to bring sinners to the Savior. You may now understand that not only are souls at risk, but you may realize for the first time, that we all will be accountable for our evangelistic efforts, or lack thereof. Therefore, I want to address a few issues with those who desire to share the faith; those who are not interested; and those who desire to, but feel ill prepared or unqualified.

For those who are willing, those who get the real gravitas of the message, a word of caution is in order. While we understand the urgency, those to whom we want to witness likely do not, or they would be believers. Therefore, a word of caution is in order: be careful of being *unnaturally zealous*. Some are simply not there yet. God may be working in their heart, but the fruit is not ready to be picked. Remember, that our understanding of the gravity of the situation, is not usually held by those with whom we want to witness. There are a number of reasons why people do not come to faith, or even want to. Here are a few basic ones to consider; but there are numerous others.

Those who are willing need to understand:

1. Those to whom we witness are spiritually blind; they do not understand the need. They are blinded by the spirit of this age. Their unbelief may be because they are blinded by Satan and/ or the world system empowered by Satan. (2nd Corinthians 4:4) Their minds are clouded, so they lack spiritual perception. This is where prayer is so key. We need to be praying that God will open their spiritual eyes so they see their need. When the Holy Spirit has brought them to the place where they see their need, their interest will be aroused; then we who have the heart for the lost, will find the door open to share. Sometimes, while they may not realize their need, our sharing will provoke that interest, which then opens the door for an opportunity to share. Sometimes our sharing causes an interest, and other times, something causes an interest, which leads to an open door to sharing.

2. There may be emotional issues that are preventing them from even looking into the faith. The evidence for the faith means little. They are angry at the world and how it has treated them. They may even be angry at God, because they feel like life has dealt them an unfair hand, and therefore, they question the goodness of God. These need to see the eternal benefits of being a believer far outweigh their temporary difficulties. We need to acknowledge that life is not always fair; but God is, and will be for all of eternity. So we pray, and we share, and we love.

3. They harbor resentment toward someone in the faith. Someone who was, or claimed to be a Christian, has treated them very un-Christ like. In this case, they need to see that the behavior of a particular Christian, is not always consistent with the one we follow: Christ. It is He who is perfect and exhibits perfect grace and love. Sadly, we Christians, are often very poor witnesses because of our less than Christ-like behavior. This needs to be

differentiated, those that identify with the faith and/or claim to be Christian, can be a world apart in their behavior, from the originator of the faith, the perfect God/man.

4. Some simply do not want to have sexual limitations or other moral restrictions placed upon them. In this case, the truth does not matter, they want what they want. Those so identified, need prayer and a dose of hard reality. They need to see the temporariness of their pursuits. They usually will not come to the faith until life changes their pursuit of pleasure to a serious experience of pain. Or, they find those pursuits have become meaningless; the emptiness of their narcissistic pursuits. In general, regardless of the sexual conquest, and the hurt caused by those conquests, there will always be a new sexual desire that seems to go unsatisfied. If it was so satisfying: why is there never real satisfaction? Why is it such a meaningless pursuit of pleasure, so ultimately hollow? It is usually pain or emptiness that changes their perspective.

5. There are those who have been deeply hurt in the Christian experience, but are real Christians. The sources for this mindset can be varied. These are those who are born again, but have abandoned the daily walk of the faith. Which can lead to deconstruction from the faith. They may feel God did not come through for them in time of great need. That God can't be trusted. Those deeply hurt, need an abundance of love, and, of course, prayer. They need a few close Christian friends who have a listening and nonjudgmental heart. These are real born again Christians, who do not need to be born again, again. They need to be restored. They need help working through the disappointments of the faith. It is often, even in their headache, they come to realize that there is no other place to turn. If we leave God: what is left? This was an observation made by the Apostle Peter in the Gospel of John, 6:68. As he observes about Jesus: where else can we go, you have the words of eternal life. The alternative is: a meaningless life in a purposeless world. They may even need to forgive God. This may sound strange, but some hold such resentment towards God, they need to

forgive; even if there is really no rationale for forgiving God. It is clear, God does not do evil. And, in time, He will make right, the pain experienced. (Revelation 22) There is a real reward for enduring pain and suffering.

6. Closely related to those who have deconstructed, because they are disillusioned with the faith, is the one who lacks adequate assurance in the faith; they do not know the abundance of evidence for the faith, nor the reasons for continuing in their faith. They are failing to see how their faith helps in times of struggle. They likely have been babes in the faith too long, and then a crisis happens, and they do not have faith in their faith. Sometimes, these are Biblically naive believers, who become disillusioned with the faith, because they were led to believe there are some guaranteed blessings, because of some faith promise, that are simply not assured to a Christian. They have a distorted view of Christianity. They may have been wrongly led, often by prosperity teaching preachers, who made promises for God that are not Biblical. When some of these promises do not materialize, because others misconstrue what is true about Christianity, they become disillusioned and may even abandon the faith. They need to work through sound theology and apologetics, and learn the real rationale for living out the Biblical faith. They need to understand the importance of finishing strong, with an insight into the Bema Seat judgment, where all Christians will give an account of their lives. This insight should foster new motivations to be faithful until the end, knowing God will reward faithfulness. It is also extremely important to learn of our Heavenly Fatherly discipline in this life, because God might need to administer strong discipline in order to get one back on track. They need our prayers, our loving encouragement, and a dose of good theology. These are discussed as we continue on in the book.

7. There are some who are not open to the gospel, since they have unchurched friends or family, who have passed away, and the thought they could be in Hell is inconceivable, even repulsive to them; therefore, they surmise that the God of the Bible is a

distortion of who God is. They can only perceive a God who is loving and kind. They have no place in their theology for a holy God who must judge sin, let alone judge someone they love. They cannot conceive of a God who would ever judge someone they see as relatively good, for their sin. Neither of these assumptions are fully Biblical. God is loving and kind. However, as we have seen, His righteousness must first be propitiated. Once this satisfaction of God's righteousness is accepted by the sinner, then God is free to be loving and kind.

However, this does not necessarily mean that their unchurch loved one is experiencing this consequence. Many have once accepted the gospel, but due to a variety of reasons, abandon the faith, even walk away in bitterness. They show no evidence of having been a believer, but maybe they are. Oftentimes, only God truly knows. There is an interesting perspective we can get from the rich man in torment, in Luke 16. He tragically understands his eternal status, and yet, he requests that someone be sent to warn his brothers. Even in his unalterable condition, he wanted the message to be taken to his family, because he now understands the eternal consequences, and is lovingly concerned. He suddenly became evangelistic, because while he could not change his situation, his love for his family left him wanting him to change the destiny of those he loved. We too should have that same attitude. The truth being unknown, since we may not always know if someone is saved and disillusioned with God, or in a state of unbelief; either way, we should not dwell on what we do not know, and have the attitude of the rich man, and lovingly want to change the destiny of those we can.

For those who are uninterested in evangelism: Let us look at why they may not be sharing.

1. Are they denying the essence of the faith? We may need to ask if they really believe? What is it they are believing? Have they come to see the realities of the faith? There is a good chance that the non-witnessing, but –identified as a Christian– may simply not be born again. They identify with the faith but are

not part of God's family. They have never been born again. They have a faith that is not an authentically placed faith. (This from a person who strongly believes in eternal security!) For these, the litmus test is a great way to start to clarify the issues central to the faith. Do they grasp the essentials of the basic gospel? They may not witness because they may have never gotten on the plane.

2. They can not accept the exclusivity of Jesus Christ as the only way; they are Christian universalists. They are unwilling to accept that those who do not believe are condemned already. (John 3:18) This pending condemnation will not change until there is an acceptance of what Christ did, the paying their personal sin debt. There is no other alternative. A dislike of Hell does not nullify the reality of it. A rejection of the essential facts of the faith, just because of a dislike for them, does not nullify its truth claims. I acknowledge that there are aspects of the faith that are hard to accept, even though the evidence is very compelling. Some may resist the exclusivity of: only Jesus.

3. They may lack confidence in the truthfulness of the faith. They are true believers but lack the confidence to move forward as developing believers. Those who are in this state of faith, need to know the faith is based on strong evidence and can be defended. If they lack confidence, they need to pursue this assurance. They often need to come to grips with the historical truthfulness of what we profess. They may be believers who are questioning the full reality of the faith. Those who doubt their salvation are not likely to have the motivation to share their faith with the unsaved. They are double-minded. (James)

4. They may see the faith, more as self-help, than eternally redemptive; therefore, missing the central message of the cross. It is true that our faith does bring us harmony and peace, but that is not the primary benefit of believing. There are countless Christian books that are full of practical insights on daily living. These are wonderful resources to have and study. They enrich our lives greatly. Since God is the designer of the

human psychic, He has tremendous insights into the struggles we face. These are treasured resources that need to be utilized and benefitted from. We need to be guided in our Christian walk, by those so qualified. But there is also a backside to this pursuit. If we stop our growth at the point of finding insights into our spiritual or emotional struggles, we may miss the cross. We may find greater peace, but miss the crucial redemptive aspects. We stop short of what Christ died for. So much of what we promote as Christianity: is really limited to Christian values and practical Christian living.

5. Many Christian are often good at talking about faith matters with other Christians, but don't take the next step and share with the non. The witnessing to Christians is not the same as witnessing to the unsaved. That is not evangelism. It is not a great commission response, if all we share our faith with, are those who already are affirming the same faith. It is generally the social stigma that is holding them back. They need a dose of reality contained in the litmus test. We all understand that faith sharing is often very uncomfortable, but the litmus test awakens us, and compels us to step out in faith; since the evidence is so compelling, and the consequences are so paramount. This is Paul's instructions, to set your minds on things above. (Colossians 3:2) As the Apostle Paul instructed in 2nd Timothy: preach the word and do the work of an evangelist.

6. There are forms of Christianity, that promote an idea of the sovereignty of God, to such a degree, that witnessing is seen as an unnecessary action on the part of the believer. They believe God is going to save who He has chosen to save. Nonetheless, regardless of theology, the commands of God remain. We are called repeatedly in the scriptures, to share the faith. As noted by Paul: do the work of an evangelist.

7. Some claim that soul winning is a gift, an office or role for only a few so gifted. (There are those who are called evangelists in the New Testament) But evangelism is also a command for all believers. Sometimes God places a call on our lives and does not relent, like Jonah. Other times, He will pass you by for the

next willing person. These are the ones who will receive the Bema Seat blessing. There are times God is looking for a man to stand in the gap, but there is no one. (Ezekiel 22:30) But that does not relieve us of the responsibility. We are all called, not to respond is simply disobedience.

8. They may be living in willful sin. Therefore, they are disconnected with their Heavenly Father. Those out of fellowship are not going to be fruitful as believers. A compromised believer is a disobedient believer. They have no interest because their minds are blinded and polluted. They are of double-mindedness, with interest in both this world and the world to come. These are often compromised with the sinful pleasure of this world. They may have even shipwrecked their faith. These may find the harsh disciplining hand of God, will come into their lives, to get them back on the path. (1st Timothy 1:19-20) We reap what we sow. God will not be mocked.

Those who desire to share but feel unqualified or afraid

There are many who desire to be life changing believers, but who feel unqualified. There are those who are simply afraid, but desire to be obedient. And those that may feel unworthy for various reasons. Let's explore:

1. There are some who believe they are unworthy to be soul winners because of their sordid past. But like the Apostle Paul, who refers to himself as the chief of sinners, these may best understand the depths of sin, and the liberation of being forgiven. Those who once so lived, often go on to become great evangelists. They have found the well of refreshing water of life. And they are now joy filled, and contagious believers. For others, they must first stop looking back, to move forward, now they are understanding their new status: New Creations in Christ. This is the Apostle Paul's perspective. He saw himself as the worst of sinners, but he also saw himself as an example for those who would believe in Christ for eternal life. (1st. Timothy

1:13-16) We who were once thirsty souls, should now be telling other thirsty souls where to find living water.

2. Every believer needs to start where they are and mature in the faith. Every believer should grow in their faith, as they learn the evidence for the faith, the doctrines of the faith, and develop the skills sets needed to share the faith. Everyone needs to start where they are and progress into who God wants them to be. Believers should grow from the milk of the word to the meat of the word; meaning, they are becoming mature discipleship making believers. It is a lifetime process, and should never end.

3. Some believers have a real epiphany. A "come to Jesus" moment. (I am using this expression in the figurative sense) They have been believers for sometime, and never really pondered the seriousness of what we believe; then they finally get it! They now really grasp the serious state of unbelievers. They go from a statement of faith to the reality of the faith. Their faith goes from a church doctrinal belief to the actual real implication of what we profess. They finally understand the message of John 14:6. It is the worst news ever, but also the greatest promise ever. For those who see the cross as foolishness, the tragic result is eternal damnation. For us who have accepted the merits of Jesus: the greatest gift ever offered to mankind. Sometimes it is as simple as coming to grips with the reality of what we believe. Finally coming to grips with the urgency of the litmus test, and then walking boldly in impacting faith.

4. For those interested, but feel ill equipped, can start by using natural contacts to bring friends and family to church or an Christian event. It has been reported that the vast majority of those who started attending church started because a friend invited them. It may be a first step in a growing process. It is understanding the essence of the litmus, and then acting in accordance with the commission given. Even if it starts as simply inviting others to church. We can be the avenue of bringing those to whom we want to witness, to others who are better equipped to share the faith. Everyone has friends or

family members they can invite to a solid Bible teaching church. A good first step!

5. Do we see ourselves as sojourners investing in the eternal, or in this world as our investment? It is a question of importance. It may be coming to grips with the reality of what we believe and acting accordingly. This life is temporary, so every investment in this world is such. Eternity is also such: everlasting.

6. Some need to stop playing it so safely, and go for it. It is like some sports teams who are too focused on not losing. It has been widely noticed that teams that are ahead in the game often play it safe so as not to lose. Often this strategy leads to losing. We who are believers are already winners. We are to be ambassadors of life, to a terminal world, with the gospel of eternal life. We can have this mindset, because we cannot lose our salvation, and our heavenly home is secure. There is no one, nor any entity, that can nullify our eternal life, your eternal salvation. As the question has been asked: what can man do to me in light of eternity? What are you protecting that you will not eventually not lose anyways? But whatever you gain by being obedient, can never be lost.

7. Paul says in Galatians he became their enemy just for telling the truth. Nonetheless, he continued on because of the love of Christ, and his love for his fellow man. He also had the insight, as recorded in Acts chapter 20: that each of us will be held accountable for our evangelistic efforts. Regardless of what we suffer, we are already winners in Christ. So we should continue on in confidence, since we can only add to our heavenly rewards. There is nothing we suffer for the cause of Christ, that we will not be rewarded for in eternity; it is part of the assessment of our evangelistic faithfulness. Therefore, a great reason is the rewards given at the Bema Seat. Who does not want to hear, upon entering heaven: "Well done my good and faithful servant."

8. A renewed motivation because one finally sees it for what it is: eternal life. I do believe after it is all said and done, we will wish we did more with the eternal, and less with the trivial. This

was seen in the movie *Schindler's list*. Where, upon the successful mission, he reflects on the fact he could have done more. This will become superabundantly obvious upon entering eternity. I strongly suspect we will all wish we did more. Unfortunately, many will be ashamed for hardly doing anything. It really is an issue of confidence in the message and a renewed sense of urgency. It is a choice between the desires we have for the temporal, and confidence we have in what we profess to believe.

I will note that this is not for the faint of heart. People who start down this road need to understand that those who step out and engage in evangelism will experience more attacks by Satan or his minions. This intended fear by Satan can be too much for some; they are afraid of the attacks and/or the personal rejection. They may fear the stigma of sharing an exclusive message - that most will reject. But we need to think about the message's implications and realize its urgency. Therefore, when we find ourselves rejected, we do not take it personal. It is ultimately Jesus Christ they are rejecting, not us. Our willingness to engage in evangelism should flow from a deep love, and a sincere concern for their destiny. They will often reject us and our message, but if we are faithful, God will reward us. Jonah did not want to go to Nineveh, but God had greater plans. Sometimes God will not relent of His call on our lives, even if we are afraid.

Always remember the reason we share the faith: the reality of Hell. If there is no Hell, there is really no need, you might as well just live as you desire. This is why we always need to be asking: why did He die? So while the best reason for the unbeliever is to avoid the righteous judgment of a holy God; for the believer, the glory of Heaven.

What can we do? In Colossians 4:3, we are instructed to pray for an open door: an opportunity. The Holy Spirit has a ministry of drawing people to Christ, but they cannot exercise saving faith, unless the message is also given, that is our responsibility. Whether they receive the message is a personal choice for each individual. It is up to each person to personally believe/accept the gospel of Jesus Christ. Tragically, some will reject it. But if we are faithful, that is tragically their choice, ours is the call to be faithful in the God given mission.

For some, they may finally see the purpose for why I wrote this book. It is to awaken a sleeping church to really understand why what we believe is so important. It should become our mission to share the message. But our mission is only worthwhile, because what we believe, is sustained by the evidence for what we believe. This process needs to continue, as we grow in the faith. And that will require us to study Christian theology, apologetics, logic, doctrinal truth, and become better skilled as messengers of the hope we have. These investments in our spiritual grow, will facilitate all of us in becoming a better witness. And this requires you to spiritually wrestle in prayer. We need to be people of devoted prayer, then proceed in gentile boldness.

This was a chapter that could be a full book. It was brief, just to highlight some basic evangelism thoughts. Those we all wrestle with. It was not intended to be an in-depth study. I wanted to cause some reflection, but did not want to dive too deeply. I am sure you could think of many more reasons.

CHAPTER 15

THE CALL OF THE CHURCH TO BE PROCLAIMERS OF TRUTH

⸺⸺⸺◈◈◈◈⸺⸺⸺

The church has been boxed in by society, by those who do not hold to our Biblical perspective. There are many voices in our society who believe the church should limit its influence to compassion outreach. To provide practical care for the poor and less fortunate in our society. There certainly is a place in the mission of the church for compassionate care for the needy. The Bible teaches that principle. In the Old Testament, this principle is discussed, for example, in Deuteronomy: chapters 15 and 26. This compassion is also modeled throughout the New Testament. The Bible also says that those who do not work, should not eat. And, if a man does not care for his family, he is worse than an unbeliever. I believe we can take that as an universal principle, even though it was written to those who are part of the local church; and its direct application is to define a standard for believers. There is a Biblical expectation for believers to care for, and love their families. There is also a needed universal application of this principle. As a society, we should expect parents to support their families. Men in particular, need to step up, and be engaged fathers. Since intact families are the anchor for healthy neighborhoods, we as a society should expect men to take responsibility. Too many men are better at procreation of children than they are nurturing them into responsible adulthood. Any sense-less person can get a woman pregnant; it is the abandonment of the responsibilities of fatherhood that is the problem. But that is not the theme of this chapter, just a little soapbox commentary. So let's return to the topic of this chapter.

A secular society will generally accept the church as long as it does not stir its moral conscience. As long as we compromise our values, our evangelsitc mission, and remain focused on charitable activities, we are acceptable. We may even be valued and appreciated for our charitable work; at least tolerated without too much objection; as long as we don't take a moral stand and try to influence society according to our Christian values. Certainly do not suggest non-Christians are lost and engage in proselytizing. How insensitive to suggest people are morally accountable to God, and therefore, need a Savior. Christians are to take care of the poor and the hungry, and leave the morals to be defined by those in the political arena, the academic halls of learning, and the entertainment world. (Good grief, how is that working for us?)

Unfortunately, this has been the appeal to the masses, by many in mainline denominations. Acceptability of all, with few of the expectations of Biblical morality. In particular, those traditional Christian standards of moral conduct; those regarding their sexuality. The expected morality that should emanate from the faith, into the lives of those who proclaim to be Christians. This altering of long-standing sexual morality has a certain appeal to those who do not hold to our Biblically based perspectives. Where love is king of all virtues. Let's just love people as they are, without too many moral expectations. The belief held in this moral vacuum is: if love is a true experience, we should not question whether it is healthy, or morally right. (We should always be expressions of authentic love, without compromising our values)

This drift from Biblical truth also includes the compromising teaching that one can be heaven bound, and not even accept the fundamentals of the faith. (Fundamentals are just accepting the faith as being true. These are not radical extreme unbiblical actions/beliefs) This is not orthodox Christianity! It is like: I am a Christian, but wink wink, I don't really believe it is inherently true. For those who hold to this view, there are elements of the faith that appeal to them: the acts of kindness and expression of love. The community of fellowship, a quasi Christian identity, but not Biblical Christianity. They promoted the theology, that general goodness, and expressions of love, will ultimately satisfy God's requirements. God's love prevails in their minds. Unfortunately, for them, this is not fully true; love wins when we accept it on God's terms, and that requires the cross! This modified message of Christianity, is not the same message propagated by their founders. This is a form of progressive thinking Christianity, but it is not Biblical Christianity. It is a redefining of classic Christianity.

Think for a moment of Jonathan Edwards famous sermon: *"Sinners in the hand of an angry God."* His preaching a fire and brimstone message, warning sinners of the sure judgment to come. Or, the bold, and life changing faith: of the Wesley brothers, Charles Finney, D. L. Moody and George Whitefield. Their profound impact on our country, because of the strong moral values that emanate from their preaching; which laid the foundation for us to become a great nation. I am not sure those fire and brimstones messages are an effective way to preach in today's culture, but there is a sentiment to what they preached. A bit of a missing ingredient in today's church, that has an, I am alright, and you're alright, mentality. A renewed move back towards those more direct confrontational preaching styles, may help us return to what's really paramount. Remember, real revival starts with prayer, and is composed of a renewed sense of the holy. A perception of God's righteous anger toward sin. A revival in our county will not happen in the environment that espouses a watering down of Biblical standards. Actually, no revival starts with soft on truth theology. We need real truth. The understanding that God is righteous God, is that foundational truth. It is not the learning of some newly discovered truth that starts a revival. It starts when something we already know is true, is then accepted as uncompromisingly true: like the claim of Jesus, in the Gospel of John, verse 14:6. This was seen in the Reformation movement, which started with a renewed understanding of justification by faith alone, and the conviction that the Bible was the sole authority for truth. These truths, and a few more, became the bedrock of that movement. Those strongly held truths, which the Reformers would not back down on, were the impetus: the beginning of restoring the truths of Biblical Christianity. They went back to the authority of the scriptures as the sole fountain for truth. They were asking: is that teaching in the Bible? Or is it a man made teaching? This is seen, as an example, in the Gospel of John, 5:39. These religious leaders were adhering to their traditions and not in the divinely inspired scriptures for their authority. But Christ says the scriptures all pointed to Him, who is the final authority, not religion. (Luke 24) He is the only one who is able to save. They were depending on their religion to save: like Catholics, the Mormans, the Jehovan Witnesses, and those who believe being religious and good will get them to heaven.

Regretfully, the truth of the matter is, most mainline churches have fundamentally drifted far from the orthodoxy of the faith. And that growing movement has even drawn the evangelical church in that direction. Some churches are even endorsing gay marriage and performing those ceremonies within the church. Abandoning even the basics of Christian sexual morality. We recently had a pastor in our community who offered to perform gay marriages for free at a local coffee house. I am sure he found acceptable interest within the liberal church community. A real hero of progress to many, but I am not sure he had God's blessing on the whole situation. (And, yes, that was sarcasm) It is noteworthy that while mainline churches have found more acceptability with those outside the Biblical perspective, those who like the benevolent mission of the church, but who only give a superficial nod to the traditional beliefs of their denominational fathers, have in the process, by deviating from Biblical truth, lost the sure message of eternal hope. Because if Christianity is not fully true, it cannot be trusted for any truth. Including the sure hope of salvation in Jesus Christ.

And while the trend towards a more liberal theology has made their faith more acceptable, the end result is, they have lost the real faith. It becomes more of a societal improvement faith, and less of an eternal redemptive faith. These churches have clearly lost much of the powerful impact that was originally achieved by their founders and early followers. Those evangelistic fathers of the faith, who had great passions for the lost, resulting in new denominations; those we still recognized by name in our communities. Their deeply held convictions are now greatly lost in this time of so-called progress; what is seen as progress by many. A progressive Christian faith. Free from the stigma inherent in Biblical Christianity. Where sexual preferences can now be chosen by the individual, and promoted in society, and often endorsed by their church bodies. (I want to be careful and very clear: kindness and Christian respect for our fellow man/women is still expected of us who do not agree with this moral drift. Grace, love and truth all together, is the model)

Furthermore, as we see their deviation from Biblical truths continued, so did their numbers, and declined significantly. The more they abandoned the Biblical standards of their founders, and the more socially receptive they found themselves with those outside the church, the less significant they became. Those who are comfortable with the benevolent mission of the church, but reject the necessary salvific aspect of the faith, have also abandoned many of the moral standards that have traditionally been the standard for a Christian. They believed being more flexible with alternative lifestyles would make them more appealing. They had reasoned that being more accepting of the changing societal values, and adjusting their own to blend in, they would be more attractive to outsiders. Some of these compromising beliefs included: embracing the teaching of evolution, denying a holy God who must judge sin, denying a real Hell, denying the full authority of the scriptures, and being more accepting of some of the world's sexual standards, they would be more appealing. Their hope was erroneously held. The leaders of this progressive thinking movement had hoped that by adapting these changing values, they would draw the outsiders in, thereby growing the church in unqualified love for mankind, the opposite has happened. Many of the insiders have left for the outside; oftentimes, to churches that still held to traditional Biblical teachings. (I did) The decline of the mainline church has been significant. The remaining faithful, who willingly accepted those denominational changes, those who found the comforting of their conscience with the softening of doctrine, now seem lost as to what to believe. They are even lost as to what their real purpose is. What they failed to understand –is that when the church leaves its strong doctrinal foundation -they no longer have attested truth. They lost their truth anchor. Leaving them adrift, without Biblical prescription for why they even exist.

The reverse of what was desired has generally taken place, with liberal churches losing members. It is the bolder, and strongly Biblical churches, that are the growing churches. People want something they can trust and believe in. They want God given truth. This is affirmed by the Apostle Paul, in 1st Timothy 3:15. He writes that the church, the recipient of God's revelation, is the pillar and foundation of truth. He earlier writes in chapter 2, verses 5 and 6, that there is only one mediator between man and God, the God/man, Jesus Christ. The only one who is able to make satisfactory ransom for man. He further predicted, in chapter 4, verses 1 and 2, that in the later days there would be a departure from truth. (My paraphrases) Is that not what we are seeing?

For sure, there are true believers who remain in these bodies. Many wonderful people. I grew up in a mainline church. I love those people. I think experientially, I could find warm fellowship there, that is comfortable, and humanly satisfying. They are generally good natured people. They are known as kind and compassionate people. Very welcoming. If only I could set aside my belief in the inerrancy of the Bible, and exclusively of Jesus Christ alone for salvation; which I cannot do, because it devalues the faith, when we do! A logical breakdown of this thought process is discussed as we progress through the remainder of the book.

(Some reflections) Early on in my faith journey, there came a period of reflection in my own life, as I started to evaluate the mainline church's message, and focus. I observed how much it had been reduced to: God is love, love all people and care for the poor. Granted, there is some value in that message. God is a God of love. We are to help care for the poor. But it is woefully incomplete, and misses the main focus and call of the church of Jesus Christ. It also diminishes the whole reason and purpose for the death of Christ. In light of eternity: this acceptance of the compromised message leaves well fed, but eternally lost souls. We should be a place of warm fellowship, and meaningful relationships, but in this environment, we cannot ignore the fundamentals of our faith, or the gospel message. It is the divine truth. What we have historically been commissioned to believe. Because when we blend in to fit in, we lose our significance. The divine standard of truth. We are no longer the salt and light. We become irrelevant as professed believers. Just soup kitchens. We become more acceptable with some liberal segments of society, but disconnected with divine truth.

I like the theme song for the old TV show, *Cheers*. It included a stanza: "A place where everyone knows your name." Indicating that this bar was a place where friends gathered, and over a few beers, they shared their lives, and enjoyed their friendship. It was a place where they belonged. They experienced life together. They laughed together. There's something appealing to that. Who does not want to feel like they belong? That there is a place we can gather with good friends, with whom to share our lives. Some safe place to share comradery in the midst of a stressful life.

Unfortunately, many churches often progress little more than that, they just add a little Christianese to the fellowship. Yet it lacks what is the primary call for the church: to be the salt and light, and truth bearers of God's message. For the evangelical church to remain true to its calling, it should create a welcoming environment, a place of authentic fellowship. (Maybe without the beer. Go ahead and smile, a little humor does not hurt) Yet without the abandonment of Biblical truth. Where, when referring to ourselves as evangelicals, means we evangelize. And we stand on the fundamentals of what we profess to believe. Because without actual divine truth, we are adrift in a world of opinion.

Notwithstanding the need for authentic fellowship, when the church leaves its greater call, it loses its unique value. It becomes a social club. Regrettably, I think this drift is becoming too universal across the scope of the Western church. The Americanization of the church. Where we confuse authentic Christianity with the so-called American dream. We don't know what we believe, we don't know why we believe, we may not even know if we believe; then why should people come to us to find the meaning of life? If we are not even sure of what we believe, why give any credence to the faith. Our faith is deduced to an existential search for meaning, like a lot of other beliefs. But if that is the case, then our pursuit is reduced to finding meaning in life; but in that process, we lose divine revealed truth, because the pursuit is reduced to finding personalized meaning.

We all naturally prefer personal comfort, stimulating music, and preaching that is focused on personal improvement. It is part of being human. We prefer chasing the vaper of the good life. There is a normal desire to want our lives to be rich, and find satisfaction in this life. Me too. But not at the cost of denying the Biblical Gospel, which is our only hope for eternal satisfaction. If we deny essential divine truths? What do we have: Soup kitchens!

I am seeing an overemphasis in nonessential issues, even in evangelical churches. Here are a number of recurring preaching themes I have recently noticed: How to get along with difficult people. How to have a healthy attitude. How to find personal peace. How to deal with conflict and emotional issues. How to move past those existential struggles that are holding us back from inner peace. How to promote social justice. There is a saying: preach to where people are hurting and you will always have an audience. There are certainly significant numbers of these hurting individuals in the body of Christ. Those that have been overwhelmed by the trials of life. We live in a broken society that needs this restorative help. This is worth preaching and teaching as long as it remains Biblically based and not a form of New Age self help. The church should also be a place where mature believers should mentor newer believers in the faith. (Remember Matthew 28:19-20 and the Pastoral letters of Titus and Timothy) We need to have mature, well ground, and seasoned saints for this to be a practical reality. But we also need to be cautious that we do not drift from God's truth into psychobabble. We need to keep in the forefront of our minds, the reason for why we exist? In light of eternity: Is what we teach, keeping with the divine call to the church? Helping those with personal struggles should be a component of a healthy church, but not the main cornerstone.

See if this illustration helps. Let's say one day after a shower you see a mark on your skin. Being a bit concerned you have it checked out at the Dermatologist. After examination, he assures you that it is normal, and nothing to be concerned about, all part of the aging process. You are thankful that this mild concern is nothing to be seriously concerned about. Then sometime later you start experiencing pain in your side.

You wisely decide to have it checked out by a doctor. After extensive testing, he has very disturbing news. It is a form of advanced cancer and you have very little time to live. Naturally you are devastated. You have been told there is no treatment and the expectation of death is in your near future. Later, sharing your devastating news with a friend, he informs you, there is a new breakthrough treatment just discovered. You see this new doctor, and he assures you that this information is true. There is a revolutionary new, and 100% proven treatment, just approved for use. Your response is now different. Instead of mild relief, you are ecstatic with the revealing news. The point is this: the church treats our situation of being lost like a mild skin blemish, and not a revolutionary and life saving treatment; one that is eternally life saving. This is the spiritual quest that we all face. Not just a temporary extension of life, or a better way to live, but an everlasting solution to our eternal destiny dilemma. A permanent solution to eternal destiny problem.

In light of eternity, we need to keep the main thing the main thing. A constant reminder to us individually, and as a corporate church body. The reminder that the gospel is the solution to man's ultimate need, is one that necessitates it being preached regularly from the pulpits, and preached with urgency and accuracy. There is only one divinely given salvific message. And because of the eternal consequences: it needs to be thoroughly known, articulated, and proclaimed in all its details. Otherwise people will go on their frolicsome way oblivious to the consequences ahead. Believing that they are meritorious on their own. Good and decent people we want as neighbors, but are not born again children of God. These unsaved are in a precarious position, since they are baselessly depending on their own insufficient righteousness, never achieving the perfect righteousness that God's justice demands. And, sadly when this is realized, it will be too late.

One of my frustrations with the church today is the over emphasis on some of the less-essentials, and avoiding the harder truths of the faith; this is often to avoid the stigma of those undesirable truths of the faith. Sorry to say, but many pastors will receive a strong rebuke from the Lord at the Judgment Seat of Christ. They were not faithful with the commission of the gospel, or were inaccurate in its presentations. (Galatians 1:8-9 and Acts 20:24-27) Many of those who sit under their ministries are unaware of what is required for entrance into the heavenly abode. They have not been properly taught. These pastors are not exactly watchmen on duty. This is becoming a growing problem within the modern evangelical church. Where are the fervent voices of pastors? Too often are looking for acceptance with the world and not Jesus. They are oftentimes mistaken regarding the essentials of the gospel. Some pastors are even denying the fundamentals teachings of the historical faith. They may not even know what is required for heaven. In that case, their problem will not be the Judgement Seat of Christ, but the Great White Throne Judgment.

The pulpits are abandoning truth to find acceptability with the masses. This is compounded by the drift of many of our Christian colleges into modernism where pastors are being prepared for a life of ministry. These compromises come in various forms: the inerrancy of the scriptures, salvation doctrines, traditional marriage, and the acceptance of evolution; all of which results in the diminishing of divine truth. When this takes place, it naturally results in churches forgoing the urgency to proclaim the gospel of Jesus Christ.

This modernism of the church is manifesting in the shabby state of our churches. Churches that are slowly becoming a mirror of our communities. I believe there are many reasons why churches are leaving the Biblical mandate. Here are a few for reflection: #1. We are being boxed in by the expectations of society. #2. We fail to grasp a clear understanding of God's holiness. #3. They are unsure what is required for heaven #4. The social stigma of engaging in evangelism is unappealing to most believers. #5. There is pressure to accept evolution as true in order to have perceived acceptability with the intellectuals of our day. #6. The inability to defend the scriptures as the infallible standard of truth. #7. The unwillingness to accept that for most of humanity --heaven is not their ultimate destination. #8. The unwillingness to accept that Hell is a real place, and is a real consequence for rejecting the salvation offered by God.

Certainly there is strong societal pressure to adopt the world's standards. Evangelism is still an activity that I don't particularly care for. What an odd thing to do: unless, Christianity is true. Then it is the most compassionate and critical activity to undertake as a Christian.

The status of the lost demands this be the highest priority. We get to this place in our churches, when we compromise the truth. The remedy is to return back to divine truth; which includes an understanding of the immutable holiness of our God, as revealed in the litmus test. This test highlights the need for the gospel.

When the church becomes more acceptable to the world, it becomes more insignificant in its purpose and call. Consequently, in the process, it dilutes God's message. I acknowledge that emphasizing this in many churches will cause some to leave for a more comfortable church in which to fellowship. There they can find worthy projects of helping those in need, and still find acceptability with the world. Or, they may just walk away. They may even be eternally saved and forever a member of the family of God, but refused to take the next step in discipleship. They may simply avoid the divine call to engage others with the message of hope. Some of Jesus' disciples did when He put forth hard truths. By abandoning the truth claims in the Bible, they have denied the very claims of Christ.

One of the hardest aspects of the covid period was the loss of fellowship. The inability to disciple and encourage fellow believers. We are created to experience fellowship. To share together corporate worship and reaffirm what we proclaim as the truth. In the meantime, what better time to engage in the great mission given to the church; when people are so uncertain about the direction of life. It is more than finding personal peace and satisfaction in this life. This was not the primary mission for the Apostle Paul. While he wrote about many of these sanctification issues, it was not his driving passion. (read the 20th chapter of Acts) He sacrificed everything to get out the gospel. That only made sense if the litmus was absolutely true.

He writes analytically about that priority in 1st Corinthians, chapter 15. He notes: If the resurrection is not true, then everything he did spreading the gospel was for not. That any sacrifice of personal comfort was for no reason. (my paraphrases) In the event the resurrection did not happen, then Christianity is not true; therefore, the agreed upon marriage arrangement in chapter 4, does make some sense, destructive sense, but is rational. But even in that scenario, what they perceive to gain is offset by the devaluing of the relationship. Is the pursuit for sexual pleasure really a meaningful enough reason to live? Studies show the opposite. Those who enjoy the most rewarding and meaningful sex lives are those who develop them in a sacred and exclusive married relationship. Without the guilt and regret that comes from those alleged freedoms. A standard that is being lost in the body of Christ. A lifetime relationship that is nurtured in love and faithfulness, is really the best foundation, and most meaningful way to live. So it really comes back to the question: is Biblical Christianity divine truth?

CHAPTER 16

CHRISTIAN LIVING IN LIGHT OF ETERNITY

Have you ever noticed while watching TV at night the themes of the commercials? In general, the theme is: you are not happy. How can you be happy if you are not driving our vehicle, eating our food, or drinking our beer. All of which they alleged will make you happy. Alternatively, if you eat and drink too much, and you are overweight, you can be slender and more sexually desirable, if you use our revolutionary breakthrough diet, beauty product, or exercise program. The next major theme is: you are entitled to compensation. Someone must have diminished your life, so allow us to sue them on your behalf. (To be sure, sometimes it is justified) But the general theme is you are not happy, nor should you be; you don't have what we are offering. This is far from the Biblical instruction to be content with what the Lord has given us as our lot in life. Not that pursuing a better life is wrong, it just needs to be kept in harmony with the mission we have been given.

We all desire the good life. We want those TV promises. We want our 2.5 kids. (I have never seen a half kid but you get my point) The house with a white picket fence on a cul-de-sac. The home that has a big backyard and swimming pool. Add in a passionate sex life, a good standing in the community, financial success, and we may believe we are well on our way to living the ideal life. Should you achieve those goals you may feel like you made it. But it is not real life, not in the real world's sense. Maybe that's why so many are so unhappy. There is the illusion, and then there is real life. And real life seldom measures up to the illusion. We have more than the majority of the world, and yet, we are among the most unhappy. There are many places in the world that are horrible places to be Christian. Serious persecution is taking place all over the world. There are vast numbers of Christians suffering unbelievable mistreatment. My own life is quite comfortable to be honest. It is my "natural" desire to keep it that way. The reality is, there are hard aspects of living in this fallen world. Life can be very hard and too often: heartbreaking.

Perhaps as I age, my desire is to return to a simpler life as a younger adult, with insignificant issues; those fond memories of my earlier days. Maybe that's why I still enjoy the old 1960's family shows. We all know that this was not real life, but certainly a life that appeals to me. A simpler life with insignificant problems and a real sense of community. I did not ponder those big questions; those eternal and/or critical and world defining issues. I just did not spend much time thinking about those serious issues. I was more caught up in enjoying a life of friends, family and personal interest. Those older shows even incorporated the church into their lives, they just don't take it too seriously. It was a religious discipline that helped them be better and more rounded people. The practice was generally expected, but they avoided the heavier themes like Heaven or Hell. It was generally a community expectation to attend church. This is just what people were expected to do on Sundays. It was a much simpler life. Unfortunately, life is not as simple as we would like it to be.

Obviously, life can be very hard for many people. Many live ominously without much perceived purpose, just living day to day. Making the best of it while waiting to die. These observations can seem a bit defeatist, but are practically true for far too many. This is often why so many televangelists are finding a harvest from the bank accounts of the deceived faithful. They promise you the illusion that your life could be like their life, if you have enough faith, and give enough money to their ministry. If you just make that "faith promise," then you will have the life they are enjoying. I have a suggestion: why not try that same principle in reverse. If it is a real principle? Give money to the struggling and less affluent, and see if those alleged promised prosperities come back to the ministry. If I offended anyone? So what! Many believers are struggling, and to solicit money for one's personal luxury is wrong: certainly unbiblical. Stop twisting scriptures! There is a saying: that for the believer this is the only Hell we will face, for the unbeliever, this is the only Heaven. This is not consistent with the illusion being promised by those spiritual materialists. (Sorry, I got off track again with more soapbox commentary)

When you think about it, so much of what we do is essentially meaningless; yet we pursue them with passion. Think of golf. I personally enjoy golf. But when one thinks about the object of the game, it becomes kinda silly. A golfer will hit a ball down the fairway, only to hit it again and again, until the objective is achieved, the ball goes into a hole. So from a meaning of life perspective, golf is not a particularly life altering activity. I find it is a good place to have some fellowship. I have enjoyed many rounds of golf with close friends, members of my family, and my wife. But never has it changed my life or affected eternity. There are good secondary reasons to enrich life via shared common interest, but these activities should never be life defining in themselves. A distraction for a while to amuse ourselves. Simple pleasures, of which I have enjoyed over the years. So I am not suggesting for a moment not to engage; because if I did, I would be a hypocrite, since I enjoy those activities. These activities can enhance the quality of our lives and give diversity to individual experiences. We should enjoy those activities as a gift from the hand of God. Since one size fits all would make life bland. A mind that is totally focused on the serious would be unsustainable. We all need reprieves from the stresses of life. We all need to take time to laugh and enjoy the goodness of life. I have long enjoyed those mutual interests with others. I enjoy sports, a good laugh, and other divergent interests. I like the camaraderie and unity of teamwork that are part of sports. Men or women from different backgrounds working together for a common goal. One of my particular interests is being a fan of professional football. Unfortunately, after too many Sunday afternoons watching a game, I find myself a bit disillusioned, realizing after my team lost, that I wasted the afternoon in futility. There needs to be a proper perspective that makes these pursuits meaningful, and also life enriching, but not life defining. (The book of Ecclesiastes)

Many of these activities are opportunities to develop lasting friendships, or create new ones. It is the unbalanced interest in these activities that lures one away from those of greater significance: like those responsibilities to family, marriage and ministry. When we become overly consumed we lose the practical benefits. Many individuals, after years of pursuing financial success, sporting conquest, or any other temporal status, realized that success in these pursuits are fleeting. If we define our worth by the win we will become disillusioned. I understand the objective in sports is winning. That is the nature of playing the game. The reality is, regardless of how good you become, there will always be someone who will surpass your achievements. Even at the top, the time there is temporary. We chase and chase and chase only to grasp the air of meaninglessness. Once again, like those reflections of Soloman in the book of Ecclesiastes. He pursued everything that could be perceived to bring meaning to life, only to reflect that in the end, that it was all vanity. He later reflects at the end of the book that for life to have real meaning: it needs to have a God focused perspective. Solomon writes a number of times that we are to enjoy the simple pleasures God gives: so enjoy. The key is to keep all activities in proper balance and perspective.

This is often why so many struggle with a midlife crisis. They feel their more fruitful days are slipping away, which can result in an ill conceived desire to recapture what remains. This happens when our minds are not focused on the promises of a life that is beyond description. The purposes for which God created us. If we lose our God given vision for living, we may pursue an ill-conceived idea, some foolish illusion, thereby, messing up a lifetime of investment in our personal relationships.

We have all known the man or woman who became dissatisfied with their lot in life; often because of the deceptive illusion portrayed by TV or movies. Then made the foolish decision to pursue greener pastures. Feeling like they missed out on something they deserved, or is missing from their lives. This with the hope that the illusion of the greener pastures would make them feel rejuvenated. It is a deceiving illusion. Sometimes the grass appears greener on the other side of the fence because the field is full of manure. (I thought of another word but wanted to be respectful) Step on the other side of the fence and see what our feet have stepped into. The false promises of a better life. But many will pursue it anyway, regardless of the consequences. That is how strong our fleshly and selfish nature can be at times. Some want the illusion so strongly, they abandon their personal vows, their personal integrity, even though it is a self-destructive illusion.

This is what illusions do, they hold out the desire that this pursuit would bring a renewed sense of meaning to the fleeting years of their lives; some renewed sexual satisfaction, a fantasy escape from the daily grind. It often does, but it is temporary, and it costs more than they ever expected. In the process, they hurt many loved ones in their lives, particularly the spouse to whom they made a covenant promise. And their children! The very ones they would have died for if needed. Now, by chasing what they *feel* are unmet needs, they abandon most everything that has real lasting meaning. They leave for a bit of temporary satisfaction, at the well of the illusion; thereby, complicating everything in their lives. I am going to be a bit graphic here. I have long enjoyed my sex life with my wife; but a boob is a boob, and even with new boobs, they will become the same boobs in time. We need to keep in focus, that married life grows richer in meaning, as we grow together throughout the journey of life. It is the richness of the relationship that makes the intimate life sacred; and truly meaningful between a man and his wife. It is the enduring journey through many of the trials of life, like the shared engagement of raising a family with a forever partner; that leaves the type of lasting memories we should all want to leave. A real legacy of honor that our children will admire.

(My warning) So avoid the damage of everything you have worked hard for and nurture your present marriage. There are ways to keep your sex life meaningful at home. It is a reflection of the quality of marriage that God intended for us, and a witness to an unbelieving world. Furthermore, the investment in your marriage is an investment in your testimony, and your children's admiration of you. Even as adult children, the stability of their parent's marriage gives stability to their own lives. A steady anchor for the whole family. It shows to our families, and the watching world, that there are God defining relationships that are worthy of honoring as a commitment for lifetime. Which are too often, sadly lacking in today's world. Let's continue.

There is something that is honorable to a lasting legacy. One that preserved through the struggles of life. A well lived life, which upon passing, leaves fond memories, and the honorable legacy we want to leave for those left behind. It is one of the true principles of living a life of honor. It is hard in today's world. There are far more temptations in today's world. The community standards are changing fast. Sex is promoted, in our faces, and then people are shocked when temptation befalls another believer. Keeping pure eyes is hard. Try to find a decent movie that does not over promote sex. Even on evening TV, what once was considered family hour, we are seeing 1950's Playboy standards, as common on prime time. Even a female razor commercial that is a bit too graphic. What was once considered erotic in its day, is now the norm. This is the lure of today's world.

The danger is that we become enchanted with the world and pursue perceived greener pastures. We throw off moral restraints and pursue the lure of temptation -which only leaves regret and pain. In the process, we damage our testimonies; thereby, forgoing the chance to leave the legacy we want. Be sure we will all stand before God as believers and give an account on how we lived out our Christian lives. We are eternally saved but still accountable. How we live does matter. The temptations may be great at times, but endurance is worthy of your commitment. If we do not keep a check on ourselves, the results will be regrettable. We may find temporal pleasure, but as most experience, great regret.

You may find this a bit humorous. I can remember playing Monopoly as a youngster, and saying Connecticut cut cut your butt, and thought it was a bit naughty. The world has changed. The church and individual believers have too. I can remember years ago when we joined a church. There were expectations that you would not attend movies or even dance with your wife in public. (To clarify, I like movies and will dance with my wife) I think some of those expectations were artificial legalism masquerading as real internal righteousness. Then again, maybe good old fashion wisdom, that protected us from sinful compromise. I have a dear neighbor who wears a dress while working in the yard. I have great admiration for her wholesomeness. A Godly lady. Not my standards of attire for work in the yard, but admirable just the same. Just contrasting how rapidly the world has changed.

This is why this reflection of the holy and the temporariness of life is needed in today's day and age. It needs to be a higher standard in all of our lives. The changing culture has also impacted the church. We normalize the world's values into our personal lives, and then accept them as normal. It is affecting our message, our communities, and our personal lives. Those worldly values have practical effects on every aspect of our society and personal lives. The consciousness of the holy is evaporating from our lives.

The drift of compromise from Biblical based truth has lessened the urgent call for faith sharing. We once understood the eternal repercussions of faith choices. Now our concern for those outside the faith is seldom heard from the pulpit. We are losing our zeal to share the hope we have in the gospel. Without the mindset of holy: everything seems okay. If we falsely perceive that we are okay in ourselves, we will not see a need for the hope of the gospel. Everything we base our morality on, should be based on God's immutable holy nature. The litmus test that has been repeatedly mentioned.

The growing compromise affects the practical aspects of our Christian faith too. Our Heavenly Father desires us to be models of the inherent goodness of our Savior; for which we will be accountable one day. For the compromising believer: the loss of blessings, prayers that are denied, accountability at the Bema Seat of Christ, and/or divine discipline in this life; to name a few. As we lose the understanding of immutable holy, we lessen our appreciation of our indescribable salvation. We may even abandon the truth, since we can no longer accept the implications of our faith being true. Satan is having a field day. That is why he is so desiring to have the saints fail. The ruining of a testimony stalls our ability to be an effective witness. When we compromise with the world to fit in, we have little to offer, but soup kitchens. We will end up with full stomachs and eternally lost souls. How tragic to imagine where our changing society is taking us.

However, when we grasp the eternal perspective, it changes our motivations. We see that choices have consequences, eternal ones. When we understand that God is not going to ever change His standards, we quit secret sins. When we understand the tremendous gift we have in our eternal salvation: we start to distance ourselves from the temporariness of this life, and look more desirably at the life to come. Our incomprehensible salvation becomes our greatest source of joy. One would think that as we age we would be more cognitive of the inescapability of death; thereby, more diligently focused on eternal issues. But that is not being manifested in many lives I know. They too have been caught by the changing culture. The acceptance of the changing culture has negatively impacted their spiritual growth and priorities. They are not finishing fruitfully. They are adapting the culture's values, and not Biblical standards or priorities. They have allowed CNN to be their standard for truth and not the Bible. It is time to reassess our temporal pursuits and refocus on the legacy we want to leave behind. Will we leave a lasting honorable spiritual legacy or pursue temporary pleasures?

What determines if a life is worth living through these tribulations and difficulties? It is when it is lived, for the purposes of God, knowing that our faithfulness will be rewarded. But not until the Bema Seat will each of us know the full impact of our lives. Until then, keep striving for the rewards that Christ is offering.

CHAPTER 17

OUR PRAYER LIFE

‹‹‹‹‹‹‹‹‹‹‹‹‹‹‹‹‹‹‹‹‹ ⌾⌾⌾ ‹‹‹‹‹‹‹‹‹‹‹‹‹‹‹‹‹‹‹‹‹

There is an area of my life that is regularly lacking: my prayer life. It does not make sense. I DO believe God answers prayer. Somehow TV gets more of my free time than it should. Not much life changing has ever happened watching TV. Generally, it is a waste of time, and wasted money on an expensive cable bill. Which is ironic, since one of the more unsettling thoughts I wrestle with, is the passing of time; the inability to recapture time that has passed. Because time once lost is now lost forever. So I need to remind myself to make prayer a priority. To set before the Lord, those priorities that I am concerned about. Particularly, that the eyes of unbelievers of whom I want to witness, would be opened to spiritual matters. Praying that they would understand the holiness of God, their need for salvation, and accept the offer of the free gift of life: eternal life. That offer is limited to time, and once passed, is lost forever. Furthermore, I need to be mindful that even in my prayer life, and yours too, holiness is an issue. I cannot walk in willful disobedience and expect God's blessing. No powerful movement of God can take place in the lives of the disobedient, nor for those who are not engaged in consistent prayer.

Yet praying often *feels* like a frustrating endeavor. To be honest: I have often felt "it appears" at times to be a fruitless experience. I have friends who have regular and effective prayer lives, not so much for me. Sometimes it feels like a waste of time; because, I have prayed for many things in my life, with little visible evidence to show. I feel like asking God, and I have, what is the use. I know God is able, but sometimes, for no understandable reason, He just does not appear to show up. I then get frustrated and want to give up what I perceive is a waste of time. And as often is the case, I find the TV an appealing way to waste time. And yet if you were to ask me, I would confess that I believe prayer moves the hand of God. A bit illogical don't you think.

Now the reasons are innumerable as to why God operates in certain ways. For me, shall I say, many are still unrecognizable. But here some are basic principles of having prayers answered. (You can do additional research if you desire greater knowledge) The Bible says if I harbor sin in my heart: God will not answer. (Psalms 66:18) Alternatively, it says that the prayers of a righteous man are powerful and effective. (James 5:16b) No doubt there are areas in my life that are lacking. Areas that need spiritual growth. Perhaps, God is waiting for me to pursue holy living with greater diligence. I also know there is a warning to husbands, that if they do not treat their wives with proper care and love, He will not listen. (1st Peter 3:7) Be clear, He is not saying that we are not born again. He is stating a principle for His children, on how to have greater intimacy with Him; which results in more favorable responses to our prayers. (I am thankful that my wife and I have a quality marriage. I give most of the credit to her. She is one of the finest people I know. A wonderful mother and grandmother. Nana to the grandkids) The point is: God is indicating there are conditions to having our prayers answered. One cannot live like the devil and expect our prayers to be answered like we are living in saintly fellowship with our Heavenly Father. As 1st Peter says: " For the eyes of the Lord are on the righteous and his ears are attentive to their prayers, but the face of the Lord is against those who do evil."

He is also sovereignly working out a plan that we may not see or understand. I understand that there is a bit of a mystery between the sovereignty of God and the free will of man. Depending on the particular theological perspective, Christians will drift usually toward one of the two. Some go so far as to say that God cannot act unless they are the initiators. Others believe God is going to do what He is going to do, so why even bother. I try to take a balanced Biblical perspective, since the Bible teaches both. And truth be told, I don't have this locked down, nor does anyone completely. Those who claim they do can be quickly exposed with a few pointed questions. There is a bit of an enigma when it comes to how and why God acts as He does.

When we try to understand the ways of God we will quickly find ourselves in very deep water. In general, I believe the Bible describes both as being true, how that can be, I don't fully understand. Yet, when I ponder it, it is clear to me that both must be true! If we are truly going to be responsible, we must be at least somewhat free to choose. However, unless God is sovereign over history, no prophecy could ever be assured. Yet, God had declared the beginning to the end, human history. And, when He commands, there is the presumption that I can obey, at least to some degree of human ability. Therefore, what He commands, I am being held responsible, even if it is beyond my full ability. He has said to be holy since He is holy. Now I can be better, and walk according to the Spirit which will reveal a more holy life, but I will never be holy in an absolute sense. This is because I was born with an inherently sinful nature passed on from Adam. Since God has revealed aspects of both, we should endeavor to understand the best we can, both Biblical principles. One perspective shows our personal responsibilities and the other gives the assurance that God is still in ultimate control.

While these are twin truths, there are human limitations to our understanding of these themes. The finite can never grasp the infinite. Understanding the ways God will always be beyond full human comprehension. We can grow in our comprehension of these revelations, but there will always be a limit to our human understanding. This is true of prayer also. When and how God chooses to respond is often beyond our understanding. I know it can be frustrating at times. There are many, beyond our knowledge, reasons why God is doing what He is doing. (Just read the book of Job) This is where the walk of faith comes in. Walking in faith, in light of the goodness of God; and trusting in that goodness, even when I cannot fully understand the ways of God.

As an example: I may pray and not understand spiritual warfare in the heavenlies, or the sovereign plans of God. This I do know, I am instructed to pray. To pray that the eyes of the unbelievers would be open so they can see the hope of the gospel. To pray for physical and emotional healing, and for struggling marriages. To pray for open doors so I can naturally share my faith. Pray for hearts to be open to the gospel. However, I must also understand that God has given us, and those we pray for, free will. I must allow God to be God in all things, even when I don't understand. So when I cannot think of any reasonable reason why a particular prayer should not be answered in the manner that I believe it should: I need to rest in the sovereign reasons of an Almighty God. For this life is temporary and answers may only be understood in eternity.

So if you have troubles with prayer as I do? Review reasons why your prayers may not be answered: Is there known sin in your life? Are we mindful that we are wrestling in spiritual warfare? Are we remembering that those we are praying for still have free will? Is my prayer in-line with His will? Am I perceiving that God is the sovereign God, even if I don't fully understand His ways? Oftentimes, it is simply that we have different timetables, or different ultimate purposes. There are my fleshly desires and there are His sovereign purposes. These are principles that I need to incorporate better in my own life. Maybe that's why I am writing this short chapter. Maybe it's not so much for you, but a reminder for me! To refresh in my mind the importance of prayer and also some of the principles of prayer; even if I am wrestling with some confusion over the results.

I should emphasize once more, if there are a few areas that should be a regular focus, it would be for the salvation of others, because Satan has blinded the eyes of unbelievers. (2nd Corinthians 4:4) This is one of the means for which God has sovereignly designed for us to impact the world. Certainly, we who have children, want first and foremost, the individual salvation of our offspring. Lastly, our prayers should also include a prayer for the movement of God in our time. We certainly need it! Since God has in His sovereign wisdom placed us in this time and place of history for a reason; He expects us to be difference makers where we are placed. Much of this will not happen if it is not soaked in prayer. A discipline that I need to personally work on. A discipline that all who engage in, will be rewarded for at the Bema Seat of Christ.

CHAPTER 18

THE PERSONAL CONSEQUENCES OF LIVING IN A FALLEN WORLD AND THE HOPE OF THE GOSPEL

I s it sacreligious to say there are times I don't enjoy being a Christian? I do not even like to be good sometimes. I believe I am generally a good person. But there are times when it is wearing trying to live up to those standards that we envisioned from a Christian; not in order to be saved, but a reasonable service unto the Lord. In light of God's mercy, it is reasonable to sacrifice some of my temporal comforts, for the advancement of the Eternal Kingdom. Actually, it would be reasonable to sacrifice all temporal pleasures, in light of eternity. This was the Apostle Paul's perspective. He gave up his high standing in the Jewish community, and privileged authority, to pursue the greater goals God had for him. (See Phillippians chapter 3) The same appreciation of what we now possess, our tremendous gift of eternal salvation, should produce a similar mindset. This would indicate by our actions, that we have a solid comprehension of what we truly have been given: an eternally redeemed life. This was the message from James, the Lord's younger half-brother. He instructed us to know and do. This is the expected life for all Christians. (Once again to be absolutely clear, that moral change is a desired expectation, but not a condition of our salvation. I agree with the Chafer Theological Seminary statement in the section on Soteriology. One can find the doctrine statement on their website) These expectations come as part of my identity as a Christian, for a watching world. For those who evaluate the merits of Christianity based on the authenticity of the Christian's walk. And for this to be realized, requires a Christian to pursue a lifestyle of consistent righteous living, even though it can seem out of touch with the world we live in.

Likely one of the reasons why I preferred jail ministry. There was very little stigma with the inmates with whom I minister. The incarcerated, those who knew I worked there, gave me some instant credibility. If an officer in uniform was willing to humble himself enough to return to the jail at night to share the gospel, then maybe he is worth giving a hearing. Since it is purely a volunteer activity on my part, it showed that I truly care. It was, in another sense, a captive audience who often had nothing else to do. (Sorry, it is the reality of the situation) I know there are many that I work with who saw my ministry as fraternizing with the bad guys. To be sure, jails house some of society's most immoral men and women, people we need to be protected from. The pod I taught in was maximum security. Many who are sex offenders. Others are incarcerated for murder or other serious crimes. Not exactly the prime of society when it comes to high moral standards, but created by God just the same. Therefore, they have worth in the eyes of God. As with all sin, it is just a matter of degrees. In light of God's immutable holiness, we all fall short of the Glory of God. Infinity short! Think of this way: If I am on the side of the rising sun, and you are on the other side of me, I can say I am closer to the sun than you, but we are both roughly 93 million miles from the sun. A few feet do not make much difference.

I tend to think of it another way when it comes to ministry in the jail -there by the grace of God goes I. I was fortunate to be raised in a professed Christian family. Had I been born into another family, or culture, my outcome likely would have been different. My inherent sinfulness likely would have led my life in another direction. Oftentimes it is largely dependent on the deck of cards we are dealt, those that we had no say in. I did not choose my parents or the neighborhood I grew up in. This is why some compassion should be afforded when it comes to those less fortunate in life. Not everyone had the same favorable cards. Had the deck of cards been different, any one of us could have found ourselves manifesting the same outcome. We all have the potential for carnal desires. And if we open that door, it can wreck our lives. (Galatians 5) Oftentimes, the difference between lust and adultery, is three drinks and the opportunity. The truth is that sin can become a master of anyone of us. The degree of sin we exhibit is often just the opportunity to express itself in an individual's lives. The degree of supporting restraint is often the difference. I recognized that I was fortunate, therefore, I try to be more compassionate. This is not to say that many don't agitate me with their nonsense and ongoing deviant behavior. Let's continue to explore this issue.

Those who are incarcerated often come from drug infused neighborhoods. They generally lack a Godly heritage. Most have educational deficiencies, or mental health issues. The moral decay in some of the neighborhoods where they grew up is rampant. It is my strong conviction that the number one issue resulting in deviant behavior: the lack of a Godly man in their homes. Men who should be expected to lead their children in the ways of life. Installing the heritage of principle living. Simply stated, many men are not being responsible in their God given duties. They are failing to be a strong presence in the home; with the desired purpose of raising their sons and/or daughters into responsible adulthood. And this brokenness of the American family has been accelerated by women who have lowered their moral standards. They have forsaken moral wholesomeness. It is clear that way too many children are born outside the God ordained design for the family. Sexual morality is not a result of economic status, since the ability to say no is not conditioned on resources; but the consequence of that morality does affect their economic status. Numerous sociological studies have shown these statements to be true. Just do a quick web search to validate the truthfulness of this statement. I personally have seen it via my work experience.

I, as have many others, have noted the societal and personal grounding benefits of those moral practices that are derived from the teachings of the Bible. Values like: honesty, commitment to marriage, hard work, sexual restraint, and personal responsibility are all good foundations for every society. I even wrote a research paper to that effect in a psychology class at a secular college. To the credit of the professor -it was well received. It was my contention that basic Biblical principles provided stabilizing benefits to those individuals who practice the faith, which inturn promotes positive mental health. These practices create stronger families, less street drug use, less violence, less crime, and encourage personal responsibility; therefore, a safer and healthier society. It is clear that nurturing those aspects of our spiritual nature generally results in being a better citizen.

That is why it is troubling when many of our leaders think those positive influences that flow out of Christian principles should be removed. They maintain that we cannot have Christianity taught in our public schools. An endorsement of a particular religion they say. But all morality must have an understructure. Some standard of truth. They fail to see that the removal of Christian morality is unstabilizing for society. That the removal of our foundational moral principles that reverberate from the faith, is not good for society. There is a strong correlation between those virtuous Christian teachings and strong neighborhoods and healthy communities. When we replace our moral foundations with Godless thinking: we have no moral standard. Godless morality has no viable moral foundation. It has no anchor of truth.

This is manifested in the growing educational push to be free from all religious principles. Think this through, since it really is quite simple. When the dignity of a man is reduced to the later stage of the evolutionary process, it is hard to expect people to see why they should adhere to ethical standards. If all we are is a higher developed animal, then why should we be surprised if some act according to this alleged nature. Animals are animals no matter how well we dress up their image. If that is the conclusion? It is hard to impress on those accepting this teaching that life has real meaning. It is the truth that we are created in the very image of God that results in a sense of intrinsic worth. This has played out in many people's lives. Read the Jeffrey Dahmer story. He placed a good part of the blame for his moral choices, on the devaluing of life, via the teaching of evolution. If all we are is an animal, then why can we not be eaten? He thought so! Crazy world we are living in. What we promote as ideas does have practical ramifications. What foundation we build upon is crucial. Ideas have consequences. Hitler had ideas of morality. So did Dietrich Bonhoeffer. They were a world apart.

I have noted it a number of times in conversations, and I am not sure if the idea was an originated idea, or the thoughts came from another forgotten source. Even if I knew Christianity was unsupported by any credible evidence, I would still want it taught in schools, and emphasized in our communities. I contend that we cannot have a healthy nation if the moral foundations are removed. Even if our faith was without merit, there are still good practical benefits, to justify the teaching of it; as a good moral foundation for a society. That is a simple truth. (Psalms 11:3) Therefore, while the benefits are the byproduct of these principles, all foundational truth needs to be anchored on something that is always true, and that is the immutable nature of God. So it is ultimately: God's intrinsic nature that is the basis for those values that make our lives grounded and meaningful. (And to be absolutely clear, Christianity is founded on very sound evidence)

Those who are extracting the Christian faith from our societies are seeing the fruit of their actions. The brokenness becomes more obvious everyday. Everyone can see we are slowly destroying ourselves with unrestrained moral freedom. This is obvious in the lives of those who are housed in the prisons and jails. This tolerance of deviance is being advanced to the rest of us as the new sacred value. It is now considered noble to be tolerant of most everything, and considered to be intolerant, if we hold to an expectation of moral wholesomeness. The foundations we build on have consequences. This is why we need the message of truth and Grace: first in prevention, and then in redemption.

Let's explore this in real practical life. While I don't teach in a womens pod, where is the hope for someone who has engaged in the drug culture? The type of lifestyle that often leads to very promiscuous living. How does one recover from the emotional stigma of prostitution? After years of degrading yourself for drugs, which often then leads to more promiscuous living, how is one to find restored hope? How does one restore a sense of wholeness, after years of sexual degradation? What can a secular counselor do to help rebuild a life, after being morally compromised by promiscuous living? You can analyze forever the root causes. Offer some practical advice for positive change, but such counseling does not lead to a renewed sense of wholeness. That can come only through the gospel of Jesus Christ; which is able to restore a person to a renewed life. And Jesus is the master of restoring lives. It was His model of ministry; validating the worth of a person, regardless of their past. And only the gospel of Jesus Christ can result in this becoming a reality. The brokenness of our world is the natural result of what happens when we abandon truth. For divine truth is the foundation for morals, and also contains the liberating hope of the Gospel, because the Gospel is the evidence of God's redeeming love.

This is the uniqueness of the gospel. Many religions teach some form of moral living. Only a belief in the Gospel gives new life. While it is true that sin is present in all of our lives, and we all have regrets, there are some, which include sexual sin and/or those actions that have hurt another, that particularly linger in one's soul. Those that result in a sense of regret, shame, and remorse. These irreversible actions are some of the most difficult to overcome. It may appear to those so scarred by these lifestyles, that the ability to restore one's life to a state of wholeness, is impossible. They therefore abandon the effort to even try. They lose their desire, because the hope of ever arriving at a state of respectability, appears to be unattainable. However, when they see that their worth is determined, not by past personal choices, but by the God who validates them and extends His love; they see that all hope is not lost. It all starts with the renewing hope of God's redeeming grace. In eternity all these sins you committed in your body are gone: You are a new creation in Christ. Actually, you are a new creation already, upon faith in Jesus Christ; the newly redeemed life, becomes a wholly new and resurrected body at death, for all of eternity.

It has been said that the value of something is the price that is paid for it. In this case, the value of a soul is of tremendous value, since God the Father paid for your soul with the blood of His Son. Therefore, you must possess profound worth. This, then, becomes our hope. The knowledge that God sees us as immensely valuable, even in our sin; since Christ died for us even as sinners. If we are loved as sinners -think how much more as His children. (Romans chapter 5:8-9) Then for those who do respond to the gospel, the understanding that they have become clothed in the very righteousness of Christ, is the impetus to growth in the Christian life. This with the desired goal of showing that transformation; because to the outside world, the inward transformation is unseen, unless the newly redeemed manifest it to the world in which they live. The world cannot see the spiritual new birth. They cannot see something life changing has taken place in one's life. That is why Baptism is important. It is a good first step in telling the world: something has changed. I am a new person.

Therefore, the newly redeemed need to take real sanctification steps to show the world that something has changed in their lives -if they want their conversion to be taken seriously by others! Since the evidence of the life changing hope of the Gospel that has been received, can only be noticed by others, by a changed life. This necessitates some real sanctification in their lives, even though they are fully accepted as a child of God, at the very moment they accept the Gospel of eternal life. But if you want others to believe a change has really happened? Then one needs to manifest it to the world by showing the newness of Christ-like behavior. Otherwise others will see only the shell of the new you. We who have been redeemed should no longer live according to our old nature. (Galatians 5) That is not God's desire for any of His children. A new life should show a new lifestyle; even though we are fully accepted at the very moment of our salvation. And that gift was received without any personal merit.

This is the hope that comes only in the Christian message: the Gospel of Jesus Christ. The hope that starts with the understanding of God's restoring love. This is the most crucial starting point. The discernment that in God's eyes, they still have indelible value. To become aware that God is a God of new beginnings. The felt need is often the desire for authentic love. This is often the first step in that redemptive process. This is the reason many first come to faith, for the emotional unmet love needs. While this may be the drawing reason, the greatest benefit is the forgiveness of all sin and eternal life. But that may not be the original draw. Everyone has a natural desire to be authentically and unconditionally loved.

For we who are redeemed, the best place to start in reaching out to those lost and deeply hurt in the despair of life, is by sharing this vision of hope. Which is the love of God being portrayed for them in the cross of Christ. Because those feelings of unworthiness are almost unbearable; resulting in a sense of deep despair, since they perceive no hope. Therefore, without this hope, they continue in those ever increasing destructive lifestyles, joining those in similar lifestyles. There is acceptance with those who too have found themselves in the despair of life. Those sharing the feeling of being unworthy of true love. It lessens the stigma of those regrettable choices. It is a world of lost hope. And to protect their fragile wounded souls, they often put up a very hard outer crude image, as though they are not troubled by their lifestyles. But the pain is real and very deep in their souls. This is why redemption in the gospel is so freeing; but it is also so hard to fully believe and accept. It is hard to grasp that no one is beyond the love of God. While He knows everything about everything, He still loves the unlovable. Just read in the gospels how Jesus interacted with the lowly of society. The unlovable, at least in how they perceive themselves in their own eyes, and most often in the eyes of society; those who have been scarred by the devaluing effects of sexual sin.

Regardless of the reality of this hope, remember that the pure love of God is often hard to convey to the one so devastated by a life of sin. There is often a long progression of drug use that leads to a lifestyle of regrettable sexual sin. Or, it can start with sexual sin, that leads to drug use to mask the pain. In either case, they have a deep desire to experience this real God accepting love; but it is an unknown love. They have a most difficult time accepting this pure love as unconditionally expressed in the gospel. Oftentimes because of the way Christians have judged them or lived hypocritical lives. These devaluing feelings also may come to the person who is the victim of sexual abuse, in which case, it is no fault of their own. However, it often leads to the feeling of unworthiness; which then leads to other self-diminishing actions, that compounds the feelings of unworthiness. A vicious vicious cycle. The feeling of being purely loved is hard to accept. Those caught up in the cycle of sin do not know what authentic love is, so they often settle for being used for love.

So how is the cycle broken? It starts with the genuine love of Christ. When one grasps the hope that they can start afresh. That a brand new identity that can be found in Christ; the first glimmers of hope start to be realized. They are already fully aware of their sinfulness, no matter how much they portray a sense of denial. What they have a hard time grasping is that God still has arms open to those so willing. A chance to start again with a new identity as a child of the living God. No longer living with the identity of a prostitute, or their history of being sexually permissive, or that as a criminal, but that of a child of the King. The first step comes by the simple comprehension of God's desire to accept them into His family. The desire of God, to every member of the human race, is that they too can be accepted as a full member in the body of Christ: fully adopted and fully accepted! But it must start where it started with each of us: the choice to accept God's love offer. When this is understood and accepted, the practical sanctification aspects of redemption should start. Then the freedom, and renewed sense of wholesomeness grows, as they come to know, and then grow in that knowledge of their new identity. Their new creation in Christ should start to be manifested with new practical aspects of a restored life. A witness to the world of the redeeming love of Christ. They then can become a walking testimony of the goodness of God's grace.

This is something that no secular counseling can offer, nor the criminal justice system. Not just the changing of their eternal destination, but by joining the family of God, they change forever who they are in identity. The chance to begin again is life affirming to the one who will accept this love. The knowledge of having been clothed in the very righteousness of Christ, adopted and accepted in Christ, is freeing. This again, is where the wisdom given to the Apostle Paul, comes again into the equation. In Philippians, chapter 3, he writes the one thing he did was putting the past behind him, and striving for the goal in Christ. (my loose paraphrase) What great wisdom from a man who once persecuted the church of the living God. Should Paul have stayed mentally in that regretful time in his life, his ministry would never have shown the fruit that it did. He would have stayed stuck in regret and guilt. This is not the desire God has for any of us. (1ˢᵗ Timothy chapter 1)

There is an offer from God that is beyond anything this secular world could ever offer: The chance to be fully forgiven. The opportunity to be clothed in the righteousness of Christ. Being able to rejoice in the fact that they have been fully adopted and born anew into the family of the Almighty God of our souls. What a wonderful promise and offer! What an opportunity for a new beginning. An opportunity that is offered freely to those so deeply wounded by the scars of life. A completely new identity, and completely new beginning. A chance to put the emotional scars of sin, and a life of bad choices behind them, and now be seen as a child of the living God! A new creation in Christ. Then they can look forward to the day when this old fleshly nature is totally gone, and they can celebrate their glorification in heaven in a resurrected body. Hallelujah what a Savior!

Our call as ambassadors of Christ

This life changing hope will only happen when we as the body of Christ undertake the God given responsibility to share this hope; the renewing hope contained in the Gospel of Jesus Christ. This message needs to be shared, then continue in discipleship. The learning of their new identity needs to be developed and explained. The motivation to share this hope comes when the believer understands the consequences, both temporal, and eternally. When we accept our ambassador's responsibility to express the authentic love of God; convinced that it really does matter both now and into eternity. No doubt we are called to be the messengers of hope to a dying world. Only Jesus Christ has the ultimate message of hope. Why are we keeping this message of hope to ourselves? The scriptures instruct us to be ambassadors of the hope of the gospel. We who are redeemed need to be messengers of the way to redemption. Because those so scared by a life of sin need to know: how wide and long and high and deep is the love of God. (Ephesians 3:18) Because the acceptance of pure love is very hard to grasp after being so deep in the grip of despair. For those who have been betrayed, and/or violated by the actions of others, which later led to their own contribution to this despair, it is the stigma of shame that is almost impossible to overcome. It is the insight into the qualifications of Jesus Christ as the God/man, and an understanding of the results of His sacrifice on the cross, that gives this aspiration to move forward, and begin again. We Christians who have been redeemed, now have the responsibility to be messengers of the way to redemption.

I am in no way suggesting that the God ordained role of government be set aside. We need protection and upheld accountability of individual actions. I am saying that there are two different focusses. There is the role of the government to protect us and hold criminals responsible. And then the role of Christians being ambassadors of Christ, for the purpose of sharing the way to a redeemed life. These two functions are part of God's plan. One is for the safety of an orderly society, the other is the life changing message of salvation, which is another way of saying less crime. (Our world is full of broken people that resulted from the devaluating effects of sin) Furthermore, once those who have entered into the criminal justice system or drug rehabs, this message becomes the first real prospect for the restoration of their lives. This is another way of saying less crime, and less self-deprecating choices in the future.

(My editorial) The abandonment of our Christian based morality by our media, entertainment industry, and our governments, results in these self-destructive outcomes; broken and devastated lives are the natural byproducts of this movement. Our government and the entertainment industry now promote lifestyles that are devaluing our society. And when the natural consequences happen, as they generally do when we abandon self-restraining morality, they cry out for more and more resources to help those whose lives have unraveled; not realizing their values created the problem. Regardless of the amount of resources we give, they are futile for the changing of lives. The very desire for freedom that is not grounded in Biblical morality, only leads to wounded souls. Lastly, the body of Christ does not help the situation, if we abandon our God given roles as ambassadors of Biblical truth. We need a stable and wholesome foundation or we will unravel. Not too hard to understand is it?

CHAPTER 19

LEGALISM OR DISCIPLESHIP

L et's start by describing our terms: a disciple is a learner. A person under the tutelage of a teacher, professor or pastor. It doesn't always mean being a Christian. One can be a disciple of another religion, a sage, or some philosophy, and not heaven bound. One can be a disciple of Christ, and not a born again Christian, like Judas. Whereas, legalism is human merit and/or man made religious rules, undertaken in an attempt to find acceptance with God. These dictates are often presented as conditions of the faith for one's salvation. Conditions that are imposed on the followers, and are often portrayed as rules or conditions of the faith that must be followed to go to heaven; like the teaching of many religions. They are man generated and not divinely given.

There is nothing so frustrating in the Christian's walk as trying to merit our Heavenly Father's love. He is by nature: loving! It is another key aspect of His nature. When we become His children, we are accepted in His beloved: that is, Christ Jesus. This is what is meant by being in Christ. Once the payment for our sins, which has been already accomplished on the cross by Christ Jesus, and then accepted by a sinner as full payment of their sins: God the Father is free to express His lavished love. (1ˢᵗ John 3:1-3) His just demands are satisfied. His wrath on sin has been propitiated. Which means: He is forever satisfied with Christ's payment, for those who have believed in Christ Jesus as their Savior.

This has been an area of theology that took me some time to appreciate. It took years to absorb the significance of these vital teachings of the scriptures. The understanding that my relationship with God was forever settled: I am His! Now and forever! This is another occasion where we need to pause and allow this aspect of the gospel truth to anchor deep into our souls. We read through pivotal teachings, only too quickly to move on to the next point, without allowing these freeing truths to sink deeply into our souls. These are some of the tremendous blessings our Heavenly Father wants us to know and celebrate. God, our Abba Father, wants His children to know, we are forever His. (See 1st John chapter 5, along with numerous other sections of the scriptures) We have been purchased by the blood of Christ. The knowledge of our permanent sonship/daughtership, is one of the key elements of our freely given salvation, that we need to know, and celebrate. (Also see Ephesians, particularly the 1st chapter) It is freely given according to His grace. And, Grace by definition: is unmerited.

For me, it was crucial to understand this aspect of our salvation. It assured me of my eternal destiny -resulting in joy. It relieved me of the anguish of conditional salvation teachings. And this confidence continues to grow as I realize the significance of this Biblical truth. This growing insight into sound theology is grounding and freeing. As Jesus said: you shall know the truth, and that truth will set you free. (John 8:32) (My paraphrase based on numerous translations) To be free, depends on knowing the truth: once a son, always a son, is liberating truth.

This leads to another facet of theological teachings that needs to be explored, and understood, to give clarity to the subject: The themes of Justification and Sanctification. If we confuse these we will be subject to uncertainty in regards to certain aspects of our salvation. This topic can be a bit complex when we start to look at these teachings in their different applications. So I am going to keep the subject matter, as generally understood, in its primary application. Justification has to do with my standing before God. To be right with God requires

100% perfect righteousness. In order to qualify for heaven: I need to be positionally perfect. This is justification: a legal declaration from God, about every believer in Christ. I am seen as perfectly righteous. A judicial declaration by the Judge of the universe. (Romans 8:33-34) There is no higher authority.

Generally speaking, sanctification has to do with my daily walk, and that will never be 100%. To try to merit or achieve this perfect standard can be maddening. To pursue this status of perfection, by human effort, will be tremendously frustrating, and full of existential anguish. Remember, justification is being declared permanently righteous because of Christ alone! Sanctification is part of intentional growing discipleship. It is becoming Christ-like in our behavior and attitude. Big big difference!

This is why legalism is so destructive. We should walk in harmony with our Heavenly Father. He wants us to be fruitful, and to live His life through us, but it will always be less than perfect. Accept that and you will be freer. You can save yourself a lot of vexation if you will keep these distinctions in mind. In justification: we are absolutely and permanently declared accepted. In our walk, our sanctification: we will have ups and down, and our lives will always be less than perfect. We have a perfect Savior, but we as Christians will always be imperfect in our conduct.

Part of the process of becoming more sanctified is being a disciplined disciple. And intentional discipleship is part of our sanctification. They are intertwined but not exactly the same. Our progress in sanctification manifests in practical righteousness, as we learn to walk by the Spirit. This is the process of learning to walk in harmony with the Holy Spirit, so we are more spiritually mature in conduct. We become progressively holier. When we are walking accordingly, we are not fulfilling the desires of the flesh. (See Galatians, 5:22-26) However, when it comes to discipleship, there is more than just our sanctification.There are a number of components. One is our righteous conduct, our behavior. But there are many who are good moral believers, but are lacking in their Biblical comprehension. They have great zeal, but lack grounding truth. They are limited to what they have been taught from the pulpit. And oftentimes that is lacking in doctrinal substance. They have not attained the Biblical knowledge necessary to explain the doctrines of the faith, so they are easily swayed by unbiblical teachings. To become Biblically literate requires diligent personal study to grasp the deeper doctrines of the faith. That only comes as the results of personal study of the scriptures and theologically sound resources. This process takes many years of discipline study. As the process continues, it should result in being both: spiritually mature and grounded in the doctrines of the faith. Manifesting Christ-like attributes, which is God's desired goal for all Christians. This will only come as the results of being a growing and learning disciple. But it also includes other aspects of the Christian life, like the spiritual wisdom we gain that can only come by the trials we experience in life. Those that test our faith in the real world. Life can be a great learning process, if we apply Biblical principles to the trials and experiences of life. Which should result in spiritual wisdom, our sanctification, and being better prepared to be a discipling believer. All of which are necessary, if we want to be fruitful believers.

But this is conditioned on gaining the wisdom God wants us to learn, so we are prepared. Much of that can be learned by studying the wisdom books of the Bible: like Proverbs and Ecclesiastes. This is a desired goal for all believers: spiritual wisdom. The sanctification of our spiritual walk, and being grounded in the doctrines of the faith. Thereby, being a reflection of our Heavenly Father, which is all part of being a disciple. It is the process of maturing in our faith. It takes time, but it is not automatic. It is a submission to the will of God, and walking accordingly. It is always by the power and presence of the Holy Spirit, but never in the power of our flesh; since the efforts of the flesh is equivalent to legalism. Which is deadly to our spiritual growth. The process and goal of sanctification is growing from a new babe in Christ, into a mature saint. This is the central theme of the second half of the book of Galatians. It is further addressed in many other parts of the scriptures.

Oftentimes, it includes learning to let go and leaving what is behind, behind. As Apostle Paul wrote in his book to the Philippians, in chapter 3. He learned to leave behind his hateful past, and even his high religious standing, and strived for the purposes of God. He wrote that to those believers, so we too can put that principle into practice. It is Godly wisdom to know that living in the past is not healthy, nor does it promote the spiritual life God desires for His children. Remember, the process of discipleship is a lifetime pursuit of learning and growing, and never ends. It always endeavors to have the mind of Christ. It is moving from the past, our pre-Christian life, to the life that Christ desires for us. The desire of God for every believer is: we go from saint in our position, and grow more saint-like in our behavior.

This is why it is absolutely crucial to learn of my forever sonship. This is the foundation of stable freedom. This comes when I stop trying to earn God's love and just rest in it. When that takes place, we find freedom. For me, it manifested as I started to reckon on my eternal status as a child, and not my behavior to have this assurance. This is why the belief in eternal security is so important. If something can change my status as a son, I have legitimate reason to be concerned about my salvation status. A potential fear that I will be anxious about. If I have to merit this salvation standing, then I will be insecure in my spiritual walk. It is the difference between living out my faith with assurance, and working to maintain the assurance of my salvation. This is what legalism and probation salvation does: It creates a fear based salvation. Yet, I understand the scriptures say equivalent to 365 times, not to fear. Seems to me like God wanted one reminder for everyday. And to fear not, would require a knowledge of my eternal security, for what greater fear could there ever be, but the fear of being separated from God for all of eternity.

This is where the body of Christ plays a major role in the sanctification and discipleship process. We need to be a body of believers, where real people can be open and honest with their real struggles. More than one person has reflected that attending church is not of interest, because they already are very mindful of their shortcomings: their personal failures. When people are already overly conscious of their regrets and shame, they are not going to be interested in attending a church that is legalistic. Those who teach a conditional acceptance based on moral goodness, instead of Grace, create this environment. We all need a Savior!

I was reflecting on this sometime back. If sermons become too focused on our shortcomings, and the need for personal spiritual achievement, then there is no wonder why counseling centers are full.

I mentally visualized this as sitting in church with a bright light being focused on aspects of our lives that are deficient. Each week drawing attention to another area. The unrelenting call to measure up to an unachievable perfect standard. When this continues, despair sets in. The feeling grows that we will never measure up to the proclaimed ideal standard. There will come a time when we just give up trying, resolving that that is an impossible goal, or we are diminished to the point of feeling worthless. But if our acceptance is knowingly secure, because we understand we are permanent sons and daughters, beloved children of our Heavenly Father, we are then in a much better position to accept challenges to grow in grace. But the key is growing in GRACE. The result is our real sanctification. The resulting natural desire is: we will want to be spiritual victors, because we know we are already victorious in Christ.

Let's think this through. The alternative is: if I think that my behavior is the basis of God's acceptance, there goes any hope of peace. This is a major difference. If I am reprimanded as a son, but know I am secure because of the Father's love and promises, I can still have peace. Even when I am living contrary to some of the desires that our Heavenly Father has for us. However, if I am presented with the idea that my sonship is in question because of some deficiency in my Christian walk, then fear is the natural result. How could it not? Consequently, if my consistent upright behavior is the condition for my eternity, I will experience recurring insecurity, to the point of affecting my mental health. Because any serious reflection, by any honest believer, will show that our lives do not always measure up to the goals of our faith: the sanctification of our lives. This is the affliction of legalism and probation salvation.

Here is the outworking contrast. Before I was a Christian, I was sinning against a Holy God. He, as the Judge of the universe, must punish every sin. However, now as a son, I am sinning against my Abba Father. Therefore, my sin issue has been fully atoned for, and there is no need to be punished. In another sense: this sin is more grievous, since it is my Heavenly Daddy that I am sinning against. I am sinning against the One who loves me unconditionally. My status as a son is never in question; however, my sin is against my own Abba Father. Which as has been noted, can break fellowship with my Abba Father, but not my relationship.

However, this does not mean that the church should accept willful defiance from regular attenders or members. The scriptures are clear that there is an expected code of conduct. Should there be a case when a fellow believer is walking in willful disobedience, there are Biblical principles to address this wayward believer. In general, the first is to confront the believer one on one; then if needed, as an elder group; if that does not bring about the necessary change, the last step is putting that one out of fellowship until they repent. Meaning he or she changes their minds on what is clearly unacceptable for a believer. During this period we should pray for the believer, and maybe even revisit, but never restore until repentance is brought about. It is the time for divine discipline. Oftentimes the only thing that will bring this one back, is harsh discipline by God the Father. (1st Corinthians 5:5)

This is why accurate Biblical theology is so incredibly important. What is taught in our pulpits will either draw, or repulse people, who may be coming through the doors. We are not Christians because of our behavior. We are Christians because we have accepted Jesus Christ as our Savior. That should change our behavior, but is not a condition for maintaining our salvation, since it would be impossible to know our salvation status, if that was the case; but God says we can know. (1st John chapter 5)

We possess divinely revealed truth. A sure foundation for living a meaningful life. A church that does not stand on this truth is close to being useless. We need to proclaim the truth, since we have it as a divine revelation. But we need to be full of grace too. Yet this can be a difficult balance to achieve for the church. It is also a problem for many to find that balance in their own spiritual walk. How to hold strong morals, and still be a person or church that shows love as an extension of God's grace, can be difficult. For churches, a good sermon is not enough, we need relationships, and faith affirming theology.

This is why strongly grounded believers should be mentoring immature believers. (Functioning like a family) We, as a church, need mature believers, helping younger believers, in their role as husbands and wives. Mature saints, teaching men to be men, and women on how to be a lady. We are so confused as a society. And this confusion is leaving men and women unsure of who they are, and their roles in life. Which leads to additional sexual identification confusion. And this is being injected into our society by those who reject the moral standards prescribed in the scriptures.

Therefore, the over-focusing on previous sinful behavior brings on unnecessary feelings of remorse. For those who previously bought into that permissive thinking, as they were led by these misguided philosophies of the world, need redeeming grace. Those whose lives have been marred by this persuasion, but now find themselves in need of restoring grace and mentoring discipleship. On the alternative side of the issue, are those who continue in unrestrained, and unchecked, sexual freedom. A permissive mindset that has lost the value of wholesomeness. It is damaging to the person, primarily our young ladies. This deviation from Biblical morality is creating confusion for both sexes. We need both: grace and truth. We can be holders of Biblical lifestyles and still be merciful to the person who is struggling with the vices of life. Like Christ, who was a full manifestation of both: Grace and Truth.

This is best seen in the Gospel of John, where Jesus is shown to be the ultimate manifestation of truth and grace. (John 1:14) But it takes Biblical wisdom for the body of Christ to know how and when to apply. We are called to be a body of believers that upholds strong morals, and also a place where sinners feel welcome. Overfocus on one will drive away the needy; those are overly sensitive regarding their past sinful failures. To be lenient on the teaching of the other brings loose morals and a lifestyle that is not acceptable for a child of God. Both legalism and loose morals can be destructive to achieving a healthy body of Christ. It is like being a spiritual coach. We need encouragement, and to be challenged, to grow in grace; with the emphasis on Grace. A teaching we can see all throughout the New Testament. The writers of the NT epistles generally established the secure foundation of a believer, before the challenges to grow in the faith. (Compare the early chapters of Galatians and Ephesians, with the later chapters) We are to be ground and then encouraged to grow.

I am thankful I have good solid Christian friends that I can share my spiritual struggles with, they keep me balanced. They encourage me like Barnabas did for Paul. A sign of mature discipleship is that we love the brotherhood of believers. (John 13:35)

Grace and truth together: a needed, but sometimes difficult balance to achieve. An additional reason to know your security in Christ. But also why we need to understand our Heavenly Father's discipline and the Bema Seat judgment. (Both will be discussed in upcoming chapters) All the while, never neglecting the need to keep the freeness of the gospel clear; this without diminishing that God is immutable holy, even as our Heavenly Father. We are now in a different relationship that is sure, a son with his Father, eternally secure. The truth is: we are eternally secure, but have a Heavenly Father who desires us to grow in sanctification. So when I need correction, I am receiving it from my Abba Father, and not from a God, who requires an undefined level of obedience for my salvation to continue. An unsure salvation that is based on my faithfulness. (Merit based salvation) This conditional portrayal of God is not the Biblical description of our Heavenly Father. (Grace relationship)

The desire of God, for all of His children, is that we grow mature as sons and daughters. We are to live according to the leading of the Spirit and never on our own fleshly power, which is often a sign of legalism. Trying to live up to some standard to earn God's acceptance will never work. We need to learn the teachings of Galatians 5; so we don't walk according to the flesh, but manifest the qualities of the Spirit, by walking in the Spirit.

(My editorial) The age we live in is very difficult. We have many in society pushing for absolute moral freedom; usually in the realm of unchecked sexual expressions. The idea that a man can use a shower in a room that my daughters or wife is in need of, angers me. Just because a man is confused about his own sexuality, does not give him the right to violate my wife, or daughters, modesty and moral purity. When this is allowed to take place, their safety is in doubt, and their modesty is being compromised. But is it being pushed upon us! To object to what is being pushed upon us often brings accusations of being intolerant. I am concerned if we will be able to object to any sexual expression in the emerging society. What happened to the long held virtue of wholesomeness: a lost virtue in today's world. Where is the wholesome lady in a dress? The gentleman who treats a woman as a lady, respectfully. The propagation of immorality, and demanding we Christians embrace what is clearly sin, is unconscionable. And if we do not accept what we see as objectionable, we are called intolerant. Maybe even punished by the government or employer. God forbid. All morality is either based on personal preferences or divine revelation. If we keep compromising on moral issues, we will eventually have nothing left that's truly wholesome, nothing sacred. This is social engineering without a moral reference point. No place to plant our feet on what is right or wrong. Keep on reading to develop these thoughts.

CHAPTER 20

ETERNAL SECURITY AND THE SPIRITUAL STABILITY OF THE BELIEVER

As discussed in the last chapter, it is essential to understand our security in Christ, if one wants to experience steady peace and joy in our Christian walk. The teachings in this chapter are absolutely crucial to have a victorious Christian walk. We need to know: not only am I saved, but can I count on being saved and secure for all of eternity. There is no more important topic regarding these two elements of our salvation. They are intertwined together, and I don't believe they can be separated. Let's start with some foundation.

I have recommended a number of very good books that I found instrumental in my spiritual journey. But seven in particular need to be highlighted in regards to this chapter: *Shall Never Perish, Forever*, by Dennis M. Rokser; *Once Saved Always Saved*, by R.T. Kendall; *Shall Never Perish*, by J. F. Strombeck; *Secure Forever*, by Thomas M.Cucuzza; *Eternal Security*, by Charles Stanley; *Getting the Gospel Wrong*, by J. B. Hixson; and *How You Can Be Sure That You Will Spend Eternity with*

God, by Erwin W. Lutzer. So I am not going to spend an inordinate amount of time arguing for the acceptance of Eternal Security. They all do it so much better than I could. My intent is to give a few solid arguments, and then leave those interested in learning more about the subject, to the reading of those suggested books. Additionally, these arguments are woven throughout this book. These are just some highlights to refresh your memory. While not an exhaustive section of the book, this is extremely important for the spiritual well-being of the believer. Unfortunately, avoided by most, because it is believed to be unnecessarily controversial. But all truth is controversial. So regardless of opinion, I believe it is absolutely crucial to have this understanding. This is essential knowledge for all Christians to have; since, it is imperative to know the full extent of our salvation; the key to having settled assurance! I can be absolutely assured because it is the promise of God that I am depending on and not my feeble efforts. Let's continue with some of the affirming principles:

Frequently in the Bible, the offer of salvation is conditioned on believing on Jesus Christ and His sacrificial atonement on the cross: which results in receiving the gift of eternal life. Seems pretty simple to me. Somehow we complicate simple issues. When this is not the accepted teaching, we drift into uncertainty about our salvation; which brings about spiritual depression: as noted by J. F. Strombeck, in his book on Eternal Security. The spiritual depression results from the uncertainty regarding the dependability of salvation. If a human contribution is required? Then confidence will always be lacking. Because any required human contribution will always be subject to uncertainty. But this is not the description of salvation the Bible describes. The Bible describes the condition for eternal salvation, and its permanent results, differently from the hopes for personal sanctification. (See the justification and sanctification descriptions in chapter 19)

The confirmation for this may be best seen in the Gospel of John, chapter 5, verse 24. Look at the progression of thought. It starts with Jesus making a promise to the one who hears and believes, with the results being eternal life, which is in the present tense. Meaning I am currently in possession of eternal life. The promise continues with an assurance of never coming into condemnation, and already crossing over from death to life. A passage that states the conditions for receiving salvation, and continues with explaining some of the salvation results. These results fall under the umbrella of the numerous salvation benefits we received at the moment of faith. Seems pretty clear, and personally, is very comforting for me. Maybe why it is one of my favorite passages in the Bible. Certainly much different from probation salvation teachings, which most often are derived as a result of not interpreting passages in their proper context. Often those that confuse sanctification passages, where a commitment or behavior change is called for, in contrast with justification salvation passages, that are presented as free, final, and complete.

As noted, for years, I was a probation officer. There were conditions of probation. Once those conditions were met, the probationer was released and set free from those conditions. They generally earned their "salvation" from probation by good behavior. This is not so with the free offer of God. The offer of salvation is an offer to receive the free gift of eternal life. Remember that the teachings from God's inspired authors have an intended purpose. Therefore, the scriptural revelations from God, are those who have believed, have received eternal life. This clearly means it is eternal in duration. That alone should end the discussion. One is not on probation with God! An unbeliever upon understanding the gospel, and believing it, has been given eternal life. It is a present possession for the one who has come to faith. A new standing of forever sonship/daughtership. It is received at the very moment of faith, and results in being granted the free gift of salvation. We don't wait to verify it with proof of good works. It is not to be earned in part as we walk out the faith. (The sanctifying aspect of the Christian experience) We are justified the very moment we accept what Christ did on our behalf. This is a full and permanent acceptance. It is not probationary, nor in any sense, conditional acceptance.

As noted, not to believe this truth, will result in an uncertain salvation status and/or spiritual depression. Furthermore, it also affects our boldness. If my salvation is conditional, I tend to live defensively, trying to play it safe. I will find myself trying to maintain or protect my salvation status. I may forgo steps of bold faith, because I am afraid that I may encounter a situation that puts the status of my salvation at risk. For example, let's say that I am put into a situation where I must choose between potential persecution and/or hardship, or the safety of a loved one, and by compromising my faith because of fear, or because of my love for a family member, I have in essence denied Christ, and therefore, I am at risk of losing my salvation. (That is an implied potential consequence of probation salvation thinking) I may therefore, instinctively, shy away from those situations. I will naturally stay in my comfort zone to avoid any chance of this dilemma. Living in protective fear. In that line of thinking, my salvation status is maintained because of my faithful endurance, and not the assured promise from God. However, if I know I am absolutely saved, and what is afforded to me is an absolute promise from God, then what do I have to fear? At most, temporal discomfort, which if I faithfully endure, will bring about additional eternal blessings. (More on that in chapter 22)

Moreover, there are numerous teachings in the scripture that reinforce this principle of our secure salvation. Consider what the scriptures teach about being born again, or becoming a new creation of God. How can one be born again and then become unborn? Or, become a new creation, then reverting back to their former spiritual un-regenerative status. This teaching is foreign to the clear teaching of scriptures. The scriptures continue to reinforce that security theme, with the teaching that we have been sealed by the Holy Spirit, until the day of our redemption. There is no one in the universe that is able to undo what God the Holy Spirit has done in sealing the new believer for the day of his heavenly arrival. Once saved, always saved. Or, once sealed, always sealed. A promise that is absolutely dependable because it is based on God's immutable perfect character. God cannot lie: it is contrary to His nature.

There is another scriptural teaching that is often not translated in most scriptures. It has been drawn out by Dennis Rokser in his book, *Shall Never Perish, Forever*. It is called a double negative. There are a number of places in the Bible (Gospel of John) where translators do not record the double negative (ou me); which in the Greek means it will never happen under any circumstance. It is not proper English to translate as such. So it is not translated in most modern translations, but very reassuring to know as a believer. It is emphasized in the

Greek, with the idea, that we will never lose our salvation under any circumstance. It may appear to be redundant grammar for us who speak English, and not the customary usage in English, but in Greek, it is an emphatic assurance. It is certainly a Biblical teaching we need to know, since it adds to the assurance of our faith walk. What a wonderful assurance, to have this comprehension of the absolute security of our salvation. That no matter what happens in life: I know that I know my eternal destiny. May I say that the book by Rokser is excellent. I have read it at least five times. Dr. Andy Woods also does an excellent series that can be found on the church's website. (SLBC Andy Woods, under the topic Soteriology. A 58 week teaching on salvation) I strongly recommend the investment of time listening to this series by Dr. Woods and the reading of the book by Pastor Rokser.

I liked to explain it this way while teaching in the jail. (Since they were prisoners this made particular sense to them) Every unsaved person will someday stand before an infinity Holy God. He, as Judge of all, knows everything about everything in one's life; even the intent of the heart. Even those that are generally noble, will be put to test. We can hide nothing from God's all knowing mind. This knowledge is the evidence against us. Then that evidence is applied to the standard: the absolute perfection of God Himself. There are no alterations to that perfection. As noted numerous times in this book, the standard is the immutable holy nature of God. And be judged. And judge fairly. And found unworthy. Unless, they have been declared righteous by the ultimate Judge, since they have become benefactors of the declaration of justification; which is, Christ's righteousness imputed to us. (Romans 5:1 and 8:33-34)

Therefore, those who accept the gift of eternal salvation have changed their forever position. The one believing - is now a forever son or daughter - of their Heavenly Father. We will never ever face God as the Judge. We have changed rooms. We no longer have a pending judgment in the courtroom of God, after this life. There is no need for the pending judgment of God, where perfect justice must be administered. We have been granted, or better said, placed into the forever family room of our Heavenly Father. The Heaven or Hell judgment is over. We no longer need to fear that someday we will face, once again, the question of our eternal destiny. There has been an irrevocable change into that of being a son or daughter of our Abba Father. We have been accepted into the forever family room of our Heavenly Father. We have complete assurance from the ultimate fear.

However, we do not escape our responsibilities with our Heavenly Father. As Christians, our Heavenly Father wants us to be living ambassadors. To behave like sons/daughters of the coming Savior. I like to explain it this way, let's suppose I have two sons. (I don't so this is an acceptable illustration) One of my sons is always going astray. He just cannot seem to avoid trouble. He is often an embarrassment to the family. As expected, our family name is important to us. We desire a good reputation in our church, our neighborhood, and with the larger community. Now, my other son brings great joy to us. He is a fine young man. He makes us proud that he has our name. We frequently hear from those in the community what a responsible young man he is. He is known for his work ethic, and for being honest in his endeavors.

Now comes Friday night. The two sons of mine come asking for money for their Friday night activities. The first son, who tends to be reckless with those expectations of ours as a son; the one who simply cannot be trusted, because, as noted, it seems that everytime I grant his request for money, he disappoints us; therefore, I deny him. (In the Christian experience this could be a loss of blessing, Fatherly discipline, or unanswered prayers to name a few) I simply do not want to contribute to another embarrassing and drunken night of shame; not when he disrespects our name by his behavior. However, the well behaved son, the trustworthy one, I gladly give him money as a reward for another good week in school. This money is given as an appreciation for his behavior; therefore, the request was granted. (In the Christian experience this may be seen a special answered prayer or some particular blessing from our Heavenly Father or those rewards at the Bema Seat) In this illustration, it may be money for pizza with his friends, since he has earned this, and I want to show him my appreciation for his representing the Miller name with dignity. Oftentimes blessings come to those who are faithful in their walk, just because God loves to bless His children.

This illustration shows why obediences is only a question of fellowship. Our degree of intimacy with our Heavenly Father is based on our walk of obedience, but it is never a question of sonship. Since eternal life is forever life, therefore, sonship is forever. Once born again into God's family, always a member of God's family. (For the record we have one son of whom I am very proud to be his dad. A really fine young man)

This teaching is highlighted by two of the writings of Apostle John. In the Gospel of John, the primary focus is on establishing the nature of Christ deity, revealing His saving work, which is received on faith and faith alone. Where faith in Jesus Christ, and the acceptance of His payment on the cross for our sins, results in eternal life. Whereas, in the letter of 1st John, he writes to established believers, about having fellowship with our Heavenly Father. How to walk in a manner that brings one into a harmonious fellowship. They do have some crossover, but the main focus is different in the two books. While the truth of our secure position is established at the moment of salvation, it does not release us from consequences. As I have experienced in my own life. God has a strong disciplining hand for His wayward children. (See chapter 12 of Hebrews) While His discipline can seem harsh, even to the point of the premature termination of our physical life, a most severe form of discipline, it never nullifies our eternal life and new birth. The discomfort that is experienced by the hand of our Heavenly Father means He loves us. He also wants us to be fruitful and exhibit qualities of His Son, our Savior. Even in discipline, God is expressing His love. Actually, this is a demonstration of His love. He disciplines those He loves. This can be done without loss of salvation, since He is fully satisfied with the payment made almost 2,000 years ago on the cross. Furthermore, always remember that we are clothed in the very righteousness of Christ; He will never disrobe us.

A few last thoughts on this subject. This relates to God's immutable holiness. Let's say one was saved but not eternally secure? What happens the very moment a believer sins? Let's say someone is saved at church one Sunday, but the moment he gets ready to leave he has a sinful thought. Then the newly saved person is distracted by someone. The sinning thought is later forgotten. Has the sin nullified his salvation? Does this sin nullify his new birth requiring him to be saved again?

What degree of sin would it take? Remember, the immutable nature of God does not ever change. I have never met one person who does not sin, even after salvation. Therefore, any sin no matter how minute, would cause God's standards to be reviolated, and thereby, potentially outside the previous salvific work of Christ; if the benefits of our coming to saving faith do not have permanent results. This conditional concept could have profound implications. What a horrible situation to consider: if our salvation is a probationary status or conditional? Any sin would be enough to nullify our salvation, and we would be in need of being saved again and again and again, you get the point.

The logical outcome of this probation salvation thinking is that to receive salvation, every sin had to be atoned for, but after salvation, God lowers His standards and accepts some sin. But this idea has no place in the scriptures. There is no place that God says you can go so far, then once you transgress this limit, you lose the benefits of what Christ accomplished on the cross. To think this way would create an uncertainty that could cause madness, or degrees of spiritual depression. If one truly considers the implications, it is troubling to the soul! The belief in eternal security is necessary for our spiritual and mental stability. And is theologically consistent with what the Bible teaches. This is seen, even from the earlier stages of the scriptures, where there are a number of Covenants. The Abrahamic is unconditional. There are no conditions, because God's promises were based on His actions alone in securing the Covenant. But another Covenant is conditional: the Mosaic. Where blessing and curses are conditioned on obedience. The first one was an absolute guarantee. The other, the Mosaic, where blessings and curses were based on their obedience to the commandments.

The expectation that there should be some moral reform after salvation is true. Nonetheless, the issue at hand is the absolute completeness of salvation. If after being saved, I enter probation salvation status, then this dilutes the holiness of God. Meaning, he modifies His required holiness for salvation to continue. It would then be a combination of His sacrifice and my good behavior, in my post salvation, to sustain the continuance of my salvation. There is no assurance there. Also there is no litmus test in the scriptures for this thinking. There are indicators of our spiritual development, but never for our eternal salvation. The key to proper interpretation is the audience. To whom are those particular scriptural passages addressing? For unbelievers, the standard is absolute perfect holiness. That is why a completed salvation is needed. We need a declaration of permanent justification. For the believer, calls for a more righteous walk with our Father; a more sanctified lifestyle as a son/daughter. And that requires commitment to walking in the spirit, because our justification has been declared, and never needs to be repeated. Therefore, behavior is a fellowship question, and not a salvation issue.

A few more thoughts on this misconstrued thinking. If probation salvation is the status of the Christian: then someone may need to be reborn again and again and again to keep rejoining the family of God. Since every time they sin: they would be once again outside the redemptive work of Christ. Or we need to clarify what sin is sufficient to lose salvation, and what level of compromise is acceptable to God. Which sins can He overlook regarding the status of our salvation relationship, and what sin causes the loss of salvation. This type of thinking would compromise the holy standards of God, and cause believers to live in perpetual fear.

Some believe the teaching of 1 John is the required solution to restore salvation after sinning. One would need to confess sin to be restored back to salvation status. However, no one is totally mindful of every sin they commit. We may need to confess known sin to restore our fellowship with the Father, as we are convicted by the Holy Spirit, or from reading the Bible, but never to restore sonship. We should walk in the light of God's revelation and confess known sins, because we want to have His blessings, and be in close loving fellowship. Furthermore, being in good fellowship with our Heavenly Father, helps us find favor in our prayer life, etc. But obedience is never required to sustain our sonship, since new birth is once for all, and so is our adoption into the family of God.

This in particular is why we need to understand our forever settled salvation to have spiritual stability. A salvation that is not subject to nullification. A secure salvation that has the very promise of God behind the guarantee. This is the freedom of knowing our secure hope in Christ. The sure hope that I am in a forever relationship with my

Abba Father. The possibility of facing the Judgeship of God is over, forever.

To fail to understand this likely means we have not thought through the implications of this teaching; as would be the case with probation salvation theology. And the fear that this belief naturally suggests. Because, if we are not thinking through the logical ramifications of the probation status teaching, with the mindset that understands the absolute immutable holiness of God, and we don't believe in eternal security, we will never have complete assurance of heaven. We would at best have a hopeful salvation. We will never have the absolute assured confidence of our sonship with our Abba Father. A sure confidence that we can always approach the throne of our Father, because of God's unending grace, and because we are His children. We need an understanding of our irrevocable gift of eternal salvation to be spiritually and emotionally anchored.

That is why the scriptures describe our salvation in many diverse terms: like being born again, declared justified, clothed in the very righteousness of God, being sealed by the Holy Spirit, and possessing eternal life. Which all indicate our acceptance and standing has forever changed. Our sonship is one that ensures our eternal future. This is the forever change of status: from a son of Adam, to a child of our Abba Father. Therefore, to doubt our salvation is detrimental to our spiritual confidence. If I can lose eternal life? What was it that I received? Our Heavenly Father wants us to have the assurance that we are forever His! (1st John chapter 5) It is the foundation for our spiritual confidence. This is why it is written in the fellowship book of 1st John. If we are uncertain of our eternal status with our Heavenly Father, then true fellowship will evade us.

I can anticipate some of the objections to this teaching; those who claim that one must be an active disciple to be a Christian. But that would mean that my faithfulness is a condition for salvation. That I must do good works to validate or contribute to my salvation. But this thinking clearly minimizes Christ's completed work on the cross. Which Jesus said on the cross was finished. (John 19:30) Furthermore, discipleship is not always a good indicator. Judas was a disciple (a learner of Christ), but not born again. (John 17:12) Even though he was a disciple for years, he was the son of perdition. (Read chapter 13 of the Gospel of John and well discussed by Rokser, in chapter 12, in his book on Eternal Security) And in the Gospel of Matthew, it was said it would have been better if he was never born. (Matthew chapter 26) Lastly, let me ask you a very serious question: can you really say you are a disciple, if you are not active in the great commission as commanded? (Matthew 28:19-20) Will you apply this principle for yourself, if you are not actively sharing your faith, and allow people to go to Hell, because you fear the social stigma of evangelism, then claim that discipleship is a requirement for salvation? We should look for opportunities to share our faith, it is commanded. But discipleship is not a condition for our salvation, because it adds fallible human obedience to the salvific work of Christ. The scriptures are clear, it is not by works, so it may be by grace. (Titus 3:5) Our discipleship should be expected, but is not a condition for salvation. If it were, then should not those sins of omission, like neglecting to evangelize, be included in those requirements? In the book of James it says to know and not to do is a sin. Are you sure this sin of omission is not keeping you out of heaven? Yes, you can, since eternal life is a free gift.

Our motivation to evangelize should result from an understanding of the implication of the faith, knowing the consequences of accepting or rejecting the faith. It is a true expression of our love for our fellow man. And our love for mankind is what moves us to evangelism. Furthermore, our degree of motivation, to share our faith, shows how much we really believe what we profess.

Lastly, as I have noted, to doubt our status is to live in spiritual uncertainty. I need to know, that I know, that I am a child forever of the living God. He is now my eternal Father. Never to be put aside as a son or daughter. That is comforting joy my friend. A real peaceful joy! NO matter what happens in this evil world, my rightful standing as a child in the family room of God is never a question. Even suicide and apostasy can not undo one's salvation. The gift of eternal life, and spiritual new birth, do not allow the undoing of what has been given by the grace of God. Because, I am adopted, redeemed, born again, a new creation, justified, a present possessor of eternal life, and therefore, I will be glorified. Guaranteed! God forgives and accepts, not just He loves us, but because the full payment for our sin has already been made. Therefore, what do I really need to fear? Hallelujah, what a Savior, to whom I am thankful for my all-encompassing salvation.

Mini Bibliography for this chapter

1. Strombeck, J. F. *Shall Never Perish,* Kregel Publications, 1991
2. Rokser, Dennis M. *SHALL NEVER PERISH, Forever.* Grace Gospel Press, 2012
3. Cucuzza, Thomas M. *Secure forever!* WWW.xulonpress.com, 2007
4. Kendall, R.T. *Once Saved, Always Saved.* Authentic Media, 2005
5. Stanley, Charles. *Eternal Security,* Thomas Nelson Publishers 1990
6. Lutzer Erwin W. *How You Can Be Sure That You Will Spend Eternity with God,* Moody Press,1996
7. Hixson, J. B. Ge*tting the Gospel Wrong,* Grace Gospel Press, 2013
8. Olson, Lloyd A. *Eternal Security, Once Saved Always Saved,* Tate Publishing and Enterprises, 2007
9. Dr. Andy Woods Soteriology series found at SLBC Andy Woods
10. And numerous other books. See some of them in my Bibliography section
11. Lightner, Robert P. *Sin, the Savior and Salvation,* Thomas Nelson, 1991
12. Stegall, Thomas L. *The Gospel of the Christ,* 2009

CHAPTER 21

ETERNAL SECURITY AND THE GOSPEL PRESENTATION

W hen endeavoring to share the gospel with the lost, it is crucial not only to be clear on what is the content of the gospel, but also, to be able to communicate the salvific results that come upon believing. It is a process of learning that takes time and careful study. But it is absolutely necessary for those receiving the salvation message to know the results of believing; so they have firm confidence in their salvation. Therefore, to share a faulty gospel has eternal repercussions. First, because a faulty gospel is often deficient information to bring one to salvation. Secondly, for one who is saved, a faulty understanding of the results of believing the gospel, results in an uncertain salvation. This is addressed in the first chapter of Galatians by the Apostle Paul. Where there is curse, an anathema, for altering the gospel message or its content. Why so harsh of a warning? Because it is a message that has eternal repercussions. In Paul's Galatian letter, he warned them that there were individuals who were influencing others by altering the Gospel. They were teaching that there were other conditions that must be met to earn their right standing: both in justification and growing sanctification. The altered message had become a confusing message. They were actually very diligent in the pursuit of self-righteousness. But it was an attempt at man-made righteousness. Which falls woefully short of the infinite righteness needed for acceptance before God; and does not result in eternal sonship. This is a grievous substitution for the righteousness provided by God; which is provided through the person and work of Christ. Later, as the book of Galatians progresses, Paul starts to address how to grow in sanctification salvation. The process of growing mature in their given salvation. How to grow from a new babe in Christ into a fruitful mature believer; which too requires a clear understanding of the faith.

Whereas, in comparison with the book for 1st Corinthians, where Paul is addressing immoral behavior, he gives a list of warnings and potential consequences, but no anathema. Why? Because it is not how people enter into a right relationship with God. It is not an eternal life issue. Serious lifestyle issues for sure, but not the altering of the message that brings eternal life. The apostle Paul, who wrote both books, had greater concern for those self-righteous alterations to the gospel in Galatians, than he does for carnal behavior in 1st Corinthians. The church of today has this backwards. While sinning behavior has significant consequences. Paul was far more concerned about the eternal consequences of a faulty gospel message, since there is only one Gospel message that brings eternal salvation. The development of Christlikeness in the life of a believer is significant, but pales in comparison, with the message that brings the gift of eternal life. Tragedy, there will be a lot of self-righteous people who will have the door of heaven closed to them. The standard does not change. It is absolute perfection that is required, and nothing less is acceptable. This is why we need a permanent solution for our unrighteous condition; being clothed in the very righteousness of Christ is just one aspect of the solution. But in light of God's holy nature, a wonderful truth to have firmly settled in our minds.

I am not saying that failing to teach the assurance of eternal security, it is not possible to present the gospel. However, there is the very real possibility that some moral reforming conditions may be implied, and that confuses the message. This is an alteration of the true gospel. This altered Gospel may not lead to eternal life. The whole reason for sharing the gospel is to lead someone into a saving faith. (This is not a special faith, but a properly placed faith) It is a message that requires clarity, and proper content.

If there are any requirements added to the freeness of gospel: it is faulty, and may lead to devastating eternal consequences. We must be diligent that what we are sharing is God's truth, and nothing but the pure truth of the gospel. Therefore, when we are presenting the gospel message, we need to make sure it is clear and understandable. This is not a trivial theological issue. We are talking about God's only plan of redemption. There is only one gospel. There is only one Lord and Savior who is qualified to bring about the salvation of mankind. It was His work as Lord, on the cross, that atoned for our sins. If you are failing to understand these principles, you are not grasping the distance between you and the infinitely holy God. You do not understand the gospel! Don't fool yourself. Pride can be very destructive, and can have eternal consequences. If you think you can somewhat help merit this standing before God: you will be eternally disappointed. That is being kind-hearted in description. An understanding of the litmus test I gave, remains a true indicator of whether you grasp the gospel.

There is more to this issue: a gospel message that does not include full assurance, is lacking in its clarity to the believer. That is, until the full message has been delivered, understood and accepted, it is subject to misunderstanding. The understanding that is necessary, is that we, upon believing, have a secure and everlasting life. Until that takes place we will naturally experience frequent bouts of doubt. This is not the same as the proper respect for God fear, that all believers need. But recurring thoughts of not really being saved. Or a fear of returning to the state of the unsaved, because of some deficient moral behavior. It is also possible that the results of a faulty gospel is: one may have never actually been saved, because there remains questions as to what is really required to be saved. A nagging fear that you are not measuring up to the requirements for salvation. Of course, if you are trying to merit salvation, either in part, or as a whole, by your own merits, then it is a well placed fear. You then have valid reasons to question your salvation. This is an dangerous and deceitful message of you cooperating with God to earn salvation, like those, to whom Paul is writing to warn in

Galatians. Which is so prevalent in many church doctrines today. And often preached erroneously from pulpits! Regardless of what aspects of your responsibility you undertake in the effort to help secure salvation, your part will be subject to defect. Woefully deficient. And the agony of misunderstanding the true gospel, will last for all of eternity.

Remember, the standing sonship/daughtership requirement before God is always 100%, or not at all. When it comes to our salvation, there is only pure white or absolute blackness, there is no gray. This failure to understand the finality of our salvation naturally leads to uncertainty; and not the peace that our Heavenly Father wants us to enjoy. And rightly so! The understanding of our eternal sonship/daughtership is the only way to have true peace. If you doubt your eternal standing? How can you possibly present a gospel that gives assurance to the unbeliever? How will they even know if they are saved, if you too, do not know the means and conditions for receiving salvation, and the results of being saved?

As indicated, we can share the salvation message without teaching eternal security, but it will always be an unreliable message. And one that is subject to insecurity for the one believing the message. My recommendation is that we include the assurance of salvation when presenting the gospel of Jesus Christ. It is always a clearer and more confident message to share. And will likely produce a more lasting assurance for the one believing. A more joyful response. A joyful response, knowing that, upon receiving the unconditional (other than faith alone) and completed salvation, granted to them in Christ, they can now rest fully assured. It comes down to this: either Christ paid it all, or we have an uncertain and untrustworthy salvation. This contrast has real ramifications. One option can affect our spiritual health, and/ or our spiritual destiny. The other, spurs us on in our walk with our Savior. To whom we are so grateful, that we want to worship, and share. This is not a trivial matter.

For what resting hope is there to a gospel presentation that is uncertain in its secureness? To present the idea that by believing you are saved, but don't count on it. A gospel that suggests that you need to prove it by your behavior is insecurity at best, and maddening at worst. Of course, if you want others to take your conversion seriously, a change of behavior brings credibility to the inward change in your life. But we also see that outward change in many cults. Outward moral reform is not always a dependable test of salvation. We need to keep the gospel clear: faith alone, in the work of Christ alone, brings forgiveness of sin and eternal life. When we as a body of believers are not presenting an assured salvation message, nor even confident in our own salvation, how can the one to whom we are witnessing have confidence?.

Have you seen the books being marketed that claim to bring assurance of salvation? Why is it that after reading them, the end result is that the reader is left so uncertain? It is because those authors add numerous subjective requirements, and then suggest these subjective litmus tests of our behavior brings assurance. Puzzling, is it not! Those subjective requirements that don't bring assurance. Keep it clear, upon simple trusting faith in the person, and sacrifice of Jesus Christ, brings forgiveness of sin, and acceptance into the forever family of God; and eternal life. Additional details may be needed to help clarify the subject, but never more subjective qualifications.

In summary, if we do not have the confident peace that we are safe and secure, how do we share a sure and confident salvation message? If we ultimately do not know if we are eternally saved without a doubt, how is the one receiving our message to know? Let's be clear with the gospel! Both with the content and results. Because when we have this uncertainty of where we stand with our Heavenly Father, our motivations for living out our faith are different; it is based on working to maintain our salvation, and not resting confidence in our salvation. We will find ourselves in a protective maintenance of our salvation, versus bold living salvation. Almost like the experience of foster homes for so many children. They are living there, which gives some comfort, but they know that it may not be their permanent home. We don't have a foster home God. We need to communicate that the acceptance of Christ results in the permanent removal from the courtroom into the living room. A permanent acceptance into the forever family of our Abba Father. Eternal security is the assurance that I am forever, and ever, His child. This is the essence of what the gospel of eternal life assures. And it is a gift in the truest sense. One that is eternal in duration. That is why the gospel is so offensive to so many. It is the claim of exclusivity by Jesus Christ; which many find unacceptable to believe. (Galatians 5:11) There are alot of gray areas in our lives, this should not be one of them. There is only one way per Jesus: John 14:6. And it is an exclusive way!

Mini Bibliography

1. Bing, Charles C. *Lordship Salvation,* Ph.D. Dissertation, 1991
2. Bing, Charles C. *Simply By Grace,* Kregel Publishing, 2009
3. Bing, Charles C. *Grace Salvations and Discipleship,* Grace Theology Press, 2015
4. Chafer, Lewis Sperry, *Salvation,* Kregel Publications, 1991
5. Chafer, Lewis Sperry, *True Evangelism,* Kregel Publications, 1993
6. Chafer, Lewis Sperry, *Grace,* Kregel Publications, 1995
7. Cocoris, G. Michael, *The Salvation Controversy,* Insights From the Word, 2008
8. Hixson, J. B. *The Gospel Unplugged, Lucidbook,* 2011
9. Hixson, J. B., Whitmire, Rick, Zuck, Roy B. *Freely By His Grace,* Grace Gospel Press, 2012
10. Hixson, J. B. *Getting the Gospel Wrong,* Grace Gospel Press, 2013
11. Hixson, J. B. *Top 10 Reasons some people go to Hell, and One Reason No One Ever Has To!* Grace Acres Press, 2020
12. Moyer, R. Larry, *Free and Clear,* Kregel Publications, 1997

CHAPTER 22

THE CONSEQUENCES OF THE BEMA SEAT OF CHRIST

There are a number of Covenants, but two in particular need some focus: the one unconditional (Abrahamic) and the other conditional (Mosaic). The former was a guarantee entirely by God Himself; the later, the blessing and curses of the Mosaic, which is conditioned on behavior and obedience. This is where I see in the Abrahamic covenant aspects of theology which implies eternal security; and in the Mosaic covenant, which is conditional, and brings blessings and discipline based on how we respond to those commands The potential for divine discipline, and/or, for rewards or loss of rewards. This is our subject in these next two chapters.

If what I have written so far is true? And I am convinced it is! (Or I would not be writing this book) I understand, and expect, that many will disagree with me on certain aspects of my theology. But I stand by what has been composed. Yet, I can surmise the objections: there are no consequences for bad living, but this is not true. There are very significant consequences, even eternal ones; but our eternal salvation is not one of them. A failure to understand this will cause some to question: why be obedient? Maybe even asking themselves why they should act according to their saved position.

These are not scholarly, but general observations, based on the in-depth reading of the scriptures and personal reflection. Here are a some for consideration:

1. New birth produces a new nature
2. Church discipline
3. The Holy Spirit living in us
4. The conviction of the Holy Spirit
5. The encouragement of other believers
6. Natural consequences of sinful choices
7. Bema Seat consequences
8. Divine discipline
9. Bema Seat rewards
10. Unanswered prayers due to sin in our lives
11. Broken fellowship with God
12. Family and/or community expectations
13. Broken relationships due to sin
14. Financial loss of blessing
15. Guilt over sin
16. Our reputation in the community
17. We can lose the peace with God
18. We can lose the peace of God in our lives
19. We can become distorted in our thinking
20. We can lose our wisdom for proper living
21. We can become spiritually blind to truth again
22. We will become spiritually misguided in our walk
23. We lose our eternal priorities; the chance to make a difference
24. We regret missed opportunities for doing good
25. Walking in sin can lead to a loss of clarity
26. Walking in sin can lead to dissolution with the faith, and then the abandonment of the faith; which leads to a sense of meaninglessness or harsh discipline

27. Walking in sin can lead to loss of purity of mind; which leads to many of the aforementioned problems, and those resulting consequences
28. We lose the joy of the Lord
29. We again find ourselves living a purposeless life
30. We find the struggles of life have become pointless
31. We can become so dispirited, we could even become suicidal
32. God may turn us over to Satan as discipline, removing His covering
33. We lose the respect of our fellow man
34. We could lose our jobs or promotions due to overt sin
35. We can lose the respect of our children and/or wife
36. We could lose our children and marriage due to sin

So you can easily see that there are abundant reasons why we should be motivated to live a life that is consistent with our standing in the faith. In the next two chapters, I want to focus on two major ones: the Bema Seat evaluation and divine discipline.

At the Bema Seat of Christ, the quality of our Christian lives will be evaluated. It will be a divine evaluation of our faithfulness as an ambassador of Christ; it will show whether we were faithful or indifferent in our God given responsibilities. Either way, the quality of our Christian lives will be revealed.

For some reason, this teaching about the Bema Seat has been neglected by the majority of pastors. And the ramifications of this subject have failed to be expounded upon from the pulpit. Yet, it is a central teaching in regards to the consequences that result from how we live out this gift of our salvation. It pertains to the quality of our Christian walk, and gives us even more motivation to live faithfully, as a child of God. The Apostle Paul writes about the subject a number of times. (See 1st Corinthians 3:12-15, 2 Corinthians 5:10, Romans 15:10, Colossians 2:18, and 1st Timothy 4:8, as examples of a few) Yet it is also seen earlier on in the scriptures. Moses, like us, had the choices of the riches of this world, or the esteem of Christ and eternal rewards. What are those esteems? They are guaranteed eternal life, divine blessing, our eventual glorification, and our potential rewards for faithfulness, to name a few. In the New Testament book of Hebrews,11:25-26, the author noted that Moses desired the riches of Christ more than the passing pleasures of this world. He looked forward to the reward. That should be our model. He understood the principle the Apostle Paul later wrote about in 2nd Corinthians 4:16-18. Simply, our present troubles are nothing in light of the exceeding glory that is coming to us; but in addition to these promises, our eternal rewards if we are faithfull.

In just about every book in the New Testament some form of warning and/or promised reward is given to the Christian, regarding the consequences of how we are living out the faith. It may also come to the faithful one, with a warning not to lose what you have labor for, etc. (Colossians 2:18) The idea being that if you have lived a quality Christian life, don't allow a temptation or moral compromise, to cause you to lose much of your testimony and/or reward at the Bema Seat. (See 1st Corinthians 9:24-27, as an example of the Apostle Paul's desire not to become disqualified or lose a well earned reward) There are both positive and negative aspects of this teaching. These are not warnings of loss of salvation, but losing grace rewards because of unfaithful living.

The idea that every believer will be given the same reward in heaven is without Biblical corroboration. To believe that the truly born again, but comfortable Christian, will receive the same reward as the missionary who sacrificially pursued the cause of Christ is just not Biblical. The Lord is a just God, and will not forget anyone's sacrificial labor. While salvation is absolutely free: our God is just, and will reward accordingly those who took seriously the responsibilities of being an ambassador of Christ. For those who lived their lives in light of eternity, and not for temporary pleasures, will find a great reward at the Bema Seat. The alternative is also true. For example, those who avoided sharing the gospel to avoid social stigma, will find they have forsaken eternal reward opportunities. Those eternal blessings that could have been theirs, if they were willing to take seriously, this key teaching of the Bible.

If a pastor wants to motivate his sheep, he should highlight the results of the gospel, and the rewards for being faithful in that ambassador mission. Pastors willingly accepted this calling to teach and preach, it should mean the whole counsel of scriptures; as the Apostle Paul wrote in the 20th chapter of Acts.

Sadly, many of the pulpits of our day are adrift with appeasement of conscience, and are too diligent not to offend. The major theme in the Sunday morning messages has emerged into the popular message of how to live successfully in this transitory life. With the emphasis on overcoming trials that naturally come to all of us. Often embedded in this message, is the idea that personal satisfaction in this life is the goal. Those under this teaching may feel better, and find greater worldly satisfaction, but those messages do not have much impact on eternity.

The results of this prevailing message now being preached: you can have your best life now. This diminishes the motivation to live with the thought that one's personal sacrifices will be remembered, and rewarded, in the coming Kingdom. What happened to the willing sacrifice for the cause of Christ? Knowing that one's labors will be recognized by God at the Bema Seat. The confidence that God will see one's good deeds, as an expression of their faith, and reward us in the ages to come. Remember, that God placed this teaching before the believer, so we can know that sacrificial labors are worthy of our devotion. This was His revelation to us! Furthermore, it reveals His fairness to each and every believer: our God is a just Heavenly Father. Unfortunately, many Christians will be greatly disappointed when they realize that by pursuing temporal amusements, which have ended at death, has resulted in forfeiting possible heavenly rewards. All because they were not diligent in the more important aspects of the faith.

How did we fall into a misguided emphasis in the church? Where key Biblical truths are neglected. We simply are not being taught key Biblical truths in many churches. This neglect to teach Biblical truth undermines our motivation for service. It also manifests in the benign impact of many believers in our local church bodies; since, if there is no reward, then soft Christianity makes sense. It is comfortable to the soul, but deadly to the mission to proclaim the gospel.

So let's explore this teaching to establish its relevance for the Christian. Remember, this is a Christian only evaluation. There is no question of Heaven or Hell at the Bema Seat. It takes place in Heaven after the Rapture of the body of Christ. The evaluation has to do with service and sacrifice. What did I do with the knowledge of the faith? Was I willing to sacrifice for the cause of Christ? Was I willing to sacrifice some of my desired social reputation to reach those who need to know about the saving work of Christ? Was I diligent in my effort to reach those that need the message, and then encouragement, on how to join the Father's family? When it comes to rewards, some of the questions are: Did I sacrifice anything for the faith? Did I manifest Christ-like attributes in my personal life? Was I a faithful servant? Did I understand the perilous situation the lost are facing, and then have diligent motivation to introduce them to the hope we have in Christ? Am I being accurate with the gospel presentation? These are just a few of the areas of evaluation.

Dr. J. B. Hixson and Mark Fontecchio, in their book *WHAT LIES AHEAD*, A Biblical Overview of the End Times, listed a number of the areas that Christ will evaluate at the judgment seat. It is a very comprehensive list. These areas are: Enduring Trials, Diligently Seeking God, Perseverance, Faithful in Ministry, Longing for Christ's Appearance, Leading Other to Christ, Faithfulness to Christ, Diligence in the Christian Walk, Stewardship of what Has Been Entrusted to Us, Enduring Persecution, Remaining in Close Fellowship with Christ, Benevolence toward the Poor, Wholehearted Service to Christ, and Ministering to the Saints. They give a thorough and detailed overview of the Christian Bema Seat evaluation. Others give a different detailed list. But in general they are the same similar areas of evaluation. That is because they come from the same source: the Bible. Depending on who is listing them, and how they are classified, will determine the number of categories. But the key point is that our God is not unjust to forget our struggles or sacrifices, in our service for the cause of Christ. Our degree of motivation also shows the degree of hope we have in Christ. We usually only go as far as we have the confidence that what we believe is really and truly, true. Hence the need to study apologetics and solid doctrine, which affirms that we are investing in what is really worthwhile. Our devotion, in the joyful service to others, manifests the degree of Love of Christ that dwells in our hearts. A sacrificial life shows that we are truly eternally minded. Our willing sacrifice for the cause of Christ shows the watching world that we really believe our faith is true. It exhibits that we understand that how we live does matter: both now and into eternity.

As you would expect, the evaluation will be different for each individual in the body of Christ, depending on the opportunities and situations. It further depends on the calling that God gave, and the obedience to the call. Not everyone has the same talents and responsibilities placed on them. Not everyone is called to be a pastor or evangelist. For those who are called to these roles, the requirements are higher. But the reward is also potentially greater for those called to these high callings, assuming they are faithful in that calling.

As an example, regarding pastors, there is a particular reward for faithful pastors and teachers. (1st. Timothy 5:17) But as expected, they are also held to higher standards. (See the Pastoral letters of Paul: 1st and 2nd Timothy and Titus) Higher expectations from the Lord are due to their elevated role in the body of Christ; and therefore, the reason for this should be clear. Should John Q Christian have a moral failure, the impact is generally limited to his personal testimony and family. It does impact the message of the gospel, but not to the degree of a pastor. A smaller impact has smaller consequences to the credibility of the faith. Therefore, it is obvious, that the role of pastor/teacher has a much greater impact on the perception of the faith. For the one who is looking for reasons not to even consider the claims of the Christian faith: obvious hypocrisy is such an excuse. They want to avoid the moral ramifications that are inherent in the faith. So hypocrisy in the life of a believer is their justification. A rationale for avoiding investigating the merits of the faith. For those who desire to continue their lives uninterrupted by the sexual standards inherent in the Christian faith, hypocrisy is their excuse. Without this knowledge, they may forgo the gift of salvation that is being offered to the unbelieving. Think of the impact it could have. They would reject the provision of what Christ offers; even though it is to their own demise, resulting in devastating eternal consequences. Hence, the high calling of a pastor comes with much higher standards. Therefore, even for those outside the body of Christ, the high calling of a pastor/teacher is crucial for the advancement of the gospel. Because someone's eternity could depend on the integrity of the person proclaiming the message. If the person proclaiming the message is not credible, then maybe, they perceive that the message they proclaim is not credible. Particularly, for those who cannot separate the truthfulness of Christianity, with the sometimes disgraceful behavior of those who claim to be Christians. Again, see the letters of 1 & 2 Timothy and Titus, by the Apostle Paul, for some of these standards to be in ministry.

Another reason why God has such high standards for pastors/teachers is the impact on those within the body. It can cause disillusionment for many. As an example, if a pastor is caught having inappropriate relations outside his marriage, it undermines every moral principle he has taught. Those who hold the pastor in high esteem may be disheartened by his failure to live what he has taught. Should temptation take down a pastor? That failure does significant damage to the proclamation of the truth. It affects the noble truth of everything the church should stand for. It discredits the truth, even though the veracity of the faith remains true. Paradoxically, the foundations of the faith are true, even if the one proclaiming it does not live up to the high expectations of the calling. The negative impact of moral failure is strongly felt by believers and nonbelievers alike.

Yet, regardless of how we practice our faith, the truthfulness of Christianity is still the truth. Take for an illustration, you go to the doctor and get your physical. The doctor then sits down with you and reviews your health status. He sees your weight creeping up. He informs you that you're getting close to pre-diabetes. He suggests you exercise more, eat better, and lose some weight. He is likely correct in His recommendations. Let's suppose that the doctor giving you the advice is overweight himself, and should take his own advice. The truth of what he is suggesting is still true -even if he is not practicing the advice himself. This is true of Christianity too. The truth of the faith remains: it is true! But those poorly practicing the faith are not the best representatives; nonetheless, the truth of the faith remains just the same. That is one of the reasons why God places such high standards on those who claim the name of Christ, particularly pastors and spiritual leaders. It affects the possible reception of the message and/or disillusions those who are part of the body of Christ. As noted, it may provide the justification for some to forgo exploring the solid evidence that validates the gospel message, even to the demise of their own eternal destiny.

Additionally, it is more than just the credibility of the message, it also undermines the desired holiness that God expects from the body of Christ. If we are intended to be salt and light, we need to exhibit those qualities. Any compromising moral failure brings old fashioned shame to everything the church is called to be: a beacon of moral truth. The divine standard of truth. (1st. Timothy 3:15) Accordingly, we should expect those who are called by the name of Christ, to exhibit lifestyles that are upright. It is even greater for those outfront, as the face of the faith. Those in the role of pastor/teacher/leader. Because a compromised church is a worldly church. Exactly what we are seeing today in our church communities. A worldly church that has lost the perceived value of those high moral standards; those that should naturally be reflected in the lives of Christians. A worldly church that is too often influenced by the standards of society around us, instead of the scriptures. The standard that is described in the scriptures, and not by our morally collapsing society. How can we be the salt and light in a compromised lifestyle? Keep in mind, as we stand for these principles, we should expect push back; since, what we should stand for, will not usually be a welcomed message from those outside the faith; and sadly, from many in the faith community.

This is in line with an insight that my wife and I have discussed. I think, at times, because it is concerning to her. She has noted some good solid Christian's lives unravel. Resulting in a fearful mindset that when we step out in faith to make a difference, and live authentic Christian lives, we become a target of the enemy. Clearly, Satan wants to do us, and our testimony, damage. He generally goes after those that are making the greatest difference. That should be expected. If you step out in faith to make a difference, beware, you become a target. Should John Q, who is inactive in ministry be overtaken by a moral failure, there is a limited impact on the message. But those in leadership, and who are trusted and admired, if they fall, the impact is much more substantial. Satan has his targets. This insight into spiritual warfare often creates fear, as it has in many Christian's lives. This is why many back away from the full commitment to the faith: it is easier to go with the flow.

Likely why the lukewarm believer is mostly left alone. Since the truly born again are not going to lose their salvation, and they are only making a limited impact with their spiritual gifts, they are little threat to this worldly kingdom. Satan is not going to awaken a potential sleeping Lion. Those who have no interest in leading others to Christ; whereby, changing the eternal destination of those who will receive the message. They are generally good people with whom you want as neighbors. They do not make people uncomfortable by active witnessing, since they falsely believe their character is their testimony. Behavior gives some credence to their faith, but so does the behavior of many other non-Christian faith traditions. It is the evidence that Christianity is true, that makes what we believe and share of such great value. Good neighborly behavior does not explain the gospel. They are good people, but their lives have little eternal life changing value. Their impact, or lack of, will be personally realized at the Bema Seat; when they realize they wasted their lives with personal pursuits, and not the causes of Christ.

This is why the calling of a pastor is so crucial. Many have a noble desire for spiritual leadership, but lack the mature stable faith that is expected in such a role. That is why the new to the faith are not to be put into such high calling positions. (1st Timothy 3:6) They may have been successful in secular life, but this does not qualify them for ministry, since they are ill equipped for the coming spiritual attacks. Since Satan wants to do damage to the cause and message, and knowing the individual weakness of the believer, he attacks where vulnerable.

I have been in jail ministry with those who surprise me with their depth of knowledge, but they are inmates. I believe many are really believers. They just have fresh weaknesses that do not allow them to be leaders. Some have even wanted to exert their influence over my class with their degree of knowledge. They feel this knowledge elevates them to such a role. I welcome them to participate but not dominate. In my judgment they do not have the standing credibility to be preaching or teaching. They first need to establish their long-term spiritual maturity to be worthy of such a calling. There is a humbling and a mastering of the fresh that needs to take place beyond just knowledge of the Bible. Also, there are established leaders that have been vetted. To be in these roles, we needed to be endorsed by our home church, giving credence to our faith, and go through a background check, showing we are worthy to be teachers.

Additionally, we had an established and well respected organization that gave leadership and oversight to this ministry. That too, gave credibility to those who taught. With each pod leader having the freedom to teach as they felt the Lord's leading. It is also my personal credibility that gives me the standing to be a teacher. Those well versed in the scriptures, but not having the established righteous foundation (being inmates), need to focus on growing, not just in knowledge, but character too. Should they develop that high moral character, they most likely would not be in jail in the first place. There was one individual in particular who was very impressive with his Biblical knowledge. Rattling off scripture verses after verse only to indicate how many times he has been incarcerated. Hard to see his credibility to be a teacher of righteousness; even though he was well versed in the scriptures. The scriptures are clear, we need to have recognized credibility to preach others; those spiritual principles of the scriptures. Since knowledge alone is not the only criteria for being in position to teach. This is crucial not only for the credibility of the gospel, but because of the coming Bema Seat judgment. If one desires a high calling: he should also be aware of the higher standards. When we are in these roles, we should model lives that are above reproach.

This is why an understanding of the Bema Seat is crucial for our motivation as Christians. If there were no Bema Seat: then why subject our lives to spiritual conflict, other than for the salvation of our loved ones! Let the world go to Hell and enjoy one's life. This is what is called Reductio Ad Absurdum. It is the logical outcome of the faith being true, but not doing anything to share that truth. If there is no accountability one day, and we are not expressing authentic Christian love by sharing the faith, that is the end result of neglecting our responsibility to evangelizing, and the faith being true. This is the outcome of trying to maximize one's personal comforts here on earth and ignoring the eternal. If the desired goal is the American dream form of Christianity? Then this reasoning makes sense: the Ad Absurdum. Sadly, this is the practical ramifications of what is being practiced in most churches today. If you are not interested in sharing your faith? The truth is that you are standing by, letting people go to Hell, while pursuing your personal quality of life. Be clear, there will be accountability one day. It will be determined by our adherence to the list above by Hixson and Fontecchio; and chronicled by many others like Harlan Betz in his book, *Setting the Stage for Eternity*; and in Erwin Lutzer's book, *Your Eternal Reward*. Living an authentic Christian life can be sacrificially tough, but the rewards are out of this world. It ultimately comes back to the question of whether what we really profess to believe, is fundamentally true or not. And, we are willing to act according to that truth.

In any war there are casualties, especially if we are not prepared for the war. We need to have the mind of Christ. We need to be praying for courage and an open door, and abiding in Christ. Actually, we must be abiding to be fruitful for Christ. This is discussed in many places, but particularly in the Gospel of John, the 15th chapter. The fruit comes not from our own effort, but by abiding in Christ; so His fruit can be produced through us. (Also discussed in chapter five of Galatians) Where we need to be walking according to the spirit to produce good spiritual fruit in our lives. This is further illustrated in Mark, chapter 4, verses 19 and 20; where the quality of the ground determined the fruitfulness. It is not just the message, but the quality of the ground that determines the results. There are too many believers who are so concerned for the cares of this world, and the deceitfulness of the riches, that their lives have become unfruitful. But there are also warnings: if we draw back from living out the faith, then we are like those whom the writer of Hebrews was addressing, in which God was not pleased. I understand it is natural to draw back. We all do to various degrees. However, how we live does have eternal consequences. For the believer, what degree of reward is determined at the Judgment seat of Christ. Who does not want to hear from Christ: "Well done My good and faithful servant." What a compliment to receive at the end of life's journey.

As to what the rewards are and how long they last, there are a number of perspectives. Some think they last only for the 1000 year rule of Christ. Others believe they last throughout all of eternity. This subject is worthy of full books. Some of which I recommended in the suggested reading section. Others address the subject as part of their books. My emphasis is limited to the overall theme of this book: the immutable holiness of God, the need for personal salvation, and how that belief is manifested in our practical lives; the eternal ramifications of how we lived. It is crucial to understand that we will be held accountable, and our present actions matter significantly: both now and into eternity. It is significant because of the rewards we receive for our faithfulness and/or the souls of those we led to Christ. Therefore, this teaching is worthy of our serious reflection; not only for our own benefit, but for the souls for whom Christ died. To respond in a positive manner shows we truly have an eternal perspective of life. And therefore, it is eternally profitable to endeavor to live in such a manner that honors our Savior. Moreover, there is coming a day when He will honor us as His children, for our faithfulness. While it is clear there are rewards, there are warnings too! See the next chapter.

There are many Christians who seem to coast through life with many temporal blessings and relatively few problems. As a newer believer, who has tried to be a difference maker, that too did not make much sense. It was not until I came to understand this fundamental teaching, that this insight came alive. It opened my mind to the fairness of God. And that insight alone does not make a difference, until we take this teaching seriously enough to engage. And our engagement is motivated, impart, when we understand there are eternal rewards for our faithfulness and sacrifice. And that insight grows when we have a personal epiphany, a "come to Jesus" moment, regarding the horrors that await the unbeliever. When we grasp these insights, a willing sacrifice makes sense: like winning souls for Christ. But be prepared for some spiritual war in the process, so stay on your knees.

And this all makes logical sense if we take spiritual warfare seriously. The enemy is not going to waste a lot of time on someone who is passive in their faith. Those who take the road of comfort and ignore the eternal ramifications of the very faith we profess. Always be mindful that eternity is dependent on what we believe, and to those we witness to, what we share. This is the central truth of the Christian faith. If we choose the comforts of this world, we will miss the rewards for sacrificial faithfulness. Which I believe lasts into eternity, but even if it is only for the 1000 years of Christ's rule on this earth, it will be well worth the sacrifice, as has been discussed.

A desire for good evaluation is a key factor in pleasing Christ. This is not in inorder to become a Christian, but the desired results of being His faithful child; just as I desire certain behavior from my own children and grandchildren. It is not some status to achieve to be my children, but desired because they are my children. They will always be my children or grandchildren; just as I am always and forever my Heavenly Father's child. This by being born again and adopted into the family of God. My faithfulness does not determine eternal sonship but it does affect eternity. The questions remain: Am I as a son, walking in fellowship and obediently with my Heavenly Father? Is my life a witness to the goodness of God's grace? Did I love enough to give up some comforts in this life to be rewarded in the next? Did I endeavor to reach the lost? Our response to these questions is also an indicator of how strongly we believe what we profess. All aspects of our lives will determine our degree of rewards, but never our salvation!

Therefore, always keep this in mind, this is not a Heaven or Hell question. If it were, it would lead to merit based salvation requirements, which undermines the very redemptive work of Christ; and removes the confidence of our salvation. Which further diminishes our joy, our hope, and our motivation to serve a response to His love.

The more the church, as a body of believers, drifts from the understanding of the immutable holiness of our heavenly Father, His ultimate justice, His fairness in all things, and the coming rewards for faithfulness: the more irrelevant we become to the world. We lose those premier reasons for the hope we are called to share with the world.

It remains the same question: either Christianity is fundamentally true, or it is not?

Mini Bibliography

1. Betz, Harlan D. *Setting the Stage for Eternity,* Falcon Publishing LTD, 2005
2. Beware Paul N. B*elievers Payday,* AMG Publishers, 2002
3. Lutzer, Erwin W. *Your Eternal Reward,* Moody Press, 1998
4. Numerous others as listed in sections of my Bibliography
5. Hixson, J.B. and Fontecchio, Mark, *What Lies Ahead,* Lucidbooks, 2013

CHAPTER 23

FATHERLY DISCIPLINE

⚬⚬⚬

There is another scriptural teaching that is unknown to most Christians, denied, or not understood. It is not understood because it is not being taught. But the truth is: God, our Father, disciplines His children. Likely another reason God is described as our Heavenly Father: since He becomes our Abba Father at the moment of salvation. From the earliest chapters of the Bible, God disciplines His children. (He judges the world of unbelievers) He disciplines His children because we are His children. A big difference. Judging is an exacting of a penalty for sin; it is an upholding of His righteousness. There is a necessary penalty for sins, and it must be administered to remain faithful to Himself. For God to be a good God, justice must be an aspect of His nature. Some of those punishments came in time: like the flood, or Sodom and Gomorrah, when God could no longer tolerate the degree of sin on earth. Other forms of punishment and/or discipline came as God determined it was necessary for Him to intervene.

For those outside the faith, the actual individual eternal consequences start at death. (See Luke, chapter 16) Later, the final individual consequences of sin will be dealt with at the Great White Throne Judgment, when exact personal sins are judged. And the final administering of the ultimate and horrifying consequences of personal sin takes place: the eternal separation of those outside the redemptive work of Christ, into Hell. Described as the Lake of Fire. Where each unsaved man and woman will be judged as unworthy, and fairly judged, as to degrees of punishment in Hell. Even in Hell, the punishment is appropriate to the degree of sin. Because God is immutable: He therefore, was unable to forgo what is required to vindicate His absolute righteousness. The punishment of sin is actually a magnification of God's holiness. He is perfect in justice because He is a perfect Being. God cannot change that aspect of His nature just because He loves, as has been emphasized throughout the book. There is no subject I dislike more than this topic. However, this is one of the compelling reasons why I wrote this book. I felt the gravity of this subject was so neglected by most Chrisitans, that it needed to be expounded upon. I reluctantly perceived that we as a body of believers needed to come to grips with this truth; no matter how vexing it is to accept.

However, the disciplining of His children has a different purpose. His anger for sin has been appeased. He no longer needs to punish us for sins. He satisfied that need on the cross at Christ's expense. We are now members of the family of God. Children of our Heavenly Father. Citizens of Heaven. Therefore, He disciplines, but does not judge us. This is the consistent pattern throughout the Old Testament. And, is further developed in the New Testament. In the Old Testament, when He blessed His chosen people, included with those blessings, were warnings. His revealed expectations for ambassador living. They were to be holy people set apart to their God. The Priest of God to a world that did not know Him as the only real God. It was God's means of revealing himself to the world, which He did in various ways and through various means. As well discussed in the book of Hebrews. (I would like to suggest a book by Dwight J. Pentecost: *Faith that Endures*, for a more thorough study of this subject)

To His own, He made clear what He expected; and as they normally did, they walked in disobedience. He would send prophets to warn them. Most prophets were faithful to the call. Others, like the Kings, were generally a great disappointment. As usual, they walked according to the ways of the nations around them; who were often notoriously wicked. After repeated warnings, He brought significant discipline upon them, even sending them into bondage, by empowering Godless nations to extract the necessary discipline. Consider that as a nation who is turning our backs on God! I know we are not God's chosen people, but we were a God honoring nation, all the way back to the earliest stages of our history. An imperfect nation, but generally, a God fearing nation. Like David characterized in the Old Testament: a man after God's heart, but who engaged in some serious sinful behavior.

He also dealt with individuals: think of Moses. There is a major covenant called the Mosaic Covenant, which is named after him. Yet, when he lost his righteous composure, God did not allow him to enter the promised land. Moses was allowed to see, but not enter the promised land; even after being predominantly faithful in his leadership. Another major covenant is named after the covenant given to David: the Davidic covenant. This great man of God, David, fell into a sexual sin. He tried to cover up his actions, by setting up Bathsheba's husband to be killed; a man who was faithful in his service to the king. Nevertheless, despite his greatness in the chronicles of Biblical history, remember the consequences for David, after the adultery and the set up murder. God struck the infant son of David and Bathsheba to death. Then toward the end of David's life, pride got the best of him, when David counted the strength of his kingdom, against the advice of his advisor. In this particular case, God granted David the choice of chastisement. (2nd Samuel chapter 24 and 1st Chronicles chapter 21) Think of Samson and the violation of his Nazirite vows. His disobedience cost him to lose both his eyes and power. Think of Nebuchadnezzar in Daniel. It is not likely Nebuchadnezzar was a child of God, but he is a good example of both punishment and discipline. His prideful attitude angered the Lord. Then the Lord punished him. Humbling him to live and act like an animal, until he repented, and was later restored by God. He was also a tool God used to discipline His chosen people. Both are illustrations of God exacting a consequence for sin: for willful disobedience and pride. If God disciplined these individuals, don't think for a moment that we are beyond His firm hand of discipline. If God will discipline two of the greats in the Old Testament, what will He do to you and me, if we walk in willful disobedience?

This same theme continues with His saints in the New Testament. (In the New Testament all believers are positionally saints) Those who do not believe our Heavenly Father is a disciplining Father need to reread much of the New Testament. The sin unto death in 1st John, chapter 5, as an example. Apparently, there were individuals who stepped over the line of God's tolerance, and were judged with the ultimate temporal judgment: premature physical death. This sin unto death resulted as a consequence of sin, without the loss of salvation. Think about the sickness brought upon the Corinthians for carnal behavior in chapter 10. Where Paul uses examples from the Old Testament, of God's stern discipline, as warnings to these disobedience New Testament believers. Then he warns these believers to expect similar consequences should they continue in those sins. There also is an expression of His loving discipline, as detailed in the book of Hebrews, chapter 12. The confort, if there is some, is that what the Father does, is done because of His love. This with the purpose of correcting wayward children so they return to the path of righteous living. His Fatherly purpose of disciplining love is like any good father: the development of Godly characteristics. There are numerous other examples that could be given in both testaments. The point is, our Heavenly Father is a real dad, and dad's discipline. This discipline is the desired goal of all good dads: they want their children to manifest righteous living.

Other times, the actions of God are for the sanctifying of His children, as through fire. The bring of dross to the top; to remove what is interfering with the sanctification process. It is the process of purifying them for greater service. He sometimes needs to purify His children to be useful in certain services. This is not so much a discipline, but a purification of His saints. It may look and feel the same to the believer. Just as a coach pushes an athlete to develop greater use of skills, God will sometimes use trouble and hardships to mature His children for greater use. By allowing them to experience tribulations and hardships - to break the lures of this world. These actions may not be the results of a particular sin, but God being interested in preparing us for the greater good, and His glory. The Apostle Peter and the Apostle James, both talk about this in their books; they write that the enduring of suffering matures us. They used the greatest example: Christ Himself. While being God in flesh, yet, even He suffered, even though He was without sin. He is to be our supreme example.

From the beginning to the end of the Bible, the scriptures are clear: God will eventually punish sinners, in eternity, or in time and eternity. He must hold true to Himself. For the child of God: He disciplines. The difficulty is evaluating when we are being disciplined, being matured, or when it is just the results of living in a fallen world. This may not always be known. It takes wisdom and spiritual insight; even then it is not always clear. The first question I would ask myself is whether there is known sin in my life that needs to be confessed and forsaken. Have I started down a path that will bring untold trouble and regret into my life? This may be God's warning to stop before the inevitable happens. It is clear, nobody likes divine discipline, but it often keeps us from bigger sins. When what we are doing may bring our testimony into compromise, expect God to act! Or, if our actions may bring harm to the cause of Christ, God our Father likely will be dealing with us. And it will likely be something we could and should have avoided. God is a jealous Father. A rod to the backside is often well deserved, and has an intended purpose. He desires our development of practical righteousness; which is His divine purpose for all His children. Furthermore, He is serious that those who proclaim His message, model it with their behavior. God despises hypocrites. Read the Gospels on how Jesus interacted with the hypocritical Pharisees of His day.

There are at least eight causes of trouble in our lives as believers:

1. It could be divine discipline. The main topic of this chapter. There were countless ways God disciplines His children in the scriptures. Sometimes shocking harsh discipline. Think of Ananias and Sapphira in Acts, chapter 5. It was a small lie. Yet, it appears that the movement of the Holy Spirit was so powerful, that any entrance of selfish compromise would diminish the movement of God. This is also seen in 1 Peter, which states that judgment starts in the House of God. In another situation, the Apostle Paul turned someone over to Satan to teach him a lesson. This is seen in 1st Corinthians 5:5; when he turned

someone over to Satan for the destruction of the flesh, so his spirit may be saved on the Day of the Lord. God may use Satan and/or his minions, to extract the discipline He desires to have us endure. This is seen in the Old Testament too. In 1st Samuel, particularly chapter 16, where God removed His Spirit from King Saul, and sent an evil or distressing spirit upon him for disobedience. God may also choose some form of hardship: like physical pain, financial setbacks, a distressing spirit, or loss of some blessing, to name a few. Alternatively, if an area of our lives becomes unbalanced, the removal of cherished things from our life that we desire more than Him. There are many examples that could be included, as forms of divine discipline. We will all face some discipline in our lives. Not to experience divine discipline could mean you are not really His. Since the book of Hebrews indicates that being disciplined is a sign of sonship. Be sure, God knows the hidden sins in your life; it is called omnisciences. He knows everything, and Dad's discipline their children! This leads me to think about the late gifted apologist Ravi Zacharias. I don't have God's revelation on this, but I may have His mind on this. But I wonder: could Ravi's chronic pain and sudden death be the hand of discipline from our Heavenly Father? If it was? It is a shame, since he was one of the most gifted men I have ever listened to. God was using him greatly, but it appears his flesh got the best of him. If David and Moses were subject to harsh, but deserved discipline, don't fool yourself by playing with sin. God knows and it will cost you! Remember most of the Bible was written to Christians. I have seen a number of believers suffer serious consequences, and while I can't say it was always divine discipline, but.... It is consistent with what the Bible teaches.

Alternatively, we can avoid some discipline, when we repent. (meaning we reconsider or change our minds) If we take responsibility for our sins, come clean, and ask God to forgive, since God has promised He will. This does not always remove all consequences, but it does restore fellowship with God, and restores joy. And, it may avoid God's need to discipline. God our Father knows what discipline is best for us. This is part of the theme of the book of Hebrews.

2. It could be the maturing process that God desires us to endure; just like training an athlete for the sports contest, or a soldier for battle. God may be training us for the spiritual game of life. (See 2nd Timothy) Our Heavenly Father may be preparing us for some present, or yet unknown situation coming into our lives, but we are not prepared for the call that is coming. A yet unknown ministry that he is preparing us for, but one for which we need to learn to depend on the Holy Spirit for the power of God to be equipped. Or it could be the need to remove some fleshly stronghold that is holding us back. He might be preparing us, so we will be successful in the mission we are going to be called to undertake. Championship teams or athletes don't become such unless they are fully trained. They need to be masters of their own facilities. Spiritual training is often for the purpose of maturing us for the coming calling. Included in this, is the idea that pressure and tribulations are often designed to create tough and deeply mature believers. Some of the most deeply anchored believers are those who have endured tremendous oppositions in life. There is a desire for spiritual maturity that God our Father has for all of us -no matter how untasteful it is to experience.

3. Spiritual battle. The scriptures are clear that we have an adversary that desires to destroy us, and destroy our testimony. It may come in the form of a direct spiritual attack. An attack on our mind or body or family. Whatever he wants to try to ruin. Whatever he can use to stop us in our service for the Lord. Or, through temptation, that has the same outcome. It destroys our witness through the lure of sin. There are other options for Satan: he may tempt us with greed for money or power, the bitterness of the heart, or resentment. Anyway he can, he wants to destroy us. He cannot take our salvation, but he can mess up our personal lives, our family life, and diminish our testimony. I would note that we are more likely to endure these attacks if we are difference makers in life, particularly, evangelistically. Satan

knows once saved, always saved. That our eternal salvation is untouchable. But if he can ruin your testimony: he stops the effectiveness of your witness.

I believe this is the avenue that he uses on many Christian leaders: the temptation of sexual sin. It starts as a little indulgence to escape momentarily the challenges of life. Before you know it, he has you in the grips of despair, and has destroyed most everything you have stood for. The consequences will be far more than you ever expected. The hurt will be beyond what you ever expected. You will be bewildered at how it all unraveled. I know of many very effective and good Christian men that did not respond to God's warning. It appears they fell by the allure of Satan. This is likely after failing to respond to the warning discipline. We all know that sex is very enticing. (That is why the media uses sex to sell) Who has not enjoyed this wonderful gift of God. But it needs to be kept in God's boundaries: one man and one woman for life. Since Satan is looking for an open door for our destruction: don't open the door!!! Keep your thoughts pure, because that is where it starts, in our minds.

4. Our troubles may simply be our own foolishness. If I get drunk and drive my car into a tree breaking my leg, that is not God's doing, it is consequences for stupid! God is sovereign, but has free will figured into the plan. Sometimes my consequences are just the doings of my own foolishness. This is where the scriptures are so helpful, particularly those of Proverbs. Godly wisdom saves a lot of trouble, and maybe a broken leg!

5. Our struggles may be the results of God keeping our lives in check. I am thinking of Apostle Paul and his thorn in the flesh. He did not do anything sinful that necessitated divine discipline. His thorn was given to cause him to be more dependent on the presence of God for his strength. God had given Paul special divine revelations that may have caused him to exalt himself with that knowledge. The thorn was allowed to remain to keep him humble and grounded. God's grace was to be sufficient for his calling. Otherwise, Paul may have gloried in his natural ability, special revelations, and not God sustaining grace. This

is seen also in Abram's wife, when Abram told pharaoh she was his sister. God intervened to prevent the King from sinning with Sarah; which would have interfered with His purposes for Abraham and Sarah. (Genesis 20) God may intercede to prevent sin in our lives. I have often wondered if He has done that in my life; cause me trouble, to protect me from sinning against Him, as a protective action.

6. There are times when even good people touch God's glory. I am thinking of 1 Chronicles, chapter 13. The Israelites were moving the Ark of God and it became unsteady. Uzzah placed his hand on the Ark to steady it, and was instantly killed. Even David was angry with God, for what appeared to be overly harsh discipline. But there are times that God's glory is such, that any intrusion, results in immediate divine discipline. This is not normative, but does reflect how God feels about His glory. This is why pastors need to be sure that their ministries are focused on giving the glory to God, and not to seek their own exaltation. Like so many TV televangelists, who are too full of themselves.

7. The Federal Headship. This principle also applies in salvation history. In Adam we all inherited a sin nature. Those in Christ have been granted imputed righteousness. The headship often determines the representative results. (See Joshua chapters 7 and 22, and Judges 2:13-20) God may allow extracted consequences due to the moral choices of leaders, like in the Old Testament; when God's leaders committed sins against His revealed will, God often extracted punishment beyond just those who sinned, as in the case of David. (2nd Samuel, chapter 24) David's sin led to the death of thousands, even though they had no participating actions of their own that contributed to the consequences. The principle is also applied to the government. When a President or leader makes decisions for the people, like entering a war, it is the people who generally pay the consequences of the decision. Like in communist or Islamic countries, where persecution comes just for holding a particular set of beliefs, that are contrary to the dictates of the leadership. Think of Hitler and the results

of his venomous hate of the Jewish people. Consider that the next time you vote. Alternatively, this applies to countries, when they become too evil. Think of all the times God judged nations in the Old Testament. Or brought harsh discipline on His own people for their evil ways. It was necessary to remove the dross (sinful and Godless behavior) from the nation. If you think God will stay His hand of discipline forever, you will likely be shocked when He does act. Our country may be getting very close to provoking God to undertake harsh discipline! It may be close to the time that He separates us from our prosperity, so He can restore our righteous foundations. Harsh discipline does that!

8. The clear fact is we live in a fallen world. The world can be a very evil place to live in. We can be the innocent victim of a crime, or happenstance, even a random, but tragic event. I work in the criminal justice system. There are a lot of evil opportunists who are on the lookout for their next victim. Many Christians were born into a world that is not favorable to the Christian faith, and being faithful, they suffer for simply loving the Lord. This also blends into the category of spiritual warfare. The list could go on and on. It is not necessary to describe them all. It is common knowledge that this world is not too friendly to believers and nonbelievers alike - oftentimes for different reasons. But negative and very painful events come to some of the best of us. See my next chapter on suffering.

(My reflections) The alternative is also true. If we are compromising with sin, and life is going well, it may be that demonic forces have deceived you. You may have been seductively entrapped, and you are being lured into destruction. The fact that there are no presenting troubles, that normally come the way to all believers, is you have been caught in deception. Sinister forces have you ripe for the destruction of your Christian faith, the destruction of your family, and the ruining of your testimony. Satan's minions may even lessen our distresses so we continue down this path of ruin. Giving you a reprieve from the stresses of life through secret sins. This lurer gets stronger and stronger until you are ruined. Satan is very deviant, whatever works. He is glad to use the lure of sin for your spiritual demise. To draw you away from your God given walk of faith, and then ruin you.

I have this suspicion that this is the path that ruins many men of ministry. When one engages in ministry, they naturally engage in spiritual warfare. Particularly, if they are actively sharing the gospel or involved in pro-life causes. The warfare can be very intense. I wonder if the reprieve of the warfare is given to the men who finds some relief of stress by engaging in secret sexual sin. They escape, then they are destroyed by the escape. There are other areas that can be tempting too, like the greed for wealth or fame. Leaders may feel that they are not being properly compensated for their work, and undertake illicit, but regretful actions. This is why a firm understanding of the Bema Seat is needed. We will get paid; but it may not be until the Bema Seat. Be warned of these seductive lures of Satan. Sometimes, the difference between lust and adultery, may be as simple as opportunity and three drinks. Satan's agents may back off the warfare and entice with the lure of temptation. This leads down a path that is only a temporary reprieve of the stresses of life, but one that ultimately leads down a path of destruction. Deception to destruction is the goal of Satan.

This is one of my concerns in writing a book of this nature. I have to ask myself if I am ready for what may come my way via spiritual warfare. If what I am writing is true: I anticipate, this will bring about spiritual tribulations. If the gospel does change forever the destiny of one's soul, what greater target could there be, than the one who is sharing this good news. I don't think a book that lays out a clear understanding of the way to eternal salvation, and the principles of spiritual life, is going to be well received by the enemy of our souls. Think of the evil of the holocaust if you think Satan is pansy. I personally need to be sure I am walking closely with my Lord. The Devil is not my or your playmate, but a deceiver and murderer, who wants to destroy us, and our testimony.

Mini Bibliography

1. Kendall, R.T. *Once Saved, Always Saved.* Authentic Media, 2005
2. Swindall, Charles R. and Zuck, Roy B., *Understanding Christian Theology,* Thomas Nelson Publishing, 2003
3. Unger, Merrill F. *What Demons Can Do To Saints*, Moody Press, 1991
4. Numerous others as listed in the recommended reading section.

CHAPTER 24

LIVING WITH HEARTACHE AND CONFUSION

⬥⬥⬥⬥⬥

I t is evident that many aspects of the Christian faith are bewildering: suffering and pain for example. Unanswered prayer is another. The understanding that God can, but sometimes does not, is a bit mystifying to me as a believer. I have many issues of concern that I have soaked in prayer, and yet, I have not received my desired answers. I was up in the hospital when a great friend of mine lost his infant daughter. One of the most generous people I know. One of the most evangelistic too. Even now, more than 30 years later, the memory can still be a source of sorrow. My dear wife lost her best friend to Covid. We all prayed to no avail. One wonders where God is in those times. Sometimes, I am too open with my feelings, but maybe, I am saying what others will not, but are thinking privately. There is always a danger that one may get so angry they want to wave their fist in God's face. I have experienced that feeling too, it is not good. But sometimes we feel what we feel, I am just being candid.

Let's look at suffering. It is almost unfathomable the amount of suffering in this world. It can be contemplated on a broader perspective, or as an individual experience. It has been the felt experience by many that God must not really care. That He is indifferent to our suffering. That is a hard thought to maintain, since it does not line up with the nature of God. At least from what I know about His revealed nature: He is a good good God! Others believe God is unable to do much about the situation at the present time, it is just a part of living in a fallen world. If that were the case, it would mean God is not sovereign. The idea that God is not sovereign is not an acceptable answer either, nor a Biblical teaching. Just look up the word "sovereign" as it relates to God.

The aspect of fairness is also difficult to grasp. Why are some born in circumstances, be it favorable or dreadful, with no moral contribution of either good or evil on their part. I see the good die young and those in the criminal system that are perpetual and long-living predators. A continuous threat to our safety, and drag on society. It is surprising how many older men are engaging in deviant sexual behavior; figure that out for me if you can. There are a few books in the Bible that shed some light on the subject of suffering. If you are interested: read the books of Job and Ecclesiastes in the Old Testament, and Peter in the New Testament. But even there, a careful reading does not really give all the satisfying answers. It acknowledges the mystery of the surmised unfairness, but no real soul satisfying answers. At least from a human perspective. Some aspects of life are just a mystery to me. Let me give a few thoughts on the subject of suffering and pain. But to be clear, there are no real soul satisfying answers to the problem. There are logical and theological answers, but few satisfying emotional ones. At least ones that entirely answer the reasons why we often experience this apparently unfair evil and suffering. While I am not able to solve the issue -I am trying to put some of these thoughts into perspective.

The experience of pain can be the result of betrayal, or an unintended mishap. It can be a significant injury or birth defect. It can be parental anguish, after being diligent to raise their children in the faith, only to have them abandon the faith; since we know the likelihood that leaving the principles of the faith, often leads to more unseemly choices. It may come from an act of violence: being victimized. Regardless of its source, those who suffer, are suffering. Regardless of the source of pain, it is real, and very personal. And it is often unexplainable and unjustified in our minds. How do we make sense of this? How is this personally fair? How do we make sense of the apparent meaninglessness of what we are experiencing? Let's look at a few examples:

I like sports. I like the competition and strategy of the games, and teamwork. Individuals from various backgrounds united for a common cause. I understand at the end of the day all sports are essentially meaningless. A mild distraction from the world. At the end of the game, whether my team wins or loses, it simply does not change my life. I may even agonize a bit over my team losing. Believe me: I have been a Detroit Lions fan for years. (My editorial note: not so much anymore with most professional sports. I don't want agendas pushed in my face while I am trying to momentarily escape from the pressures of life. People are welcome to engage in any cause they feel is worthy, on their time, but not mine, since few agree on what is agenda worthy) Most others could care less what happens on the sports field, it is unimportant to them.

Just like many who have no interest in sports, people are often indifferent to my suffering and yours. Perhaps, because they are caught up in their own struggles; therefore, focused on their own presenting issues. Maybe that is why pain is so difficult. It is so private and very personal, since we often suffer privately in silence. It is often unknown to most, if not all, what many are privately enduring. It shocks us when we hear of someone's suicide. How badly they wanted to escape the emotional pain. Unknown to us the suffering they were experiencing. How unbearable the world had become to them. So they take the ultimate escape, not keeping the finality of the decision in mind, including the pain they leave behind, because of the decision.

It has been said that living with pain is easier than living with meaninglessness. But pain can be almost unbearable too, especially emotional pain. We live in our private world occupied by our own struggles, fears, and pain. Most people naturally want to avoid thinking too much about other peoples troubles, since too focus on others, leads to the awareness that similar suffering may come their way. It heightens their own fears. This is one of the reasons I don't watch too much news: they sell fear. And, they don't tell the full truth anyways. They avoid reporting news that is not favorable to their preferred moral or political perspective. But they do know that reporting bad news draws interest.

Oftentimes, it is helpful to gain some new perspectives on the theme of pain and suffering. Give me a chance to reflect, and see if some of my reasonings make sense. Consider football and the unintended consequences of playing a very brutal game. As is the case with football, it is played with no redeeming value, just for the thrill of winning. I too have suffered injuries playing football. I was recently watching a news special on Alex Smith: a QB who played in the NFL. A professional football player playing for Washington. It was gruesome to see an injury he suffered after being tackled. It took 17 surgeries and almost cost him his leg from infections. When I saw the multiple compound breaks of his leg, it made me cringe. It was disturbing to watch. Even though I did not even experience the pain, I knew it hurt tremendously. His leg was broken into shapes it was not designed to be. Anyone watching the injury take place knew it was excruciatingly painful; as it was to see his reaction to the injury. It was even more painful to experience for sure. I could surmise the pain he was experiencing. So how does this relate to the theological reflection on the subject of suffering? Let me explain:

Pain is universal to all mankind, but it does differ in degrees. God being omniscient knows the pain we are suffering. Just as everyone watching Smith get injured, we all knew he was in serious pain. God knows what we are going through. He cannot not know, it is part of who He is as God, you remember: omnisciences. Just like the Smith experienced, and all who watched, it was obviously excruciatingly painful.

God knows our pain too. What does give me some comfort is that He not only knows, He too experienced pain. Think about that for a moment. This is not a God who is distant from suffering. God entered humanity and experienced real rejection and pain. God, in the person of Jesus Christ, lost His legal dad as a teenager. He would never marry or live the expected life. He was actually born with the divine purpose to die a specific death. A purposeful death. Not just to die, but to experience the most excruciating death imaginable. The brutality of the crucifixion is beyond comprehension. But even before that, He was scourged, beaten half to death. Not only did He suffer, He did it willingly. A lot of people suffer. It is beyond their ability to resist. Christ did it by divine design. He fulfilled His mission as a fulfillment of prophecy. He had the ability to stop the cruel process of crucifixion at any point. But He was on a divinely designated mission. The salvation of those that would believe and accept the benefits of the cross. If you want to question the Love of God, look at the cross.

Even more difficult to understand is what he experienced when He was separated from God the Father while accepting the payment for our sins. For all eternity, until that point, He was in perfect harmony with God the Father. But not when it came to paying for our sins. God the Father needed this payment for sin so His righteousness would be satisfied. (Remember: propitiation) And, in the most difficult moments in His life, He was also abandoned by most of His family and closest friends. And God the Father allowed Him to suffer without rescuing Him from the experience. There was a divine plan that most did not understand. So before I raise my fist in protest, I might want to do a comparison of pain experiences. Has anything I have suffered come close to what took place on the cross. While at times we contribute to our own pain, Christ undertook a mission of redemption, that was voluntarily accepted because of His love. Add a thought to magnify the situation: I suffer as a sinner in a sinful world; He suffered as the creator of the world and was without sin. Perfectly God in flesh, and yet, was willing to suffer for us. Being simultaneously: fully God and fully man! Yet, loving us enough to suffer willingly to give us an opportunity to come to the Father. Because that is what it took to provide for our salvation: an act of sacrificial love.

Furthermore, remember, no matter what we are suffering, it is temporary. Think of suffering in light of eternity. The scriptures do give that insightful, and therefore, helpful perspective of suffering. The Apostle Paul references that in the book of Romans, Chapter 8, verse 18. Where He compares our present sufferings with the anticipated Glory coming our way. Elsewhere, we are told to consider our pain in light of eternity; with a mindset that considers those suffering as our example, like Christ Jesus. (The Apostle Peter's letters) That is why for believers, death is a blessing. To undergo endless suffering with no hope of it ever ending, would be maddening. So regardless of the degree of suffering, there is an ending. There are even blessings for us who will endure suffering for the cause of Christ. No doubt, there is pain in this world: unbelievable pain! If the pain is for this life only, then I can rest in the assurance that it will end, and have the confidence of my coming resurrection body. Because there is a day coming when every tear and every pain will be recompensed, and perfect justice will be melted out to those so deserving.

A few last thoughts on this subject. His justice will be distributed to those who have dispensed injustice to others. So we should leave room for God to care for those injustices. It will come, either here, or in the age to come. Never forgetting that we too were deserving of His justice, because His standard never dissipates. Always remembering that for those of us who have been redeemed: there is the sure promise of eternal hope. And hope in the Bible is the assurance it will happen.

Therefore, this is the undeniable reason to be absolutely sure that we have joined the forever family of God. So required justice, which has been satisfied in the person of Jesus Christ, does not become an offer rejected, and one comes under that ultimate eternal justice. Eternity is a long long time. No present pain can be compared to that pending justice that faces the unbeliever. The one who insists on standing on their own merits, before the perfect justice of a holy God, will find despair that will never end. I am not sure what will be the greatest consequence of being lost for eternity? The actual punishment for sin or the mindset that there will never be an ending to it; it is horrifying even to consider.

These thoughts may not lessen the pain we are experiencing, but they remind us that it is temporary. I am not sure how those who reject the revelation of God live in a world so full of hopelessness and suffering. It comforts me to know that my Savior too experienced pain. He knows what I am going through. So when I cry out to Him, He knows both as a real experience, and omnisciently, what I am going through. Therefore, no matter what suffering I am presently experiencing, it has an end, that ends in glory. When the end does come to us, our present troubles will show themselves to be imperceptible, in light of eternity. If God does not presently resolve our pain: He will reward us in heaven for enduring it.

It is very hard to understand suffering, without the insights of the

Bible; but our hope comes down to: God knows, He too experienced, and He will make right.

Without the hope of our salvation, we all would be without recourse in this evil world. Simply, a meaningless life, in a meaningless world, that leads to declining health, and ultimately, to death. Where sex and personal achievement may give some momentary pleasure and enjoyment, those pursuits lack the sustaining reason to live with all the suffering that this life brings. Where is that hope? It is not in the purposeless world of the evolutionalist. Who have no answer or hope for those suffering. It is the understanding that we live in a world that has God given purpose, that ends in a promised glory, even when I don't understand all the details.

CHAPTER 25

TYPES OF CHRISTIANS

This chapter came about after considering the response to my first addition. I started to reflect about how different individuals, who identified as Christians, responded to what I wrote. This led to pondering the personality types of identified Christians. Be sure this is not a scientific study, just some personal and brief reflections. To be honest, it was astonishing to me after my first addition, how little some long-time Christians grasped the logical implications of my litmus test. The disconnect between being true and the ramifications of being true. The disconnection between being true, and how little of a response it evoked. The gospel is an offer and a promise of immense magnitude. What did Jesus Christ die for? He died to save sinners from Hell: first and foremost. This led me to wonder what it is that most of Christianity think the Christian faith is all about? Why are so many who identify as Christians, so unwilling to take the exclusive claims of Christ to their logical conclusion? It does beg us to ask an important question: Why is there so little interest in sharing the faith, if the faith is dependably true, and the consequences are such? Let's explore the identities of Christians to why this may be:

There are the comfortable Christian, who are real Christians, but don't want to give up those comforts we enjoy here in America. They don't want to take their faith to its logical conclusions. Those responsive actions that should naturally come as a result of being a Christian. If Christianity is true, it is clearly an evangelistic faith. These may be the majority of whom we share the faith with, in the average American church. They are good people, but avoid the implications of Heaven or Hell. Yet, Jesus says both are eternal. (Matthew 25:46) They never take believing in the death and resurrections of Christ anywhere close to what one would expect from a genuine believer; one who understands the eternal implications. These often speak Christianese as part of the Christian culture, but often lack a grasp of the deeper things of the faith; the indispensable, the eternal destiny of each person.

The shallow Christian. They may further be described as superficial Christians. I know many who read this perspective of mine will find it offensive. But I believe my descriptive assessment is accurate. Their passive response to my contentions, just do not add up to the Biblical claims of the faith. My descriptive assessment of these believers is my most confusing to understand. It is like they are wallowing in a state between belief and unbelief. They may be in the beginning of becoming a progressive Christian, the deconstruction of their faith. They may have never really pondered what it is we really believe. In all these cases, their faith profession does not correspond with the reality of what is claimed by the faith. It is a questionable faith. They are lazy thinking Christians. It is likely they have never once read the whole Bible, they're either uninterested or want to avoid even thinking about the ramifications.

There are culture Christians: I was born in the USA so I am a Christian. Some declare they are Christians by being born into a Christian family. As previously noted, God does not have grandchildren. Each person must become a child of God by personal faith. There is no other option. These may or may not actually be born again believers. Their identity as a Christian is because they were born into a Christian country or family.

We have orthodox Christians, who are politically liberal. They adhere to classic Biblical theology, but don't apply the standards of the faith to their voting, social values or sexual morality. They will often vote for godless politicians and then are puzzled why we are developing into a godless country. They often vote for their pocket or career benefiting candidates. They separate their morals into religious convictions and personal benefits. They lack a coherent and consistent application of their Christian convictions. They confess orthodox beliefs, but practice an aberrant faith in voting and practice.

The naive Christian. The one who believes anything put forth by another alleged believer, without Biblical collaboration. These too, are likely to have never to have read the Bible, even once, although they have identified as a Christian for years and years. We live in a world where most Christians still are living on baby's milk and not meat. They believe what they have been told to believe.They are not students of the word. These Christians in my life are the ones I gave my book to, but never read. They are not Bereans -if you do not know who I am talking about, you are likely not a Berean.

It is a good way to raise your children, Christians. They see Christianity as a good means of installing values and morality. They may have come from a Christian family and want to pass on the heritage of the faith. They may or may not be born again. Either way, their faith is not an evangelical faith. They attend church primarily because they believe in the derived benefits: the moral development of their children and/or the moral stability of our nation. They recognized the beneficial lifestyle attributes that are inherent in the Christian faith. They are Christian values Christians. Those who believe that living their values is sharing their faith. That is not the gospel that brings eternal life. They may be born again, but limit the faith to the promotion of Christian values. The evangelistic aspect of the faith is limited, or absent. Generally, they are strongly grounded in the culture of Christian values, and want those values promoted, and rightly so.

Some identify as Christian, but who may not be. They come from a variety of quasi-Christian backgrounds. We know them as: Mormons, Jehovah Witnesses or 7th Day Adventist, even many Catholics. They have connections with the identity of the Christian faith, but who deny key requisite doctrines of the faith. Some of these may be born again, but have serious doctrinal deviations; those that differ from the revealed Biblical faith. Others are wrongly practicing what is perceived as an authentic version of the faith, which is not Biblical, nor is it salvific;

since, there are fundamental truths that need to be understood and believed to be born again. Take a look at all the requirements Catholics must endure, hoping to merit heaven. And very concerning is how close some Protestant Christains are starting to require the same. A merit required hope, instead of the assured hope because of the finished work of Christ. The grace of God hope. By joining hands with those who have accepted these deviations from the Biblical faith, they are denying Christ alone, by faith alone, for the free gift of eternal salvation. A free salvation already paid for by Jesus Christ; which they devalue because they add personal merit or religious ritual.

The non-evangelizing, evangelical identified Christian. We have Christians who refer to themselves as evangelicals, but who have never personally evangelized anyone. They stop at the creed of the faith. Many have never even attempted. They attend a church that claims to be evangelical, but only because the pastor occasionally gives a salvation message. They are born-again believers who never get around to being evangelistic themselves. These are non-evangelizing Christians, who think they are evangelistic. They do not engage personally; at least to the point of actually evangelizing. This group are those I had hoped would read my book, because I think it may cause them to reconsider their lack of action, and step out in faith.

The universalist Christian. This perspective is confusing. It is an identification as Christian, but denies most of the essential elements of Christianity. The requisite acceptance of the core doctrines of the faith, and the personal faith necessary for the salvation of one's soul. I know many in this camp. They are good people. They profess to love Jesus. But fail to connect the dots. They are compassionate Christians, who are motivated to fix societal ills. They offer the loving and compassionate care that many need, but miss the absolute necessity of the cross. They often hold to the belief that most everyone will eventually make it to heaven. Their identity is with the compassion expression of the faith, but not the necessity of the salvific aspects of the faith. It is the promotion of the love of God, but lacks the understanding that the holiness of God must be satisfied first.

The compromised Christian. These are often very vocal about their faith, but often their faith does not translate to their morality or behavior. They love Jesus but don't adhere to some of the standards of Christian sexual behavior. For example, they attend church, are expressive in their faith, but live with their boyfriend or girlfriend. They may be born again, but not living consistent born again lives. This may be true for a lot of believers, to various degrees. We live in a world saturated with sexual images, with enormous amounts of easily available porn. We are inundated with sexual images. They are often greatly influenced by the new standards of sexuality being embraced by culture, so being a pure minded believer is very difficult for these Christians. They need to read the letter by James about being double-minded.

There are non-Christians who falsely believe they are a Christian. I know of a person who claims to be a Christian, but denies both the deity of Christ and the authority of the word of God. That is not the definition of a real Christian. They identify as Christian, but never come to accept the absolute necessity of Jesus Christ as God in flesh, who is the only source of salvation. (John 14:6) Jesus says if you do not believe *I Am,* you will die in your sins.

The struggling Christian who does not look like a Christian. Some Christians fully understand the nature of a sin, because they struggle mightily with the nature of sin. They are personally aware of its destructive nature, because the struggle has been so damaging to their personal lives. They may fall repeatedly into the sin nature, even though they are born again. They struggle mightily against it, but are often overtaken. They often can be vocal in speaking against a particular sin, because they know its power to diminish lives. Those who witness their behavior, will see them as hypocrites, or even deny them being a Christian. But that may not be the case. They are struggling with their sin nature, but it still has a controlling grip on them; they have not found victory, yet. There are numerous areas that come to mind: it could be alcohol, drugs, pornography or unbiblical sex. They know its destructive qualities, so they warn others, and take a vocal stand, even if they are personally wrestling with its destructive consequences.

There are progressive Christians, where the love of God is celebrated, but the moral expectations of the faith are subject to each person's preference. This is a byproduct of denying the full authority of scriptures. It is a recreation of the faith, where their perspective is given greater weight than the scriptures. They may have started as Christians, but left the full authority of Biblical teachings, because they now want to engage in actions that are outside the moral standards of the faith. They may have started to compromise with sin, and find in the progressive view of Christianity, the freedom they want. This new view of Christianity minimizes guilt. This is often driven by a desire for sex outside the Biblical mandate. Others may have never really come to accept what it means to be a Christian, in the classic sense. They were never born again. They embrace the love of everyone as they are aspects, but minimize the God is righteous aspect. Is that not what we are seeing in the American pride friendly churches? They promote taking pride in being a Pride church. Others are non-Christians, who identify culturally as Christians. They feel liberated as they celebrate their unbiblical, but liberating faith. It is driven by being pridefully accepting of this sexuality; even if it denies the historic teachings inherent in Biblical Christianity. Their fleshly preferences have taken priority over the classical teachings of the faith.

There are the very enthusiastic Christians who are driven by emotion, but they lack a thorough understanding of the doctrines of the faith. They are very zealous Christians, who seek the emotional experience of the faith. The clear doctrinal aspects are preferred to be ignored. They see this as too divisive. They promote the desired spiritual experiences, and focus on the less significant aspects of being a Christian. They want unity to the degree that they are willing to compromise truth, for the unity of fellowship. These too talk the Christian lingo, but are poorly equipped to explain clearly what and why they believe.

The angry and resentful Christian, but still a born again. They were born again, but now no longer want to be identified with the faith. They are born again, but due to tribulations, the feeling of unanswered prayer, or disappointment with God, has led them to abandon the practice of the faith. They have walked away disillusioned. They need lots of love; strong Christians who will come alongside them, and mentor them through the anguish, the pain, and back into the walk of faith.

Some identified as Christians who see their faith in God as a spiritual guide; Jesus is seen more of a guru and less seen as Savior. They go to church to find meaning in light of the existential struggles of life. They feel a lack of purposefulness and are looking for meaning in their lives. These types avoid the absolute necessary salvific aspects of Christ. In some circles, they have so digressed from the Biblical truth, and reduced Christianity to believing that God's role is to help them find meaning. Or, they are looking for a God, whose primary mission is to give a problem free and blessed life. Yes, Christianity will give one proper foundational perspective, and often a blessed life, but that is not the ultimate reason Christ died. It is like a back rub for a terminal cancer patient; it may make them feel better, but it ultimately does not change anything.

Go with the flow Christian. They are wonderful and very congenial believers. They prefer not to make waves. They submit their conviction for harmony, to avoid conflict. They seldom take a stand on moral or divisive spiritual issues. They seldom share the salvific aspect of the faith; since they do not want to offend. These are good decent people, but they desire harmony to the degree that they abandon truth for peace.

The disinterested Christian. They proclaim to be Christian, but have little to no interest in the implications of John 14:6, or deeper Christ like development. They possess little interest in pursuing essential aspects of what we profess. The substitutional death of Christ, and those implications, are of little interest.

I am a good person and believe in God, so I am going to heaven: Christian. These may not have ever come to saving faith. They do not hold to faith in Christ alone as the exclusive source of salvation. They believe they are Christians because they have general faith and perceive themselves as good. They are the religious lost of the Christian community.

There are Patriot Christians. These are similar to culture Christians. These share many of the moral values of evangelical Christians, but the focus is on being free as a patriot. They are often seen as focusing on being a freedom loving American Christian. The gun, guts and God made our country great, Christian. A constitutional believer. Some see the faith as a ritual of being an American, but their faith is often very shallow or undefined. Unfortunately, many are very good citizens, but not born again. We as a country need these for a healthy foundation for our country, without denying the necessary salvation requirements of the faith.

The double-minded Christian. This believer may be very devoted to the faith: even evangelistic minded. However, their lives are compromised by the things of this world. They have dual passions that compromise the fruitfulness of their walk. (A warning of James in chapter one) They are strong in their convictions in the faith; and often still controlled by the flesh.

Unsure if I am a Christian. They are Christians, but wrestle with recurring doubts if they really are saved. They may have trusted in Christ alone, but continue to doubt the promises of God. They believe, but are weak in assurance. They are on the plane, but very unsure of the trustworthiness of the plane. But the scriptures claim we can know. (1st. John chapter 5) God is a God of promise. He promises if one believes in the substitutional death of Christ for the forgiveness of their sins: they are saved! A subcategory of this group doubts their salvation and rightly so, since they never exercised saving faith. In both of these groups, they need someone mature in the faith, to walk them through the elements of the faith, to understand their spiritual status. And good sound apologetics.

A Christian, who denies the expectations of being a Christian, Christian. They know it is true, but want to ignore the implications of the faith; the exclusivity of Jesus alone claims in John 14:6. They don't want to abandon the faith, they just cannot emotionally accept all aspects of the faith. They are stuck in the new babes in Christ stage, and never grow, and don't desire to. They are unwilling to grow in their sanctification. They know the call, and what it means to be a Christian, but don't want to accept the logical ramification of what Christ did on the cross. It is a refusal to progress in the faith, because they do like some teachings of the faith; even though they believe them to be true.

There are Christians that now identify as non-Christians. They often were raised in the faith. They once accepted the offer of forgiveness and the gift of eternal life. They later got off track, and deconstructed from the faith. The reasons for this abandonment from the faith are vast and complex. If they were truly born again, then they are in an apostate state, but still born again. They are disillusioned believers. Or, the alternative is: they only once identified as a Christian, but were never born again. They never experienced the new birth required. There never was spiritual life present in their lives. These are not real apostates: these are the never-beens. It was an identity only, but they never experienced the new birth.

Then there are Evangelistic Christians. They get the essence of the faith. They grasp what I am writing about in this book; that is, Christianity is an evangelistic faith at its very core. They know what they believe and they want to be different makers. They understand the reality of the faith. They know that Hell is real, and are diligent to make sure others know the way of salvation. They know there is only one way and it is an exclusive way. They are devoted enough to have read my book. They read it because it affirms what they believe to be true. And they found some additional illuminations of the faith by what I wrote. They want their lives to make a difference, so this book was helpful. It encourages them to continue on because they get it! They want the affirmation from Christ.

These very unscientific observations show that Christians differ greatly in their mindset. It has long puzzled me why such clear statements of our faith: Jesus is God in the flesh and came to pay our sin debt, is not compelling a greater response to these truths. This is due to numerous reasons. This deviation is seen in a status of religion study by Ligonier Ministries and LifeWay, for the 2022 year. Their study reports that 42% of proclaimed evangelicals do not believe Jesus was God in flesh. Further results of their polling showed: 56% of evangelicals believe God accepts worship from non-Christian faiths. Not only are these identified Christians, they further identify as evangelicals. This is shocking! How can this be? To be identified as an evangelical, means there is a reason for evangelizing. That study is deeply disturbing, and undermines the whole of what Jesus said in John 14:6. He self-claims: He is "the" truth and He is the "only way" to the Father. The data polling and this claim by Jesus simply can not be reconciled. It appears these self-identified as evangelical Christians are really culture Christians, or they are denying the reality of the faith. These compromised beliefs are inconsistent with what many identify as. It does cause one to wonder who we are as professed Christians. One thing for sure, it does show why there is so little impact by Christians: both evangelistically and morally. If any religious belief can be accepted by God: then evangelism is not needed. If they were correct, it does create an unnecessary urgency for the believers. However, if the statement by Jesus is the truth regarding the only means for eternal salvation, then it is of the utmost importance. We need to come to a decision: either our faith is fundamentally true, or let's move on with our lives! Those claims by Christ are of the utmost seriousness, or they mean little at all. If we are talking about a real Heaven or real Hell, then this magnifies the question. It cannot be ignored. The consequences are too paramount to ignore.

Here are a few that I did not put in the list but should be briefly commented on:

I did not include the atheist. I personally don't believe someone can be a real atheist. To be a fully honest atheist is impossible. To justify being an atheist would require total knowledge, and only God possesses that. So the only honest alternative is being an agnostic. But there are serious problems with being a comfortable agnostic: that is, the question is never answered. And to me, that is a willful avoidance of the most important question ever asked: where will I spend eternity? Therefore, the pursuit for the answer is the only reasonable quest; one that must absolutely be answered, because of the implications of the question. Not being diligent in resolving the question, is to me, an escape from reality of life: you will die one day, then what? It is usually not a question of evidence. It is the desire to be free from the moral implications of being a Christian. It is the uncertainty of the truth: the exact definition of being an agnostic. Since the evidence is unquestionably strong, and the question of one's eternity still remains, it is absolutely the one question that must be answered. .

Many of these aforementioned categories could be blended together since they are very similar. These are loosely defined and offered just to promote some thought.

This was the biggest surprise for me upon the completion of the first printing of my book; it was the unwillingness of most to wrestle with the significance of what I wrote. They likely have a comfort level with their faith and have little interest in taking what they profess to believe to its logical conclusion. They do not want to consider the full implications, because the full reality of being true is too hard to accept: Heaven or Hell. It is not that they necessarily disagree with what I wrote, they just don't want to entertain the full reality of it. To tell you the truth, it is a bit mystifying. It just does not add up: the truth that we profess to believe and the disconnect with the reality of it being true. Too many Christians are really pragmatically: Christian agnostics.

CHAPTER 26

SPIRITUAL TRUTHS IN 8 MINI CHAPTERS

Here are some topics that do not justify a full chapter, but can be abbreviated to arrive at their central point. So this single chapter is a composite of a number of mini chapters.

Mini #1 Many have noted that my original book leaned a bit heavy on sexual issues. As I explained to one who raised this observation: this is because our world has gone sexually crazy. This is why the Bible warns of the lust of the flesh, lust of the eyes and pride of life. The issues of lust and the lack of sexual morality is breaking down our families, and destroying the lives of the once innocent. What once would have been considered unthinkable, is now the norm. History repeatedly shows this deviation away from Biblical sexual morality is a key factor in the downfall of many societies. This is exactly what we are seeing: the unraveling. When we walk according to our fleshly nature, we diminish the value of everything God calls sacred. This is addressed in Galatians 5: where the instructions are to walk in the spirit so we don't walk in the flesh, because when we do, we reap the consequences of the flesh. For example, a free life of sexual experience before marriage, de-sanctifies the later marriage. Since sex has lost its unique value, it is easier to abandon this standard after marriage too. This is one of the principle reasons why I have emphasized the immutable holiness of God. Sexual standards are established as a command, not to limit our sexuality, but to sanctify it; to give unique meaning to the union between a man and his wife. An experience that should only be shared between two people for the duration of their lives. As the scriptures noted: God created, in the beginning, male and female. God has not changed His perspective on sexuality. The sexual union is different from all other relationships. It is almost spiritual between man and his wife. That is why it is to be sacred, and needs to be protected. When casual, it loses its uniquely divine designed value. There should be a natural progression of a marriage. It starts with alot of sexual passion, but later matures into a deep abiding love. Sometimes we inordinately pursue youthful passion, and miss the deeper aspects of the union between the man and his wife. This is not to say that we do not continue to embrace this aspect of our marriages, but we expand on it.

Mini 2. Only when you love deeply can you be deeply hurt. This is the experience of many parents who have raised their children in the faith; only to watch them walk away from the faith. To watch them break God's standards can be heartbreaking. It is because we know the stabilizing benefits of living according to those principles.. This is very difficult for those of us who know the reasons for these principles. When parents started the parenting process, they held out hope for a lifestyle that is often not being manifested by their children. Parental heartbreak results from seeing the consequences of poor decisions. The devaluing of their lives. The latter regrets. The children we once would have died to protect, are now breaking their parents hearts. Even a greater concern than this, is the eternal consequences of those who have rejected the gospel. For those who can take comfort in the fact their children were saved, there are still the consequences as discussed in chapters 22 and 23, and will be discussed in chapter 28. Even beyond those consequences, it is the loss of the aspirations we had for our children. As stated, our greatest love and headache are both powerful parental emotions that come because of our deep love for them.

Mini 3. Oftentimes it is puzzling why parts of scriptures are so hard to understand. If God wants us to understand these truths, why do the scriptures appear so confusing at times. If they are written under the inspiration of the Holy Spirit, why not make it easier to grasp the crucial truths He wants us to know? Let me offer a few reasons why this may be so. In my limited manner of understanding, there are a variety of reasons why this may be. The first is: God wants believers to dig deep into the word of God, and when we do, He rewards us. He wants serious students. He wants disciples who want to be serious disciples. The word generally becomes clearer as we grow in faith, and maturity. Secondly, we may have a bias, or there insights not revealed, because we are not in tune with the Holy Spirit. We may be blinded because we are not walking accordingly. If you are frustrated in your pursuit to understand the scriptures, it may be that you are out of fellowship with God. He reveals those deeper truths to those who are friends: not every believer is a friend with God. It is actually possible to be born again and not a friend with God the Father. If you want to be a friend of God, and not just a child, be an obedient believer. (1st John) Then God will open your eyes to see greater truth. (John 12) This was the case with Abraham who was saved, then became a friend who could be trusted. Thirdly, we may be culturally blinded to the Jewish nature of a text, or we are missing some details in the text, that make what is difficult to understand, understandable. Fourly, oftentimes, we gain spiritual insights, as we experience life, then the principles come alive. This is particularly true of Biblical types and prophecies. Later upon fulfillment: the understanding comes upon fulfillment. For example, as seen in John's Gospel, chapter 2:18-22, and this reinforces our belief in the scriptures. Again, this is not an exhaustive study, but a mini commentary. God reveals more to His friends than He does to those out of fellowship, or the never were.

Mini 4. A Lot of seasoned Christians have a sanctified imagination. They are deeply connected with the Spirit. They can see how and where God is working. And there are a lot of spiritually immature Christians who have imaginations that they try to self-sanctify to give credibility to their views. These are not anchored in sound theology. Their imaginations give them their theology, and the Biblical text is secondary to their beliefs. They lack Biblical wisdom because they are not grounded and have deviated from the humble mission given. They are glorifying themselves and not God. Their ego has taken them off the road of sound Biblical doctrine. Not everything a Christian says can be held with confidence as being Biblical. They may simply be self-serving and self-deceiving believers. Like some prosperity preachers; who seem to be serving their interest and not God's.

Mini 5. Sex for a married couple is like a meal: for the man, sex is like dinner, a needed nourishment. He will not die if misses it, but the desire can lead to resentment if withheld too often. For a woman, sex is more like a desert after a good dinner. A nice add on, but not as necessary. This in my opinion is why a woman needs to understand this need in her husband's life. The man needs to know that loving nourishment is needed before desert. So men need to nurture their wives, and love them, so their wives see sex not as a responsibility, but a loving expression of their marriage. For the wife, she needs to understand that sex is part of the identity for a man. It can be a pure need. In either case, when it is withheld or denied, it becomes an avenue for Satan to enter a marriage. This lack of satisfaction on either part can lead to resentment and contention. So the clear teaching from 1st Corinthians, chapter 7, is not to withhold. Because when it is, it becomes an avenue for Satan. (See verse 5 of the same chapter) God understands our needs, He created us. If Satan can get a foothold, tragic consequences can happen. All sex needs are to be satisfied at home, before temptation overcomes the believer. Because any sex outside that divinely commanded union is strictly forbidden; this is a divine command. This is because sexual divergence outside the marriage never leads to lasting satisfaction: it only temporarily satisfies lust. But once you open that door, there is no end to the next temptation, and then the next. Once the door is open it is hard to close. The end of the pursuit always results in regret, the unraveling of the family and a diminished character. It leads to guilt, loss of personal integrity, the loss of one's testimony, and exhibits selfishness. If staying married is a commitment of a lifetime, then that is your only option. You do whatever it takes to make it work. It is a total investment. Furthermore, once you open that door to sex outside of your marriage, the act diminishes the investment in your marriage. If you open that door, which usually starts in the mind, the heart wanes at home. When it wanes at home, it leads down a path to trouble. That is why the scriptures warn about withholding sex: it is a sacred union established by God. Again, this emphasis on sex is due to the saturation of it in our society. It is destructive to our personal lives, nullifies our Christian testimony, and can devalue us as image bearers of God.

Mini 6. This mini is just spiritual wondering. Do you ever wonder why Satan does not give up? Why does he not give up this hope of de-placing God? He can't win. I have often wondered why Satan keeps adding to his own judgment in the Lake of Fire. He may be banking on God's loving grace; believing if he can get enough people to turn against God, God may relent and alter His plan. Satan may surmise that God loves so much, that if He was willing to die for us to save us from Hell, He may now relent and alter His redemptive plan. But that is wishful thinking. God's immutable nature does not allow that option. There is no other option for the redemption of mankind or the angelic world. But this may be Satan's only hope, since his doom is already declared. It is his only desperate option. Even though he is only adding to his eternal torment. I may be totally wrong on these thoughts, but just wondering.

Mini 7. Our Christian faith is a moral standard, a code of conduct. It is a worldview. It is how we measure our lives. It defines our standards of morality. We try to be good Christians, but we too often fall short. Even more difficult is when we walk away from the faith and then return to the faith. (Discussed in chapter 28) This awareness of moral failure can lead to a tremendous sense of guilt and remorse. When we reassess our previous moral behavior, with the new standards expected of being a Christian, we can become very remorseful. When we become a Christian, or return to the faith, it is natural to reassess those previous choices, with the wholesome standards of the Christian faith; this can lead to a sense of remorse, shame and guilt. The Bible reveals that our lives did not always measure up. This is needed information to know our status, which reveals a need for a Savior. But this knowledge can have an unintended consequence too: an unhealthy sense of remorse and regret. A few healing thoughts: One, we should expect our lives to not measure up, that is why we needed a Savior. We are sinners by birth and deed. We needed a new birth, the washing of regeneration. We need to be clothed in the very righteousness of Christ. We needed a new identity: that is what we have in Christ. Secondly, we need to live with an awareness of that forgiveness and newness of life. We need to move on in the grace and love of our Savior. We need to rejoice in our forgiveness and not wallow in regret. So while our faith is our *standard*, it is also our new *standing* of life. We need to have the mindset of Paul: who claimed he was the worst of sinners, and yet, he became the great preacher of hope, grace and forgiveness. The proclaimer of grace, our standing as new creations. So the key is not to focus on who we *were,* but who we have *become,* and who we *are* in Him. Then act according to God's perspective: declared righteous children of our Heavenly Father, clothed in the righteousness of Christ.

Mini 8. Christians and worry. Worry is an issue that is frequently discussed in the Bible, by Jesus and many others. Jesus simply says: do not worry. (as discussed in Matthew 6:25-34) A pretty simple command. Yet, so many believers are consumed with worry. We all will have periods of worry. For some, it is manifested as mild intrusion. For others, they are so burdened by these periods of worry, it can be debilitating. Worry so consumes their life, that all joy and peace are gone. They are prisoners to their fears. Some worry more than others because they are more aware of the realities of life. They clearly know how easily circumstances can devastate a life; so they are more mindful of potential heartache. The causes of worry are varied. For some, it can be a real physical issue, maybe caused by chemical imbalances. For others, it can be our spiritual thinking, or their emotional makeup. Oftentimes, some have faulty theology, and therefore, it is simply a failure to apply the principles of truth. As Jesus said, it is the truth that sets one free. (John 8:31-32)

Here are some brief thoughts about worry for a Christian to consider. First, this life is temporary. The concerns of this world should not consume us. This is not our home. We enter this world like a ray, we have a starting point, but continue on into eternity. If this life was our only life, fear would be understandable. If we were potentially losing all we would ever have, or ever will have, then this fear is justified. But as Paul says to Christians, in 2nd Corinthians 4:17-18, "For our light and momentary troubles are achieving for us an eternal glory that far outweighs them all. So we fix our eyes not on what is seen, but in what is unseen. For what is seen is temporary, but what is unseen is eternal." NIV So we need to ask ourselves: do we have an eternal perspective? Are we holding on to the belief that Heaven is beyond description? Secondly, we do not follow the instructions of Paul. He says do not be anxious about anything, but in every situation, by prayer. He continues with the instruction to present your request to God, then the peace of God comes. Are we really praying? I mean really praying. God may be using these issues to draw us closer to Him, or to strip away our worldly attachments. Thirdly, are we trusting in the sovereignty of God? Do we really have faith that God is in ultimate control? If we don't, then this is a faith issue. We are simply not trusting God as instructed, or have a distorted understanding of God. (a major theme in this book) Fourthly, are we worrying about things that never happen? If we are, then we are stealing from today, the joy God wants us to experience, for a fear of the never. This worry only adds to our distress. It never resolves it. Fifthly, are we taking every thought captive to the Lord. This is an instruction of the scriptures. Take those thoughts captive so they do not steal our peace. Don't meditate on them. Sixthly, this is a chance to model to the world the difference between those who have the hope of the resurrection, and assured eternal life, with those who are worldly; those who have no hope beyond this world. It shows our faith, and hope, as the difference. We should always be living in light of the hope we have in Christ. Seventhly, there are struggles and hardships we must live with, as did the Apostle Paul. He prayed three times and there was no deliverance. God had a purpose for Paul to share this suffering, this thorn of the flesh. So we know even the greats of the faith struggled with the why. Eightly, when we do endure, we are rewarded. God will make all distresses right in eternity. We Christians are not exempt from tragedies. It is how we respond that should be different. Do we have the mindset that we are living in God's purposeful world, or like the atheist, in a purposeless world. Are we thinking like a Christian atheist? Lastly, if there is one real issue to be worried about, it would be the salvation of loved ones; actually, the salvation of everyone. This should be our only real concern. This is the one concern that is real, everything else is temporary. This needs to be an area for all Christians, intense prayer. Prayer for God to soften the heart and open the ears to the message of salvation. So by sharing the hope we have in the resurrection, they are receptive and accept the hope we can have. This is truly the only issue that has no remedy after the grave. All other concerns have an eternal solution: not this one.

Obviously, this short mini could be a whole book, as they have been by more qualified authors. This is only intended to be a quick reflection, suggesting that we Christians are often too anxious, which should not be the case, since we have the sure hope of the only thing that will truly last: a glorification that will be beyond anything we could have ever imagined.

CHAPTER 27

REFLECTION ON CULTURE

I do not want to get too political, but a few reflections on our culture are necessary due to our rapid moral decline. I have spent considerable time thinking about the culture divide. We are not in a good place. There is little trust in our government, with politics being treated like sports, whatever can be done to win. We lost the foundation for truth. But the truth is the truth, even if denied. The media compounds the problem with their neglect of what is true, or a simple distortion of truth. It is hard to believe much of anything they broadcast. There is a common theme on TV that degenerates the image and role of a husband. This is not good. We need to promote the necessity of a faithful man in the home. They are unwisely transforming our county. If someone objects to what they believe may not be helpful to our society, they are shamed for not endorsing what the Bible clearly defines as sin. Simply to suggest that people are pragmatically better when basic Biblical principles are endorsed, often brings name calling, some ….ism is the characterization. This allegation without even considering if there is some real merit to the perspective. A real conversation on what is noble and good for our country is hard to achieve. The government has dug a very very deep ditch of debt. No one appears to understand the consequences to future generations; the inability to actually pay back the debt. Few in Washington appear to be willing to make those hard decisions. They keep passing the compounding debt onto the next generation. Our young people will be stuck with our greed and our waste. Then again, they are often the ones who have been told that they should expect everything for free. The only real free gift is our salvation, and even that was paid for: Thank You Jesus.

But think with me for a few moments. I am not saying all was well sixty years ago; The *I Love Lucy, Leave it to Beaver* and *Andy Griffith* shows period. The old black and white TV programs many of us grew up watching. You might remember in the *I Love Lucy show*, it was inappropriate to even mention that Lucy was pregnant. Compare that with the declining moral drift that we are now seeing. It is alarming. What would once have shocked people years ago is now normalized. This is why God's ordained model of society is so helpful. There are three primary units: the family, the church, and the government to restrain evil. Each of these complement and support the other. Have strong families and Bible teaching churches and you usually have a healthier society. But with the growing demise of the family, and the compromising church, you get an overbearing government. A government that now promotes evil and threatens those who call sin: Sin. We have gone from the original intent of government, that government was ours, to the idea held by those in government, that we are the government's. This is a compounding of the problem: When the government becomes promoters of unrighteousness, instead of righteousness.

Visualize this scene: A man is waiting at the altar for his bride to be. Both have kept themselves for this day. They marry with the full intent to stay so until death. The investment is the family, not the selfish illusions of personal pleasures. Respect is the norm, and is expected. Kindness permeates throughout society. Dad employment provides enough income to allow mom to stay home and attend to the responsibilities of the home and children. Almost everyone attended church on Sunday. It was a true day of rest. Very few businesses were open, only the essential. There was a general wholesomeness to daily living. Men would never swear in front of a lady. A lady was just that: a lady. Hard work was expected and ingrained in our children. The kids played ball down at the local park, or in our backyards, and were safe playing there. You get the picture. A very simple, more wholesome life. We should be shocked by what we are seeing, instead we accept it as the new normal. (This illustrative portrayal is not to indicate a standard for women: my wife, sisters and daughters all have successful professional careers. The point is simply the contrast in our changing culture)

What we now call freedom is really sexual bondage. The decline accelerated in the 60's with the removal of Bible reading and prayer in public schools. This resulted in the loss of truth and our personal awareness of our dependent relationship on God. In its place the government took the role of the dad. Women could have children without regard to many of the consequences, with the assurance that society would care for the needs. Our responses were noble in caring for the children, but that came with unintended societal declining consequences. This led to the freedom to act irresponsible and without personal responsibility. Government has failed to understand the full impact of abandoning these foundational values. Godly dads are desperately needed. Every fair study shows that the absence of a dad in the home usually leads to devastating consequences to the next generation. Which is then compounded to the next, and on and on it goes.

This also leads to the declining mental health status of our socie That issue alone is very troubling. The problems inherent in the de of morality continue to manifest. The divorce rate both in and the church reflects the lack of commitment to the promise m the altar. This breakdown of society has led to full jails, pris treatment programs. There is way too much violence in th Drug and alcohol abuse are destroying our young people before. There are neighborhoods in some cities where it is travel. People killing each other for drugs or territorial imp You think we could use a little old fashioned return t morality. To Biblical standards that many call outdate need to rethink our foundational standards. Some Bi prayer back in schools would not hurt. Seriously! society gained with the removal of those practices?

wholesomeness would be more than welcome; I think we would find true freedom, and sleep better at night!

In regards to jail ministry and working in the criminal justice system, I take some pride in the fact that when I had the authority, I exercised respectful restraint. Hopefully mixed with compassion. I am a politically and religiously conservative person who did jail ministry. I am sure some of my colleagues saw my ministry as fraternizing with the enemy. But a little research into the lives of many who are serving time is enlightening. They generally lack a good moral education. Many have learning limitations and/or they lack the support of a stable home. A large percent have mental health issues. In my opinion, the biggest issue is the lack of well-grounded Godly fathers in the home. This too is an indicator of the digression of our morals. These thoughts have compelled me to try to make a difference. I know I am not to the degree that I should be; maybe my emphasis in this book will motivate me more too.

There is also the devaluing factor of what is being taught in our schools and universities. The perceived value of life is diminished when evolution is unchallenged and the only theory taught. You can't teach someone that their ancestor is a monkey and then claim they are worthy of dignity. The foundation for seeing ourselves as having intrinsic worth, is that we were created in the image of God. We have in many of our public schools that have abandoned the virtuous character building that historically built our stable society. There are still many good schools, and a growing moment of Christian schools and a homeschool movement, that give us hope. We can also see this digression away from our righteous foundations, when we remember that the majority of universities, in the early stages of our country, were founded as distinctly Christian. They were established as highly principled and Biblically grounded, exulting the greatness of God. Those principles are now largely lost to Godless imposed viewpoints being propagated by those in control of our educational system; and generally, the views of concerned Christians, and those more conservative views are stifled. They are not even allowed to be expressed in an open dialogue.

But this decline in our society also angers me. We are all paying the price for our progressively declining moral values. One starts to wonder when will people ever learn? How long does society put up with such nonsense? How long will God put up with this nonsense? Unfortunately, prison and jail do not seem to help much. It does provide some protection, but little change. (check out the recidivism rates) Think about the investment we as a society made into the lives of those now incarcerated, now generally wasted; not to consider the wasted resource protecting society from their deviance. The significant monetarily cost to the rest of society. We are broken people. Remove those moral self restraints and see what happens. What is happening! The removal of these Biblical principles, in an unguided pursuit of freedom, has only led to emotional and spiritual bondage. Break down those foundational morals and you see what we are experiencing. There is not enough money that can fix this situation. No responsible parent would reward a child for bad choices, but many of our leaders in government believe we who are responsible, should be obligated with our hard earned money, to pay for their irresponsibility. Therefore, individuals know that regardless of their actions, the government will care for their needs. It is the freedom to keep having children out of wedlock, and expect everyone who acts morally to absorb the cost. Society has resources to help, but when the system is overloaded, it collapses. Yes, we need to care for the children, but we also need some accountability too. We need a revival of traditional Biblical values or we are going to collapse. Our constitution as John Adams noted: was conditioned on us being a moral and religious people. Very little of those values are manifesting anymore. God help us!

This can be seen in the strengths and weaknesses of two main governmental structures. Socialism plays on equality, and welfare of all, but leads to laziness, irresponsibility, and strips the reasons for motivation and hard work. Capitalism plays on greed, but promotes hard work and personal responsibility, and taking a chance on success. Christianity promotes the better of both: compassion and expectations.

The Bible was once the bedrock of our society, now it is ridiculed and mocked. In its place are the godless and immoral foundations that history clearly shows: leads to societal unraveling.

Yet the present direction is anything but the return of good solid family values. Those Biblical values that resulted in the greatness of our country, are the same values that are desperately needed for the rebuilding of our foundations. Regretfully, the opposite is taking place as a movement. There is an acceleration into moral chaos. You cannot destroy the foundations and not expect the unraveling of our society. There are core values that hold society together; our common Christian faith for one. Even when the validity of faith was not personally held, the values that emanated from the Bible were practiced as social norms. We were not perfect, but much better off before the removal of the Bible reading and prayer in schools. We are now seeing a degradation of the value of life. Everything wholesome is being forsaken. This is principally due to the loss of truth. Particularly the Biblical truth of the immutable holiness of God. There are consequences: both in our personal lives, and in eternity. There is only one hope: The gospel of Jesus Christ. There is only one ultimate source of ultimate truth: The Bible.

CHAPTER 28

WALKING AWAY AND COMING HOME AGAIN

S ome suggestive restorative thoughts for those who have once been part of the faith community, walked away, and now reflect on the aftermath of that choice. It generally starts because of one of two reasons: seeds of doubt over the truthfulness of Christianity, or one becomes disillusioned with the faith, because they no longer see the merits of living according to the faith. In either case, the faith was no longer of practical value for them. It is a good part of the reason so many young people are leaving the church. They have lost faith in their faith. And the church owns much of the blame. We are simply not equipping young believers in the foundations of the faith; giving them solid reasons why the faith is worth their adherence. We are pretty good at telling them what we believe, but we are deficient when it comes to showing our youth why they can trust in what they have been taught. When challenged later in life, usually in college, they become disillusioned with what they had believed, and abandon the practical aspects of the faith. They are ill equipped when it comes to knowing why the Christian faith is well attested, and can be defended, and trusted, as a foundation for living. A sure foundation in a world of confusion. Without that confidence, they leave the faith. They abandon the practice of those values that flow from the clear teachings of the faith. They become deceived by the philosophies of this world, which leads to becoming disenchanted with what they once were taught. They only hold on to a shadow of their moral anchor. Once the anchor is dislodged, they pursue worldly satisfaction to fill the void in their souls.

Therefore, it should be of no surprise that many leave for a season. They are no longer able to trust what had been taught to them. They no longer see the usefulness of the faith; it is too old fashioned. This is one of the deficiencies of the church not providing the grounds for that assurance, or teaching the immense value of living out our beliefs. If the church made this a priority, and equipped them before leaving, more would continue on in the faith, knowing their faith was well founded and relevant to real life. Otherwise, the allures of this world, those that are presented as consequences free, often in the form of sexual temptations, will be too strong to overcome when tempted; this leads to engaging in sex outside marriage. And that has a devaluing effect on the sanctity of the later marriage union. Later, in reflection, they will realize those choices have become memories of regret: with shame and guilt as the natural consequences. This is the victory that Satan enjoys: devaluing the person, diminishing the sanctity of marriage, and discrediting the message.

I think this is an experience that many Christians have. They were once a part of a stable church, then in their later teens or early adulthood, they take a vacation from the faith, or abandon it, because of the philosophies of this world, or because of peer pressure. They act on their normal sexual desires, and indulge in sexual experimentation. Then later they return to the faith, wanting to return to their spiritual foundations, sensing that something is missing in their lives. For others, it comes when they start a family, and they want that spiritual foundation instilled in their children's lives, as it was in their lives.

Later in personal reflection, they reassess those choices they previously made, with the moral expectation of the faith, and find regret and remorse as the end results. They now wished that part of the journey had been avoided. It often weakens the sanctity of the bond of marriage. Because deep down in their hearts they knew better. It devalued the sanctity of their sex lives. Sex went from a sacred union to an experience to be explored. They thought they had found freedom, but it never was freedom. It was the temptation that led to remorse. It was giving in to the fresh. The resulting feeling is they have lost something precious because of those choices. A feeling of the loss of wholesomeness. This is a natural guilt feeling, because they knew what it was, and what God sees: unsanctified sex. That is why that act of sex outside of marriage is regrettable: it does not have God's blessings. If this is true of you? Go back and reread this book. It really is a book of hope. It is a warning for sure, but ultimately, it is the restoring hope of the gospel message. First in ultimate salvation, and then in practical restoring sanctification. A reminder that we who have accepted the salvation offered by God, are now children of our Heavenly Father. We are clothed in the very righteousness of Christ. Then putting the Apostle Paul's instruction to use, as he wrote about in Philippians, chapter 3. The wisdom put forth by Paul: to put the past in the past. Forgiving ourselves and living out the redeemed life we have in Christ; our true identity in Christ; not allowing that regret to steal anymore of our joy and peace. This was also the prayer of David after he grievously sinned. He did not ask to be saved again, that was unnecessary, but the joy of his salvation would be restored. (Psalms 52:12) Because when one is living in sin as a child of God, their fellowship with God is broken, and their joy is lost. Therefore, accept God's gracious forgiveness, and move forward in the restoring blessings God has for you marriage. Because God has blessed the sexual union of a married couple. Sex is intended to be a freely given expression of a sanctified union. (1st Corinthians, 6:11 and 7:1-7) Accept God's cleansing forgiveness. First in justification, and then living sanctification. Seeing ourselves clothed in the very righteousness of Christ. Stop trying to merit God's forgiveness, and accept as true, that the payment has been made. Our sin is forgiven, not because we have earned it, or deserved it, but because He loves us, and the payment has been made by Jesus Christ.

As part of the creative order, marriage sex is seen by God as sanctified sex. Therefore, it is encouraged as an healthy expression of the love that God intended for married couples. A freedom to enjoy to the max.

We are even told not to withhold from each other because this is an avenue that Satan will tempt. (1 Corithians chapter 7) We are to find satisfaction in the breast of the wife, so says the Bible! (Psalms 5:18-19) This is why we need to be anchored in the teaching of our faith, and put to practice the principles of the faith. This is the insight we gain by being grounded in the faith. It reveals why the holiness of God has practical ramifications now, and profound ramifications into eternity.

So, as strongly as I can, I suggest taking the time to study those who have written so persuasively on this subject, it will anchor your faith. And put your moral foundation on solid ground. (Many of those books that have helped me are included in my reading list) A sure confidence in what we believe is the result of this investment. And, may save a person from the illusions of this world, which is often manifested later as sexual regret. Then being assured in our faith, we all are prepared to be eternal difference makers. This is the desire for all of God's children: a meaningful life, an eternally purposeful life, a joy filled life! Fully forgiven and fully accepted.

The question remains: is it true or not? Was Jesus telling the truth as recorded in John 14:6? Have YOU taken advantage of the offer of eternal salvation? Faith alone, in Christ alone, based on His finished work on the cross alone, brings the forgiveness of ALL SIN, and eternal life! Then we need to move forward in restorative righteousness, by applying those Biblical principles. I hope it will cause some to repent (meaning they changed their mind about what they are trusting to get them into heaven or how they are living) and trust in the gospel of Jesus Christ for eternal life. For recovering believers, to understand all fall short of the glory of God, but are fully forgiven, and are now clothed in the very righteousness of Christ. So take David's prayer to heart: ask God to restore the joy of our salvation. And stop holding on to regret, it serves no Godly purpose, it only steals our joy. Be like Paul.

CHAPTER 29

TEN AND TEN

I want to suggest ten responses to ten issues

#1. We, as an society, are abandoning our moral anchor. As an example, this was seen when a recent nominee for the Supreme Court did not believe she was qualified to define what a woman is. If she is not qualified in this very simple matter, how can she make some of the biggest decisions for our nation? There is a repudiation of natural and divine truth; even most elementary students know there is a difference between a male and female. We have entered a period of time when people feel they can determine their own truth; where what was historically believed to be virtuous, is now seen as narrow-minded thinking. Actions that once were considered morally wrong, or sexually immoral, are now seen as liberating freedom to be. When we leave God given eternal truth: any value or sexual expression is reduced to personal preference. Do a contrast study on the decline of students since the early sixties, when Bible reading and prayer were ruled unconstitutional. This is a byproduct of leaving our Biblical foundations, and therefore, abandoning truth. The resulting deterioration of our society is due, in great part, to the sexual revolution. The sexual moral chaos that has ensued in our nation, is being manifest. This results in the brokenness of our families units and the rapid growth of out of wedlock children.

The explosion of sex crimes and growing prison populations. This is further seen in the high degree of drug abuse; often to hide the pain of our brokenness. We need a dependable standard of truth. Take away the Bible's standard on moral issues, and you lose the basis for morality. When this takes place, we no longer have a cohesive standard of truth. The result is we have lost much of our virtuousness. The Bible warned there was coming a time when even believers will not put up with sound doctrine. Unfortunately, that time has come. In 2nd Timothy 4:3-4, the Apostle Paul writes about those who will not put up with sound doctrine. They want to hear what they want to hear. Is this not the prevailing view today? People want what they want, even if it is not healthy, nor a sensible way to live. The abandonment of revealed divine truth leads to what we are seeing: the brokenness of personal lives, and the unraveling of society. We need a standard of truth that is always true. It is as Jesus said in John 8:32, It is the truth that sets one free. (these scriptures are my loose paraphrase) It is Satan who is the deceiver, destroyer, and origin of all lies, and we have brought into them.

R: We need to return to the full authority of the Bible. In 1st Timothy 3:16, it says: All scripture is God breathed. This is the consistent claim by the writers of scriptures. This is why good sources of apologetics and the various defenses for the trustworthy authority of the divine truth needs to be pursued. This foundational authority of truth needs to be reinfused in our lives and churches. It needs to be boldly proclaimed in our churches, long before our youth, in particular, leave the home. Since the scriptures claim full authority for issues of our faith, morality, and the purpose for our lives. If one wants an understanding of our origin, our value, our meaning, our purpose, and our destiny: the Bible is the source for that knowledge. This is what the scriptures consistently proclaim. For example: the Apostle John, say in Revelation 22, not to add, nor take anything away for this book. In Jude, verse 3, he writes that the faith was once for all entrusted to the saints. As recorded, in Matthew 5:8; Jesus says not a smallest letter, not the least stroke of the pen would go unfulfilled. As Jesus explained to the traveling disciples on the Emmaus walk in Luke 24; all the Old Testament pointed to Him. In 2 Peter, chapter one, Peter writes: that men spoke from God as they were carried along by the Holy Spirit. The Apostle Paul writes in his last book, 2nd Timothy: that All Scriptures are God breathed, and useful for teaching, etc. This is consistent with the whole of the Bible. If we compromise on the source of our authority: we nullify the supremacy of the Bible as the source of truth. We would therefore have an unreliable faith, because we would be denying the trustworthiness of God's truth. What happens when we leave this standard: we have nothing of substance to offer to the world. The lack of assurance in the truthfulness of the Bible, is a major issue in the church. If we are not sure what we believe, or the reason why we believe, there is not much left to believe. How can the church be a defender of truth, for example, if we compromise with the truth and can not even agree with God on what is a marriage? When we abandon God's truth, we are left swimming in a sea of uncertainty and make believe. (These verse were taken from the NIV or I paraphrased of them)

We Christians can rest assured that our faith is well attested and can be strongly defended. We do not need to concede our beliefs. A major point I have been trying to make throughout this book is that God is not swayed by public opinion. He said what He has said; and He will not adjust His standards to suit ours; He cannot because He is unchangeable. Just because the world is pressuring us to abandon the truthfulness of the Christian faith, should not sway us who know the truth, just to find acceptability with culture, even for those we love.

#2. We have abandoned divine revealed truth, by accepting the theory of evolution. When we accept this erroneous theory, we lose our foundation for intrinsic worth; since we are then devalued to the status of the animalistic world. In this belief system, there is no rational for life, since life does not make sense without a God given purpose for creation. We are simply at a higher level of evolution. A vein of reasoning that naturally results, if this theory is true. This is how important this question of origin is. Our place in this universe is determined by whether we are divinely created with purpose or the random results of an evolutionary process. Which, if evolution is true, signifies we are meaningless in our existence. We have real worth only if we are created in the image of God. Otherwise, we are reduced to purposeless entities in a biological unguided world: meaningless entities in a meaningless world, with no real purpose.

R. We need to defend the truth that this world is a God's created world. That we are divinely, and uniquely created, in the image of God. God alone is our conceived origin. There are numerous creation ministries, that we need to immerse ourselves in their resources. These resources will affirm our beliefs; which allows us to defend our faith, and validate our divinely given worth. There is a world of difference between being a unique creation of God and the random results of an unguided biological process; as alleged by the humanist. Simple common sense indicates that we have personalities. And those personalities can only come from a personality: God Himself is that person. Evolutionists can't explain self-awareness. This clearly points to humans being more than biological beings. We have a soul and spirit that makes us unique in all of creation. We are either divinely created or a byproduct of evolution. Your origin is either a monkey or Adam!

#3. The acceptance of abortion, which devalues the intrinsic worth of all human life. If life can be chosen or denied because of convenience, or perceived worth, then we really don't have intrinsic worth. Either life is endowed with divinely given meaning, or life has no meaning. This designation of our uniqueness by God is strongly connected with the previous sections.

R. There is a view that is deeply disturbing to me, not just the acceptance of abortion as lamentable, but sometimes a necessary choice in some people's minds. But the act is now actually celebrated, as some are doing in our culture. Whereas it should be seen, for what it is, an act that devalues all of life. An act we should grieve and fight to stop. But this does not take place until we first come to grips with the revelation that all of life is treasured in God's eyes, and so should it be in the eyes of His people. This is another byproduct of abandoning truth; and results in the devaluing of the sanctity of all of human life. When life is devalued for some, it is devalued for all. For those who once succumbed to these lies, who were erroneously led by worldly deception: the restoring, and forgiving hope of the gospel remains available to whosoever. This is where the Apostle Paul insight in Philipians chapter 3, is so crucial to understand. The understanding, and then the acceptance, that we are new creations in Christ. The past sins can be forgiven as far as the East is from the West. (there is no East or West Poll: so this means completely) This is the bedrock of restoring one's joy.

#4. We are steadily removing Christian foundational truths from our society. This is an offshoot of the first principle discussed. The difference is: this is more focused on the re-entrance of those truths back into our society. I fail to understand how the 10 commandments, which teaches us not to kill, steal, be honest, honor your mother and father, etc, can be seen as the source of the problem, and not the necessary part of the solution for our moral crises. We treat problems in our society like diabetes. It helps to have medication to treat the disease of diabetes, but it is far better when we lose weight, get some exercise, and eat better. We are like that as a society. We want to correct problems by programs, instead of preventing the dysfunctions in the first place. When moral foundations are removed, this is the byproduct. It is the reason for most of our society's ills. We are abandoning a righteous foundation on which to build a healthy society. Walk out some of these ill founded ideas or beliefs, and it is easy to see where those ideas take you: societal breakdown

R. We need to start with the restoration of Biblical truth back into our society. We were strongly influenced in the origin of our country by those strongly held beliefs. We need to return to the acknowledgement that God has spoken, and His ways are always the better way. This is why the Bible's teachings are so critical; it is not just the truth of the matter, but practical application of the truth that brings the benefits. (See the book of James as an example) Those teachings promote expectations of personal moral responsibilities.. For the Christian, the key is to be an authentic Christian where you are planted. It is usually not some grand ministry. It is being grounded in the word of God, and then living out those priorities. Our country was founded on those principles. As noted, when we take away prayer from schools, we lose dependance on God; when we remove the Bible, we lose truth. We no longer have a righteous foundation, for which, to base our moral standards. God is the only reason we have meaning in life. If we deny God, we abandon any possibility for morality, or have a foundation for meaning. If the foundations are destroyed what can the righteous do? (Psalms 11:3) Alternatively, people can rejoice when the righteous lead. We need to promote the leadership of righteous men and women; those who lead in the way of righteousness; then we will not have the magnitude of problems we are experiencing. And this starts by reintroducing the eminence of Biblical morality back into our society. Giving logical reasons why they are necessary, and defending our rights as American Christians. Our God gave us the command to use our influence for good, to be salt and light.

#5. The breakup of the American family. The foundation of a stable and healthy society is the family unit. The consequences have been explored, and are, the subject of numerous books. And since this book is not addressing this as the main topic, I will only address briefly; but it needs to be addressed, because the breakdown of the family is one of the major causes of the decline of our culture.

R. It starts with re-establishing the expectation that marriage is a sacred union. A unit that needs to be promoted, protected, and defended; since it is crucial to the wellbeing of our country. This is strongly connected with the idea that those who father a child should be responsible to care for the child, not society. When one takes responsibility and pours his life into his children, the benefactor is often not just your children, but your grandchildren, and the generations to come. A strong and healthy society is the result. We are seeing the real consequences that result because of the brokenness of the American family. We need to reassess the decline of commitment to marriage, and the need for stable families, by re-established the message: the God given standards of intact, and strong family units. The health of our nation, and wellbeing of us individually, are dependent on the strength of this God conceived unit. The alternative leaves numerous sociological problems; those that contribute to the growing number of broken lives. In Malachi 3:6a, the scriptures record that God hates divorce. He does not hate divorce people, nor does this lead to a loss of our salvation; but for Christians, it will lead to divine discipline, loss of testimony, and the likelihood of generational dysfunction. For everyone, the breakdown of marriage and the family unit, naturally causes problems that ripple down throughout society.

#6. Unbiblical sexuality. All sex outside of marriage is forbidden for the Christian. Actually, it is forbidden for all, but we children of

God are particularly instructed, as we are to model our Christian lives. It really is simple: God says the marriage bed is sacred. We live in a society where every sexual temptation is promoted and often celebrated. The proliferation of pornography is destructive to the wholesome sex lives God intended for couples. Sexual temptation has become a source of spiritual warfare for many believers. But the choice to deviate from God's instructions is not just spiritual warfare, it is also simply spiritual disobedience. Those who have opened the door to this are devaluing the very virtuous lives God desires for His children. He knows the devaluing effects. So how do we live in an over sexualized world? Where various sexual perversions are often celebrated as liberating freedom; then Christians are often chastised for not accepting those alleged freedoms.

R. We start by taking God seriously when He speaks about the lives we are to live. Do not open the door to that option. Violate that standard and expect God to bring serious discipline: this is God's promise. The author of Hebrews, writes in chapter 13, verse 4: that the marriage bed is honorable among all men, but fornicators and adulterers God will judge. This was reiterated earlier in 1st Thessalonians 4:6, when Paul wrote: God will punish all such sexual activities against another brother. These warnings were written to believers. It is also the best universal standard for all of mankind. When violated, it leads to enumerable consequences to our lives, and for society as a whole. Those unbiblical actions are not pure and edifying for the believer. God set the pattern for marriage: in the beginning, God created the marriage union, when He created it only for one man and one woman. This concept is reinforced in numerous places in the scriptures; where we are instructed to live lives that are above reproach. We Christians are called to stand out in our communities as having strong and loving marriages. The world needs to see that our faith is exhibited in our pure lifestyles. We need to be the models of fun and Godly marriages. Ones that show the fruit of righteousness that comes from those marriages. Furthermore, we need to be a voice of reason for the sacredness of traditional marriage, and promote those benefits to our society. And that starts with the private lives and thoughts of each believer. Know that God knows our very thoughts, and He will hold us accountable. Furthermore, the thoughts are where the seeds of sin start. If you don't think about it, you will not act on it. If you are thinking about it, you may act on it. Be Careful.

#7. We have changed the intent of our country from: *We the People*, to unelected judges, who have re-manufacturing our moral standards by judicial decrees. For example, we have court decisions outlawing prayer and Bible reading in our schools, and additionally, redefining marriage and giving unconstitutional rights to abortion. Neither are found as rights in the constitution. Where in the constitution is it granted to judges to create unconstitutional rights, when the very oath of judges is to defend the constitution. Furthermore, we permissively stand by and allow the government to abuse the rights of the American Citizens for exercising their given rights. This abuse is coming from the FBI, IRS and DOJ: where prosecution is biased against conservatives and prolife citizens, and often ignores the misdeeds of those who walk according to the values of the Washington DC mindset; which is very liberal. We have gone from, *We the People*, to being bullied by our own government, *our* government. That was not the original intent of our constitution: which gave the *Bill of Rights* to protect us from the government. These were God given rights. For example, life is a God given right.

R. We the people need to hold OUR government responsible for the leaders decisions and demand equitable treatment of all people. We need to support groups and politicians that defend the family, our Christian convictions, and the constitution. We need to advocate the mindset that is color blind, where each individual is seen as a unique creation of God. We need to understand the *Bill of Rights*: are for our protection from the government, and not the rights of government officials to deny some of our God given rights. We need to demand that the government is to equally protect our interest, not promote their personal political preferences. When you vote for godless politicians, you get godless policies. Then over time you get a godless country. This is what we are seeing. It has been noted that man is either governed by self-restraining principles (Biblical morality) or a strong overbearing government. One that abuses its authority and power. We have a government that frequently rewards irresponsible choices, those that contribute to the breakdown of our society, then want the more responsible to pay the bill for the resulting outcome; often because they are their voting base. The same with the promotion of godless behavior by the Liberal Hollywood. They reap the financial benefits, we who are influenced by these values, reap the whirlwind.

#8. Moral compromising Christians and confused thinking world. Those who are compromising with the world to fit in, are finding these compromises are becoming increasingly destructive to all of us. As an example: those who will accept a lie that males or females can be other than who they were created to be. No matter how it is sold, a person can never be other than the DNA they were born with: you either have X or Y. Even with surgery, it is only an altering of the body, not the creation of an alternative sex. A man is a man and a woman is a woman. Even so, we are being demanded to embrace numerous lies. This type of thinking would have been seen as absurd years ago. Those who promote this thinking, want to normalize it as a value to be embraced, and not a sin to avoid. The celebration of godless behavior leads to broken lives. Which often leads to alcohol abuse, higher suicide rates, drug use, and sexual deviant behavior. All these results further weaken the sacredness of God ordained sex and God's created order. This loss of wholesomeness often leads to more abuse of substances to mask the pain. Observed the decline of the nation's mental health, the rising crime rates, and brokenness of lives we are seeing in our country. Think about the evil that many non-Christian governments bring upon their people for ideological reasons. If you are a woman, do you really want to live under an oppressive regime of some non-Christian governments? People in many countries are pushing back for their freedom, even to the point it causes them their very lives. They want their freedom so badly they will die for a chance to have it. We are giving it away.

R. We need to return to the simple reality of real life. This is the view of life that corresponds to the nature of reality as we know it. The same view we are given about the nature of life, as described in the scriptures. We need to return to the one and only God who created life: the very creator of life. We have started to live in a bizarre world. Where some allegations about the nature of life are simply foolish. Furthermore, we are implored to endorse those views. Those who identify as Christians, and are going along with this thinking, may need to be rebuked (according to the Bible), or simply enlightened on the reality of what is true. This is the Biblical mandate: to rebuke those who walk according to the world, those who are compromising with the morals of this world to fit in with the world. The Bible gives direction on how to deal with unrepentant believers. It needs to start within the body of Christ. The Biblical expected standards of Christian conduct, and it must first start within the church. Then we move outside the walls of the church, to influence the world as the salt and light of the world. We need clear voices and bolder Christians, who are able to articulate obvious truths. We need an old fashion spiritual revival within the body of Christ. I have long reasoned that even if Christianity is not true, the church's moral influence puts breaks on runaway immorality. (Be clear that I strongly believe in the evidence for the Christian faith) There are good solid practical reasons to promote a Biblical based foundation for our county. Real Biblical Christianity brings freedom to women, equality to all, righteous lives, less crime and substance abuse; and a needed moral foundation for the wellbeing of all. There are clear causes and effects of what we believe. We need the truth, and defend it. It is God's revealed truth. Evil can only be restrained by righteous truth. And righteous truth can only come from one source: the immutable nature of God. We, who are citizens of this country, need to demand our rights.

#9. The unfiltered influence of the media, education and government, as they promote Godless morality. In my opinion, the liberal media is very godless and slanted. For example: when those of the liberal persuasion have obvious moral failings, the media generally ignores the failings, or they are even celebrated. However, when the conservative or Christian has a moral failing, one that is inconsistent with the dictates of the faith, the liberal media pounds away day after day. This alone shows there are two standards because we live by two different values systems. This is an area where the writer of the Bible (Holy Spirit), and popular media differ. The Bible is very honest in exposing the fault of the saints. Whereas, the present day media hides or minimizes the dirty secrets of those who are like minded. It is as though, if they want some perspective to be true, they promote it as true, regardless of its credibility. However, if you have values

237

that are different from those of the liberal media, they will diminish the foundations of your perspective or beliefs. It is an almost endless pursuit to destroy one's view point. This minimizes the impact of your perspective. However, if someone holds the same political perspective, their private sins, their political connections, their financial misdeeds, or political indiscretions, are often just ignored, or quickly noted, and then passed over for a story they want to emphasize. We are often left trying to determine what is really true, because those who bring the information have lost their honorable call to report honestly the truth.

R. We need to be very careful of who we trust and depend upon for our news. We need honest reporting, and even handed treatment of news. I am not sure this is possible at this point, since the decline of megamedia has altered the reliability of most reporting. We need to have dependable news resources, and stop supporting those that distort the news because of their political biases. Those that devalue our beliefs and want to alter our understanding of what is virtuous. We Christians need to view life through a Biblically grounded filter, and not through the Godless filtered viewpoint of those who reject our values. But for this to be known, we need to be strongly grounded in the teaching of our faith. Since we cannot consistently live out our faith, if we do not have a world view consistent with the faith. We cannot act on what we do not know. We also need to set those standards high in our personal lives. It starts with what we watch, listen to and think about. Who we fellowship with is also clearly articulated in the scriptures. We must have a clear Biblical filter. (Our World view) If there is one continuous theme throughout these chapters, it is: what is the basis for truth? And then have the wisdom to immerse those values into our private lives. This is more than a personal integrity issue, it should be our worldview that is consistent with our faith; sadly missing in today's world.

10. Even if we make all these rectifications, which will help re-establish our moral foundations, even then, at best, they are temporary improvements. The adaptation of these will improve the quality of our lives, but they do not necessarily impact our eternal destinations. Therefore, this last one, is the only one that brings about an eternal change. However, we have a major problem, when a third of pastors in the USA now believe one can earn heaven by being good. We have

lost our way in the evangelical community. So while today's preaching reaches people where there are, and that is helpful for daily living, one of the deficiencies is that it often misses the central reason for the faith: the reason why Christ died: the eternal deliverance of one's soul. I had someone say to me the other day, that "you cannot dance with the devil forever." I responded: this should be true, because if you do: the penalty is Hell. This above all the other issues, is the main issue. Therefore, the first nine need to be kept in perspective with number ten. Even if we find the golden age of utopia, this does not discount the absolute need to be assured of one's eternal destiny. If you do not see the priority of this truth? I am not saying you are not a Christian, but your failure to grasp the significance of Jesus as our only substitute, indicates a deficient understanding of God's only plan for the eternal redemption of mankind; which is paramount over all other issues.

R. The main goal is not the salvation of society, but the salvation of the soul of man. The whole of scripture is God's loving plan to restore mankind, and creation in general, back into harmony with Himself. This is the prevailing message throughout this book. What I did understand from the beginning of my faith journey, was that if the faith was true: it was an evangelistic faith. That required being shared. It is the most compassionate action a believer can undertake. The implications of John 14:6 remain. The basis for this claim was voiced earlier by Jesus, in John 8:24, when He claimed His deity was the basis for salvation; and then in verse 30, the same author reports that many believed. Have you believed? If you have? Are you sharing that hope? Those who denied Jesus deity, His sacrifice on the cross, and/or the resurrection, die in their sins. It is as simple as that. The Apostle Paul was certainly captured by these truths. It changed everything in his life. While most of us do not get this type of revelation as confirmation, most of us also do not suffer for the faith as he did. One truth I hoped that I made absolutely clear: one who is saved at the moment of salvation, cannot be more saved than they are at that very moment. However, they can be more radically saved in their sanctification, which results in a greater glorified salvation. There is real evil in this world and it starts in the heart of each person. What the world needs is the same for each and every person. We all need the renewal of the new birth. Since, while we can taper down our sinful impulses, it will still raise its ugly head, since we are a fallen race. We can strive for a better life, but we still need eternal life. There is the clear teaching in the Old Testament that proclaims that when they return to God, He will often restore what has been lost through disobedience. The good Lord is a restorer of what the Locust have eaten: Ezekiel 34 and Joel 2. The idea is that of restoring lost blessings due previous disobedience. We need to return to God and He will return to us. It often starts as we become a people of prayer. We need to be on our knees praying for our country before all is lost. If we do not do it soon, we will lose our country. We need to have an old fashion revival in our churches that resonates into the world around us. We need to step forth with the hope of the gospel: it is the truth that Jesus came to save the lost. We need to undertake that mission with gentle boldness. So we can say on that day, as Apostle Paul said: "I have fought the good fight and finished the race." He continues in his letter to Timothy: preach the word and do the work of an evangelist. (The general theme of 2nd Timothy 4:2,4,7) We can never understand the love of God until we understand the cost He undertook to satisfy His immutable holiness.

CHAPTER 30

SUMMARY THOUGHTS

I acknowledge that much of what I have written has been enhanced by what I have learned from the labors of others. I took what I have learned, modified it, and advanced my themes. As they too took what they learned, modified it, and advanced their themes. We all build on the learning of those who preceded us. In my case, I perceived there was a very deficient appreciation of some key attributes of God, which needed to be revisited. In particular, the immutable holiness of God, and its ramifications. I hope my insights into these crucial truths has enabled me to make a contribution for the cause of Christ, no matter how small. If only one person reads, and then comes to saving faith, then the whole effort will be well worth my time.

I am not fully sure why, but for some reason, the immutable aspect of God's nature had been weighing heavy on my mind. It is likely because of its tremendous significance. The insight into the nature of God, being absolutely perfect, and unable to change, was profound to me. Never able to moderate who He was in His eternal essence. His nature was intrinsic to who He is: the immutable Holy God. The more I pondered, the more I understood the wonders of God's plan for the salvation of mankind. I understood better, the need for a permanent, and complete salvation plan; one that would fully reconcile me with

God. It was very clear that our human efforts, trying to measure up to God's infinite holiness, seem rather absurd. This insight resulted in even greater gratitude for the provisions and promises of God. He, as my Savior, was the source of my assured salvation.

These insights also highlighted the woeful neglect of good sound presentations of the gospel. A confusing gospel message is often a deficient message to bring about salvation. We need to be clear on the content of the gospel; it is the only means for eternal life. Our only hope! Therefore, the neglect by individuals believers and churches to make this the premier priority, is puzzling in light of eternity.

This book, hopefully, will lead us to reconsider our priorities. Too often focused on the pursuit of the temporary pleasures, and too neglecting of the undeniable, the eternal that is coming to all of us. The emphasis on finding satisfaction in this life, with too little regard for the next, seems to be a misplaced priority. That was not the mindset of the Apostle Paul or that of the other Apostles. I understand from church history that 11 of the 12 apostles died for the faith. (Not sure that can be completely proven, but it is very clear a vast number of followers of Christ died for their convictions) Something moved them to sacrifice all. I suggest, the evidence for the resurrection, the knowledge of the coming judgment, and the peril the lost were facing, were some of their prime reasons. Furthermore, they knew their sacrifices for the cause of Christ, would be honored one day at the Bema Seat.

God is a just God, and His righteousness must be satisfied. When I reflect on the lack of attention it receives by most Christians, and non-Christian alike, it is confusing. Since for both groups the consequences are tremendous. Yet it is sadly absent in most Sunday morning messages. The message that is sadly lacking, is the vital message, that all believers are to engage in the greater call to the church, the making of disciples, who can make disciples, who can make disciples. That is God's plan for the church. (Ephesians chapter 4) Discipleship is the development of the spiritual life of individual believers within the body of Christ. The development of the newly born, but immature believers in Christ, into mature believers for the propagation of God's salvation program. To be messengers of the Gospel; Christ atonement on the cross. For what reason did He die? Not to make us happy, healthy and prosperous, but sons and daughters. This with the hope that birth into the family of God would lead us to grow into seasoned and mature children. The problem is that many never grow much beyond initial salvation. They begin as babes and they die as babes. Salvation benefits may have been received as a gift, but growth is sadly lacking. Of even greater concern, is not only do some not grow, they are carnal (wordly) in their Christian walk. (1st Corinthians 3:1-3) In both cases, it is most likely they want the illusion of American prosperity Christianity, or they are desiring the things of the flesh more than the things of God. They do not want to entertain the clear reality of the faith: that there is a Heaven to gain, a Hell to avoid, and possible rewards for faithfulness.

For the non-believer, they will not pursue God forgiving grace, if they failed to understand their hopeless status, before an unalterable holy God. The horrors that await them upon their death. Yet so ignored or denied as a real possibility. However, when they understand this reality, the gospel becomes priceless. The insight that they too can escape the just consequence of their sin, and become a child of God, through a simple act of faith, in the gracious offer of God; since His Son already made full and complete payment. When this is understood, there is jubilation. There is no contribution by the sinner needed, foolish to even try, since it is a gift that is only merited by faith alone, because of what Jesus Christ did alone.

This, in my opinion, is all due to our failing to understand some essential truths. The failure to understand the gravity of the situation. The actual connotations of what we believe. Most Chrisitians simply have never thought through the implications of what we believe. This neglect to grasp the seriousness of the faith, results in a willingness to accept a soft form of Christianity, or even accept an unbiblical message. This is sadly due to the soft pedaling of Christianity by pastors who want to promote the best life now. They, like me, have a natural desire to be liked. To be socially acceptable to those both in the church and out. Enhanced, and maybe even a little embarrassed, by the call and responsibility of evangelism; which should be modeled by all pastors. But since the unsettling reality of God's holiness is hard to accept, with its natural connotations, and even harder to find the courage to proclaim, most pastors simply avoid it. They often have a hard time reconciling the actual implications of the faith, with their desires for the lighter Church atmosphere they prefer. A fun and exciting place to be on a Sunday. So they just avoid the issue. It simply comes down to one word: Hell. So instead of advancing the message, we all shrink back from sharing the faith, since it is easier to ignore. When was the last time you heard a message on Hell? Yet the Bible says this is the future for the majority of humanity. Which is why world evangelism is still God's heart. And the great commission is still the great commission. A commission given to the body of Christ to fulfill. (Matthew 28:19-20)

This is why our apathy does not make sense; it really comes down to the unwillingness to accept the implications of Hell. I understand this reluctant acceptance, nobody should like this reality. However, if there is no Hell, then Christianity is reduced to myths, legends, and social good programs. It would nullify any reason to share our faith. It devalues everything we proclaim as classic Christianity. It would mean Jesus Christ died in vain. Therefore, the Christian faith is a full package faith; either it is fully true, or we are practicing a man made religion. Since our convictions are based on solid evidence, this renewed knowledge should motivate us to live out the faith, in light of eternity. If Christianity is true, this is real Christianity, even if we do not like some of the ramifications of the faith.

We know that emphasizing the hard truth of God's infinite holiness does not necessarily create a warm fuzzy church we all prefer. But it is necessary to grasp the urgency for the sharing of the gospel. It is not for those who want a feel good message on how to find personal success. I understand that discipleship, as clearly defined, while Biblical, is hard to impress upon the body of Christ. The expected response to the message of truth. The duplication and multiplication of discipleship. The spiritual maturing process that is necessary for God's plan to be successful. If we are not being trained to be disciplers, we are not being equipped for the ministry God has intended for the body. (Ephesians, chapter 4, indicates this is the responsibility of spiritual leaders, to equip the saints for the ministry) When we are not training others in discipleship, we are simply passing on information. We are Biblically informed, but too often mission neglecting. To be equipped requires a good strong Biblical foundation, and, intentional, purposeful, discipleship training ministry. As often has been used as a descriptive expression: "A soul winning ministry." But this divine commission is generally neglected for more acceptable messages. Those spiritual enrichment messages most want to hear. Truth be told, we all naturally want that soft message. I will say it again, I shun the idea of evangelism, it is not my nature. The immutability of God's holiness troubles me. And the idea of Hell troubles me. But the faith is well attested and true! It just makes logical sense, even if I don't like some of the ramifications of it being true. There are no other options, other than walking away and ignoring its truth claims. But Jesus says: I am "the" way, and "no one" comes to the Father "except" through me. (my loose paraphrase) Did He tell the truth? No One! Except through personal acceptance of what Jesus Christ accomplished on the cross! As he said on the cross: "It is Finished." (Gospel of John 19:30) There is no other way, even if I don't like it.

CHAPTER 31

WHAT ARE OUR OPTIONS?

⚬⚬⚬⚬⚬⚬

Lying in bed one night, unable to sleep, I was thinking about why I felt compelled to write on such a difficult subject. This is not superficial reading; not that it is significantly profound writing. Actually, these are many of the areas of my faith that I have wrestled with for sometime. The idea of wrestling best describes what I was feeling. I was struggling with two aspects of my life that were hard to harmonize. There was my easy going nature, having fun, hanging out, enjoying time with my family and friends; that part of my life that I really enjoy. I enjoy good laughter. I have found I am good at one-liners. I like finding humor in the moment or contrasting ironic thoughts of life. While I am in law enforcement, which tends to draw political conservatives, I have found I like a good conversation with some defense attorneys. I am sure we do not see much in common, particularly in regards to religion and politics; I just like people, and find those from different backgrounds interesting. Their perspectives are sometimes insightful. They force me to think through subjects. I find that true of most people from divergent backgrounds. It is interesting to see through their eyes what I may not normally see. So engaging in these conversations allows me to see life through a dissimilar set of eyes; It doesn't feel like the appropriate time to share my faith. I want to enjoy the relationship and conversation, without thought of their spiritual condition; or those eternal repercussions that I have written about in this book.

Then there is the central theme of this book. The urgency of the gospel. That Jesus was telling the truth in John 14:6. That the validity of which has been discussed was of extreme importance. That this subject was more than how to have a meaningful life; it has real eternal significance. I was also becoming more aware that this journey of mine was slowly winding down. Life was slowly escaping me, and there was nothing I could do to recapture those passing days. There were chapters of my life that would never be re-lived. These thoughts created a time of renewed reflection, so I wrote a book. A summary of years of introspection regarding many aspects of the faith. Issues of extreme importance that I wanted to record and pass on. Hopefully, someone may even read it, hopefully, my family and friends. It was like a lasting spiritual will. A passing on of these spiritual truths. Those truths that I wanted to pass on in a permanent record; particularly, for my family. Most importantly for me personally: my wife, our children, and our grandchildren. I wanted them to know what I know. Some lasting legacy of what I have learned in my spiritual journey. The gospel that I know they must perceive and believe.

So where do we go with these thoughts? What to do with the dilemma? The preferred lifestyle of my easy going and fun loving personality. One that would prefer to ignore the harder realities of life. And then, there is the inescapable of what is true: there is a holy God, the temporary nature of life, and the contingency of our eternal destination. The ramifications of the central message of the Bible: in particular, the decision everyone must make about the claims in John 14:6. The exclusive claims asserted by Jesus Christ, the only Savior. The only source of hope that the world so desperately needs: the gospel of Jesus Christ. This is the dilemma, and there are three options: dilute or walk away or understand that truth is often hard to accept, but true.

DILUTE

This is the choice of most churches and individual Christians. Not the denial, but the watering down of the implication. When this continues on its natural projection, it is called progressive Christianity. It greatly minimizes the key points that I have written about. The cross is still part of their theology, but its significance is greatly reduced. In its enhanced form, it evolves into universalism, where most everyone is going to make it into heaven regardless of what they believe; God is a good God, and never judges. This diluted form of Christianity is so modified from its origin, it is almost unrecognizable. It becomes a quagmire of inconsistencies. The end result of this progression is it becomes a version of the faith that only exists in the mind of the beholder. It is a denial of the evidence for the faith. It is a contrived faith. There is no sound reason to trust anything contained in this mindset. It becomes a bit of postulation, which exists only in the mind of one holding the belief. Ultimately, it is basically worthless. Only the authentic faith passed on from the Lord and His apostles, is worthy of trusting in for one's eternal future. It is the only one. Then we have a trustworthy faith that gives real hope. A verifiable faith. It is then that the cross of Christ becomes so priceless, because the reality of Hell was a very real possibility. It is all important, because it is the foundation for our eternal redemption. This is the natural progression of diluting the faith. You lose what is most needed: an absolute assurance. The worth of the Christian faith is greatly diminished when we start to compromise. When we leave the verbatim revelation from God, we lose the assurance of the promise: eternal life.

However, it is my firm conviction that there are compelling reasons to believe we are on solid ground with the trustworthiness of the Christian faith. It makes sense. The evidence is very compelling. The person who denies the faith is like a man falling off a building and denying gravity. He may deny it, but will soon be hit with the ramifications. Upon death, the denier will find out they were horribly wrong about their assumptions. Their wishful expectations were not based on the credible message contained in the scriptures. The truth of the Gospel. It is likely they are avoiding the question, because they dislike the truths contained in the Christian faith. They don't want to know the truth of the matter. They so desire the temporal pleasures of this life, those pursuits that are only temporal, that may cause them their soul. This is also because there are aspects of the faith that do not agree with their idea of fairness or personal desires. They want a God of their own ideological creation, not a holy one. They like the kindness and goodness of God, but not the holy. They see an incompatibility between love and holiness, in the God they envision, so they minimize the holy. They dilute the holiness of God.

There is an appearance that the attributes of God conflict with each other. Actually, in a sense, they do. But God had a plan that would allow a full expression of both. Yet, harmonizing God's absolute holiness and unending love, can be hard to reconcile in our minds, without minimizing one or the other. The natural response is to dilute God's holy standards. But that is not a true understanding of who God is; because when we do, we minimize the insight we need to understand our need for personal salvation. The diluting of this aspect of God's nature, then dilutes the need for the payment of our sins by Christ on the cross. These are the major reasons I wrote this book. There is a necessary understanding that opens our mind to this tension. It is not to dilute God's holiness, but to elevate the person and work of Jesus Christ. It all comes together in God's plan of redemption. God maintains His holiness and yet found a way to show His love. He was fully satisfied in the work of Christ on the cross. It really is profound when one spends time considering it. So we should pause and find sweet relief from the uncertainty of what happens after death, knowing that for us who are saved, our future is secure. Having the firm confidence that one who believes has been fully and eternal accepted by God the Father. To dilute, is to nullify the urgency of the gospel, and minimize everything true about God. In light of God's immutable holiness, we need a full and complete salvation: an eternal redemption.

WALK AWAY

This one has appealed to me at times: just live and let live. Moving on from this emotional agony and enjoying the life that has been granted to me. I don't want to be known as one of those radical, overly religious people, who are always trying to proselytize others to their point of view. The Christian who makes people uncomfortable by bringing up their need for personal salvation. I want to be the person who is enjoyable to be around. So I could discount the faith. I could walk away. I had that preferred thought more than a few times. It seems so much easier. A few beers at the local pub and enjoy my time with my friends. I have often desired to put these thoughts aside and just live. My life is starting to wind down, so I could make the best of the years I have left. We did the hard work of being parents. We have earned our pensions. We could enjoy the remaining years of our retirement with adventure and new experiences. The good life we all hope for. I even could remain quasi religious, but just ignore the eternal ramifications. Be spiritual, but avoid the whole notion that there are rewards for one's faithfulness. That there is an evaluation even for the eternally saved Christian. The pushing aside the idea of a real Hell, which is a real place of consequences for sinners; for those who forgo the gracious offer of a pardon, that can be found at the foot of the cross.

These preferred thoughts become unsustainable thoughts, when one starts to reflect on the repercussion of those outside the faith. While freeing the mind by ignoring the implications of the faith, the obvious is still true: there is a date with destiny for all of us. The hard reality of our eventual death, not only for me, but for everyone. Realizing that to pass by an opportunity to share this message of salvation would be most unloving. It would indicate that I have a greater desire for my personal comforts than I do for their eternal destiny. The reality of the subject can be too agonizing even to the pounder. I feel it, and it is not my personality; I really like to be liked.

It is a struggle at times; the feeling that I can never come to full peace with this dilemma. The struggle between the two: my preferred lifestyle, and the ultimate reality, we all have a destiny with death, then there is a judgment. Regardless of my desires, the fact remains: we all desperately need a dependable answer to the question of where we will spend our life after death. The moment of death will eventually come for all of us. We better not be wrong in this decision! There is a free offer from God, with profound eternal implications. Since the consequences are so epoch, I will continue the walk, but that does not mean I don't find this as a desirable option. It is just not a rational one in light of the fact that death is a universal problem, and there is an unavoidable judgment. Therefore, I will continue to wrestle with my dislike for some aspects of the faith; all the while, I am thankful to God for His indescribable gift of salvation, in the person and work of Jesus Christ on the cross.

CHAPTER 32

TRUTH IS TRUTH EVEN IF HARD TO ACCEPT

⬥⬥⬥

Since the Christian faith can be strongly defended, with compelling evidence, there is a strong rationale for sharing the gospel. It should have the highest priority. There is simply no reason for this not to be the premier call for all Christians. The alternative is simply a denial of the evidence. Because if it is not true, what the Apostle Paul wrote in 1st Corithians, chapter 15, is a reasonable conclusion. His conclusion was that if the resurrection did not happen, the alternative is much preferred, get on with life. Because any personal cost incurred, living a committed Christian life: is senseless. Like he said in verse 19: "If only for this life we have hope in Christ, we are pitied more than all men." NIV. Why? Because we are living a lie. We are giving a false hope. And those who are sacrificing personal comfort for the hope of the gospel have been deceived. Why suffer for a lie, when there are no personal or monetary benefits for doing so? Moreover, there is no reason to make our relationship awkward by imploring the unsaved to come to saving faith. Furthermore, without the resurrection, those that have passed on from this life are just gone, it is over with. There is no hope for the dead: just nothingness. He continues the logic in the same chapter, in verse 32 b, that also makes deductive logical sense: "Let us eat and drink, for tomorrow we die." NIV If we lose the hope of the resurrection, which undergirds the salvation message, then what is left? We are still going to die. Life without the hope of the resurrection is meaningless. (Yet, is that not the strongest yearning of all men; a hope when standing at the grave of a loved one, or when facing one's own mortality) Therefore, without the assurance of the resurrection, there is no real hope! We might as well drink a few beers and enjoy those fleeting years that remain. Logic dictates that we even dance with the dark side of the world. Why not? What is there to lose? It is all transient anyways!

But since the Christian faith is true; there is no denying the strong evidence! It is therefore a message of great urgency. While some aspects of our faith are emotionally and intellectually hard to accept, it is also the greatest message of hope ever to have been given to mankind. The ultimate hope! Eternity is a long long time. So the gospel message shared is the greatest act of love. It clarifies the eternal consequences of the message: the good and bad. For those who believe, the good news of our acceptance into the forever family of God. Eventually, free from the effects of sin, death and pain. The bad, if you neglect the offer, the holy standards will be satisfied by the judgment of your sin: your eternal consequences. Since your lack of personal righteousness can never measure up to the infinite and eternal holiness of the immutable God. The facts remain: people go to Hell because they have been diagnosed as sinners, and don't accept the payment made by the Savior, so they are judged as sinners. Far too much is at stake to dilute or walk away. Death is so final. The consequences are so final. Even if it is hard to accept all of its implications. It is our secure hope of redemption. Therefore, it should become our mission to share the way of redemption; the eternal is coming, and death is final, we need to continue on in the faith. Since the equation is still the same: one out one will eventually die.

This is even manifested in the way we consider death. My good friend George has remarked that God sees death differently than we do. I believe he is correct. The perspective is with the beholder. The truth of the outcome is according to the scriptures. God sees the continuance of our lives. We go from being saints that remain in sinful flesh, even after becoming a Christian, to saints in His presence. For the believer, the entrance of death into our lives is just the changing of location to a much better place. We leave our sinful flesh for unfettered glorification. Which is the removal of our sinful tendencies. Finally free of sinful impulses. Free from pain and suffering. Life in the very presence of our Heavenly Father. This perspective of God's should be that of our own. Death should not be feared. Glory is our guaranteed future. As it is written in 1ˢᵗ Corinthians 2:9b, "The eye has not seen, nor the ear heard, nor entered into the heart of man, the things God has prepared for those who love him." NIV This is our future, guaranteed.

For the non-believer, it is absolutely devastating. The end of this life was the final chance for salvation. The uncertainty of what happens after death is realized. The baseless hope of meriting salvation on their own is found wanting. It is forever, too late! The eternal is set, and results unalterable. Please do not put this book away until you have resolved this question of your eternal destiny. It is that important, it really is!

I tried to keep the subject matter as general deductive conclusions of key Biblical principles. If this is true, then.... If not, then.... I felt it was worth bringing into focus what is often neglected in most churches: a message of eternal significance!. I have read in a couple of places that around 95% of all "Christians" never lead one person to Christ. That just does not conform with the central truth claims made about Jesus in the scriptures. Many will be disturbed by the suggested implication of the book. It is not the message they want to entertain. They like their lives, and so do I. I like to be liked. It is my nature. Most likely those who do not care for this book, will be those whose lives are going quite well, or the truths contained herein, are too extreme in their opinion. They don't even want to think about these matters. They are happy with their quality of life. They want to continue the illusion that it will last. It won't, I am sad to say. Each man is appointed to die one day and then a judgment. The Bema Seat judgment for the child of God, where our lives will be evaluated for quality. The Lake of Fire for the unbeliever, where the unmitigated righteousness of God will be revealed.

Was this book worth reading? I hope so. I know it is not a popular topic to discuss. But it is a message I felt that needed to be reconsidered. The bringing back into our thinking, the urgent need for the salvation of the lost. A chance to reflect once again on the implications of God's absolute pure holiness. It was a message needed for both the saved and unsaved. The coming to grips with the immutable perfect nature of God. In Romans, chapter one, the Apostle Paul says he was not ashamed of the gospel; neither should we. It is truly the greatest message ever given to mankind. And the most paramount message ever given to be shared. The salvific message that is professed to believe, but ignored by the majority of Christains. This is because we have a growing worldly church that is trying to find approval with the world and not from Christ. (See the rebuke of many of the churches in the book of Revelation) For those believers who are lacking in their faith walk, they need to remember that there is a day when all believers will stand before the Bema Seat of Christ. A time of reckoning on what was really important in light of eternity. For the unbeliever …. It is hard to even consider.

Since it is true, it therefore has immense implied responsibilities for the believer. To fail to respond evangelistically is a denial of everything we profess to believe. Christianity at its very core is an evangelical faith. If you do not grasp that insight, it is likely your eyes are being blinded by Satan. (2 Corinthians 4:4) Therefore, one more time, it is important to consider these themes: the immutable holiness of God, and the finality of the work on the cross by our wonderful Savior, Jesus Christ, and the coming day of reckoning. A message of real hope that is urgently needed in a hopeless world. These realities should cause us to pursue more eternally purposeful lives. Hopefully, this book has stimulated a renewed interest in the everlasting and less on the passing.

I know this was not a professionally written book, that is beyond my ability. I am a very flawed writer, as you have seen, but God specializes in using flawed people. Therefore, I am convinced, He can still use me to bring others to faith. It was my desire to write a book that took these essential and divinely revealed truths, and explored the significance of what the faith really means, because it is absolutely and dependably true. And I believed by being real with my limitations, it would have more meaning. My book was, as intended, a heartfelt book, and not scholarly work. While it may appear at times that I was babbling on and on, yet, if I was able to make the points I wanted to make, and instilled them in the reader's memory, by repeating key truths over and over, I can live with my lack of proficient writing skills. What is really important, is impressing upon the reader, the obvious implications of Biblical Christianity being true! Hope you gained some benefits from my thoughts. With that, I will close the book. God Bless You!

The truth as claimed by Jesus: is still the truth, John 5:24, 8:24 and 14:6.

It is an eternal destination question: either it is true or it is not? It is: so get on living it!

THE AUTHOR

Steven lives in Michigan with his wife of over 40 years. They have three adult children and a growing number of grandchildren. He retired after a 30+ year career in various forms of law enforcement. He presently works part time in a law enforcement role. He served as Mayor and Mayor Pro-tem of the City of Port Huron, where he has lived the majority of his life. He has served as a Vice President of a Charter School for troubled youth, on a board for a nonprofit halfway program for criminal offenders, and has served on a number of other boards: both Christian and secular. He was very active in coaching his children's various sporting teams. He spent 7 years doing jail ministry and was involved in a number of other Christian related activities. His heartbeat is personal evangelism. This is an updated version of his first book.

There is no implied endorsement, by any association, organization, boards, ministries or employment (past or present) for this book, or its content. The opinions in this book are solely mine.

I do not necessarily agree with every detailed teaching in the below listed books. But I have found real value in all of them. They are all well worth reading. There are dozens and dozens more in my library, but these are more than enough to ground you in your walk.

BIBLIOGRAPHY

Batterson, Mark, _The Circle Maker,_ Zondervan, 2011

Betz, Harlan D. _Setting the Stage for Eternity,_ Falcon Publishing LTD, 2005

Beware Paul N. B_elievers Payday,_ AMG Publishers, 2002

Bing, Charles C. _Lordship Salvation,_ Ph.D. Dissertation, 1991

Bing, Charles C. _Simply By Grace,_ Kregel Publishing, 2009

Bing, Charles C. _Grace Salvations and Discipleship,_ Grace Theology Press, 2015

Chafer, Lewis Sperry, _Salvation,_ Kregel Publications, 1991

Chafer, Lewis Sperry, _True Evangelism,_ Kregel Publications, 1993

Chafer, Lewis Sperry, _Grace,_ Kregel Publications, 1995

Cocoris, G. Michael, _The Salvation Controversy,_ Insights From the Word, 2008

Cocoris, G. Michael, _Repentance. The Most Misunderstood Word in the Bible,_ Grace Gospel Press, 2010

Cucuzza, Thomas M. _Secure forever!_ WWW.xulonpress.com, 2007

Evans, Phillip M. _Eternal Security Proved,_ Published by Lulu.com, 2008

Eaton, Michael, _No Condemnation, A New Theology of Assurance,_ InterVarsity Press, 1995

Gromacki, Robert Glenn, *Salvation is Forever,* Moody Press, 1973

Halsey, Michael D., *Truthspeak,* Grace Gospel Press, 2010

Halsey, Michael D. THE GOSPEL of GRACE and TRUTH, Grace Gospel Press, 2015

Hixson, J. B. *The Gospel Unplugged, Lucidbook,* 2011

Hixson, J. B., Whitmire, Rick, Zuck, Roy B. *Freely By His Grace,* Grace Gospel Press, 2012

Hixson, J. B., Ge*tting the Gospel Wrong,* Grace Gospel Press, 2013

Hixson, J.B., and Fontecchio, Mark, *What Lies Ahead,* Lucid Books, 2013

Hixson, J. B. *Top 10 Reasons some people go to Hell, and One Reason No One Ever Has To!* Grace Acres Press, 2020

Jones, Brian, *Hell is Real (But I hate to Admit it)* David Cook, 2011

Kendall, R.T. *Once Saved, Always Saved.* Authentic Media, 2005

Lightner, Robert P. *Sin, the Savior and Salvation,* Thomas Nelson, 1991

Lindsey, Hal, *Satan Is Alive and Well on the Planet Earth,* Zondervan, 1972

Lindsey, Hal, *Amazing Grace*, Western Front, 1995

Lutzer Erwin W. *How You Can Be Sure That You Will Spend Eternity with God,* Moody Press,1996

Lutzer Erwin W. *One Minute After You Die,* Moody Press, 1997

Lutzer, Erwin W. *Your Eternal Reward,* Moody Press, 1998

Lybrand, Fred *Back to FAITH Reclaiming the Gospel Clarity in an AGE of INCONGRUENCE,* xulonpress.com, 2009

Mansfield, Stephen, *Killing Jesus,* Worthy Publications, 2013

Moyer, R. Larry, *Free and Clear,* Kregel Publications, 1997

Olson, Lloyd A. *Eternal Security, Once Saved Always Saved,* Tate Publishing and Enterprises, 2007

Pentecost, J. Dwight, *The Joy of Fellowship,* Kregel Publications, 1977

Pentecost, J. Dwight, *Faith that Endures,* Kregel Publications, 2000

Radmacher, Earl D. *Salvation,* Word Publishing, 2000

Rokser, Dennis M. *SHALL NEVER PERISH, Forever.* Grace Gospel Press, 2012

Rokser, Dennis M. *Salvation in Three Time Zones,* Grace Gospel Press, 2013

Rokser, Dennis M. *Don't Ask Jesus into Your Heart,* Grace Gospel Press, 2014

Ryrie, Charles C. *So Great of Salvation,* Victor Books 1989

Shea, Ronald, Booklet, *The Gospel,* Grace Gospel Press, 1988

Stanley, Charles. *Eternal Security,* Thomas Nelson Publishers 1990

Stegall, Thomas L. *The Gospel of the Christ,* 2009

Strombeck, J. F. *So Great of Salvation,* Kregel Publications, 1991

Strombeck, J. F. *Shall Never Perish,* Kregel Publications, 1991

Swindall, Charles R. and Zuck, Roy B., *Understanding Christian Theology,* Thomas Nelson Publishing, 2003

Tam, Stanley, *Every Christian a Soul Winner,* Thomas Nelson Publishers, 1975

Tripp, Paul David *Forever, Why You Can't Live Without it,* Zondervan, 2011

Unger, Merrill F. *What Demons Can Do To Saints,* Moody Press, 1991

Unger, Merrill F. *The New Unger's Bible Handbook,* Moody Press, 1984

Vandergriend, Alvin, _Love To Pray,_ Prayer Shop Publishing, 2003

Yohannan, K. P, _Living in Light of Eternity_. Chosen, A Division of Baker Book House

SUGGESTED READINGS TO SUPPORT MY CONTENTION OF THE REALITY OF GOD AND RELIABILITY OF THE BIBLE

Ankerberg, John and Weldon, John, _Ready for an Answer_, Harvest House Publishers, 1997

Comfort, Ray, _Evolution A Fairly Tale for Grownups_, Bridge-Logos 2008

Cross, John R. _By this Name_, Goodseed, 2014

Davis, Max, _The Insanity of Unbelief_, 2012, Destiny Image

D'Souza, Dinesh, _What's so Great About Christianity,_ Tyndale House, 2007

Geisler, Norman L. _Christian Apologetics,_ Baker Book House, 1976

Geisler, Norman L. and Turek, Frank, _I Don't Have Enough FAITH to be an ATHEIST,_ CROSSWAY, 2004

Johnson, Phillip E., _Darwin on Trial_, InterVarsity Press, 1993

Limbaugh, David, _Jesus on Trial,_ Regnery Publishing, 2014

Lutzer Erwin W. _Seven Reasons Why You Can Trust The Bible,_ Moody Press, 1998

McDowell, Josh, _Evidence that Demands a Verdict,_ Here's Life Publishers, 1990

Moreland, J. P. _Scaling the Secure City_, Baker Book House, 1987

Murray, Abdu, _Saving Truth_, Zondervan 2018

Strobel, Lee, _The Case for Christ,_ Zondervan, 1998

Strobel, Lee, *The Case for Faith,* Zondervan, 2000

Strobel, Lee, *The Case for a Creator,* Zondervan, 2004

Swenson, Richard A. M.D., *More Than Meets the Eye*, Navpress, 2000

Wallace, J. Warner, *Cold-Case Christianity, A Homicide Detective Investigates the Claims of the Gospels,* David Cook, 2013

Wallace, J. Warner, *Person of Interest*, Zondervan, 2021

Zacharias, Ravi, *A Shattered Visage, The Real Face of Atheism,* Wolgemuth & Hyatt, 1990

Zacharias, Ravi, *Can Man Live Without God*, Word Publishing, 1994

Podcast and Internet ministries I recommend

Assured by Grace, Pastor Phil and Danny

Dr. Andy Woods found at SLBC Andy Woods

Dr. Thomas Cucuzza found at Northland Bible Baptist Church

Stand Up for the Truth, with David Fioraso.

The John Ankerberg Show, with John Ankerberg and guest.

Wallbuilders, With David Barton, Rick Green and Tim Barton.

Cold-Case Christianity, with J. Warner Wallace.

Stand to Reason, with Greg Koukl.

The Alisa Childers Podcast.

NBW Ministries WWW.NotByWorks, By J.B. Hixson

I Don't Have Enough Faith to be an Atheist, With Dr. Frank Turek.

BibleThinker with Mike Winger.

Printed in the United States
by Baker & Taylor Publisher Services